Making Every Vote Count:
Federal Election L[egislation] in the States

Andrew Rachlin, Editor

Essays and commentary sponsored by the Policy Research
Institute for the Region at the Woodrow Wilson School of
Public and International Affairs at Princeton University, the Brennan
Center for Justice at New York University School of Law, and the
Fels Institute of Government at the University of Pennsylvania.

The Policy Research Institute for the Region was established by
Princeton University and the Woodrow Wilson School of Public
and International Affairs to bring the resources of the University
community to bear on solving the increasingly interdependent
public policy challenges facing New Jersey, Metropolitan New York,
and southeastern Pennsylvania.

The Policy Research Institute for the Region
Woodrow Wilson School of Public and International Affairs
Princeton University
Robertson Hall
Princeton, NJ 08544

Cover design by Leslie Goldman
Printed by PrintMedia Communications, Anaheim, CA
Produced by the Office of Communications, Princeton University

ISBN 0-9778531-6-0

Contents

Previous Publications in this Series

BEYOND POST-9/11: The Future of the
Port Authority of New York and New Jersey

Edited by Keith S. Goldfeld

STATES AND STEM CELLS: The Policy and Economic
Implications of State-Funded Stem Cell Research

Edited by Aaron D. Levine

JUSTICE AND SAFETY IN AMERICA'S
IMMIGRANT COMMUNITIES

Edited by Martha King

THE RACE FOR SPACE: The Politics and Economics
of State Open Space Programs

Edited by Keith S. Goldfeld

FROM CAMPAIGNING TO GOVERNING:
Leadership in Transition

Edited by Udai Tambar and Andrew Rachlin

CONSENT AND ITS DISCONTENTS:
Policy Issues In Consent Decrees

Edited by Andrew Rachlin

THE POLITICS OF DESIGN:
Competitions for Public Projects

Edited by Catherine Malmberg

NEW DOWNTOWNS:
The Future Of Urban Centers

Edited by Jonathan R. Oakman

Preface

Famed playwright and armchair political philosopher Tom
Stoppard once wrote: "It's not the voting that's democracy;
it's the counting"—an observation that seemed especially wise
after the debacle that was the presidential election of 2000.
However one felt about the outcome of that election, it was
more than clear that the process had fallen short. Quite simply,
we needed to work on our counting. The straightforward act
that we all learn on our fingers and toes in kindergarten becomes
monumentally complex when expanded to the tallying of tens of
millions of votes for thousands of candidates cast by citizens of
diverse abilities and language backgrounds on voting apparatuses
that are anything but universal across jurisdictions. The 2000
race showed that these strains had pushed our electoral system
beyond its capacity, undermining the connection between the act
of voting and the outcome of elections.

Enter the Help America Vote Act of 2002 (HAVA), a much-
touted bipartisan attempt to improve the administration
of America's electoral systems. It gave states a set of goals:
improved poll worker training, the installation of new voting
machinery, and the establishment of statewide voter registration
databases. It gave states money to accomplish these goals—more
than $3 billion in total. But it also gave states a lot of leeway to
determine exactly how to implement the bill's prescriptions,
which has led to important variations in impact state to state.

Our region—New York, New Jersey, and Pennsylvania—has
been at the center of this reform effort. With some of the
nation's most complex voting systems and large populations, the
region's states presented special challenges to HAVA implementation. And, with over $300 million of HAVA money allocated
for the region, we have also been some of the prime beneficia-

ries of the Act's largesse. For these reasons, we were extremely pleased when we formed a partnership with the Fels Institute of Government at the University of Pennsylvania to take part in a project that they began in 2003 to assess the progress of HAVA implementation in the region.

2005–06 was a crucial period for HAVA—a period to take stock after the 2004 elections and see how early phases had worked, and also a period of important next steps, as deadlines for implementing major pieces of HAVA's mandates came due. The partnership of the Policy Research Institute for the Region with Fels was thus a fortuitous one; to their focus on state and local administration, we were able to add ours on state and local policy. Our combined efforts led us to expand on Fels' original project to examine both nuts-and-bolts implementation questions and overarching policy questions. The result was a series of writings and discussions that serve multiple audiences. Scholars, policymakers, and election administrators will all find new and challenging material on HAVA in this volume, from Edward Foley's bold attempt to reframe our understandings of appropriate goals for the reform of election administration to Ray Martinez's pragmatic take on the need to improve voter confidence in election results.

Critically, these different perspectives are not isolated from one another; the contributors took advantage of the election reform conference we convened in April 2006 to share ideas and build on common ground. The depth and breadth of their work here reflects this all-too-uncommon meeting of scholars, policymakers, and administrators.

Our work on HAVA, however, is only a part of this volume. Early in our project, the Institute and Fels took on a critical third partner: the Brennan Center for Justice at New York University School of Law. The Brennan Center is one of the nation's most respected centers for research and advocacy on election reform, and they convinced us that talking about HAVA in isolation is really only telling a part of the election reform story. Two other critical pieces of federal election reform legislation are also shaping the way our country selects its leaders: the Bipartisan Campaign Reform Act (BCRA) and the Voting Rights Act (VRA). We came to agree with Brennan that a consideration of these two bills' impact on election reform in the states had to be a part of our work as well.

The Bipartisan Campaign Reform Act (BCRA), also passed in 2002, reshaped campaign finance regulations, drastically reducing the impact of so-called "soft" money in national elections. It was an attempt—not, of course, entirely successful—to limit the influence that wealthy groups and individuals can exert on the electoral process. As Stoppard no doubt understood, "counting" in a democracy is not merely about being marked down; rather, it is about mattering, and mattering equally.

Like election administration, campaign finance reform is an important and timely issue in the region. On the one hand, the region is home to some of the nation's most sophisticated campaign finance reform efforts, from New York City's and nearby Connecticut's public finance systems to New Jersey's recent "pay-to-play" restrictions. On the other, the region also presents unique challenges to campaign finance reform, including a seemingly endless number of wealthy, self-financed candidates who undercut public finance systems and set the fundraising bar ever higher for their opponents. As Richard Briffault's piece in this volume makes clear, BCRA has both direct and indirect effects on the states' responses to these challenges.

The VRA, then, may seem the odd bill out. It is much older than the other two pieces of legislation we consider here, and many of its most important provisions concentrate their impact well outside the region. Yet in some ways, the region offers an ideal context for thinking about the VRA and the basic principle at its core—the need to offer special protections to minority voting rights. To begin with, with its significant and growing immigrant population, the region tests the limits of the VRA's minority language provisions. But even more importantly, it is precisely the way that the region's problems with minority voting don't fit within the VRA's protective confines that makes this the perfect

place to talk about its future. As Richard Pildes, Guy Charles, and
Luis Fuentes-Rohwer note in their contributions to this volume,
modern impediments to minority voting are not geographically
isolated; they are as prevalent in New York or New Jersey as in
Alabama or Mississippi. Problems with ID requirements for voting
and felon disenfranchisement, he argues, require a new approach
to protect minority voting rights—one that works as well in
Newark as it does in Selma.

Democracy demands not only an accurate counting of votes and
assurances that all votes count equally, but also equal opportunity
for citizens to submit their votes to be counted in the first place.
That the current Congress renewed the VRA without addressing
this crucial point makes the discussion in this volume all the more
valuable. To whatever extent fostering scholarship and debate on
improving protections for minority voters helps build intellectual
and political capital in support of that goal, we hope this volume
will play its small part.

We would like to thank our partners at the Brennan Center and
the Fels Institute for their hard work and thoughtful counsel, and
to laud them for their ongoing work to improve elections in the
region and beyond.

Anthony Shorris
Director
Policy Research Institute for the Region
Princeton University

Introduction

Justin Levitt
Brennan Center for Justice, New York University School of Law

In November 2000, the signs of strain in the American election system grabbed the attention of the nation. Record amounts were spent on controversial "issue ads"—often unregulated or financed by huge contributions to political parties from wealthy special interests. Glitches at the polls produced chaos. Voters tossed from the rolls and harassed in the streets reminded the country that the legacy of discrimination was still very much alive. A photo-finish made the background rules of the election process suddenly salient. And under intense scrutiny, they were found wanting.

National efforts at reform centered on three major federal statutes. In 2002, the Bipartisan Campaign Reform Act ("BCRA") changed the rules for funding federal election campaigns for the first time in three decades. The same year, Congress passed the Help America Vote Act ("HAVA"), the first federal law focused entirely on the administration of elections. Finally, the fight to renew expiring provisions of the Voting Rights Act—the nation's hallmark civil rights legislation—launched a national effort to re-examine the Act's continuing vitality.

These profound federal developments have, naturally, caused waves in the states. National laws create local obligations. But they may also spur local innovation. As Justice Brandeis recognized long ago, "a single courageous State may, if its citizens choose, serve as a laboratory"—and in the last few years, there have been many laboratories of democracy. States have used the three major federal models as points of departure for their own regulation of the election process, to mixed effect. And the experience of states, counties, and municipalities under these regulatory regimes will certainly guide the next wave of national election reform.

It is time for a thorough examination of the rules by which our elections are run. Our recent experience under the three major federal election statutes—the Bipartisan Campaign Finance Act, the Help America Vote Act, and the Voting Rights Act—will help us evaluate best practices for the future.

We chose to focus our study on the experience of three states in particular: New Jersey, New York, and Pennsylvania. These states are engines of the national economy, with high per-capita income, and a history of confronting political corruption and related thorny campaign finance issues. These states are also among the most populous in the country, and thus among those with the largest voter rolls, the most precincts, and the most polling places. They have received more than $300 million in funds disbursed under HAVA for new voting machines and registration database systems. Finally, these states are also extremely diverse, with racial minorities and language minorities protected by the Voting Rights Act. Jurisdictions in all three states have been involved in election-related litigation with the Department of Justice in the last decade.

What can we learn from this state experience to guide future reforms of the rules by which elections are conducted?

To help answer this question, we asked several nationally renowned experts to comment on the federal developments and their impact in the states.

First, we start with the money pouring into the system, and the states' experimentation with campaign finance regulation in the aftermath of BCRA. Professor Richard Briffault of Columbia Law School—and a 2005–06 Fellow in the Program in Law and Public Affairs at Princeton's Woodrow Wilson School—briefly surveys the state campaign finance regulation currently in place, the impact of the new federal developments, and the potential for future innovation in the states.

Second, we look to another source of money pouring into the system: the federal HAVA disbursements to the states, and what the states have done with the funds. Professor Sarah F. Liebschutz of the State University of New York–Brockport and Professor Daniel J. Palazzolo of the University of Richmond offer a detailed examination of the states' HAVA compliance, drawing out lessons from each state's attempt to grapple with HAVA's specific mandates. Next, Professor Edward B. Foley, Director of the Election Law @ Moritz resource at the Moritz School of Law at Ohio State University, takes a longer view of the election administration reforms that HAVA demanded and the expectations that the statute created. Professor Foley's paper canvasses the mechanisms, within HAVA and beyond, by which we might improve our ability to ensure that valid votes are reliably counted—without sacrificing our ability to ensure a reliably final election result.

Finally, we turn to the Voting Rights Act. In particular, we examine Section 5 of the Voting Rights Act, which demands preclearance of election laws in certain jurisdictions, and the lessons of the battle over its renewal. Professor Guy-Uriel E. Charles, of University of Minnesota Law School, and Professor Luis Feuntes-Rohwer, of Indiana University-Bloomington, criticize what they describe as the "mechanical" renewal of Section 5 in its current form, without addressing the limitations of its substantive standards or its enforcement mechanism. And Professor Richard H. Pildes, of the New York University School of Law, questions whether future voting rights legislation should follow the Section 5 model—aggressive federal oversight of the racial impact of changes to existing laws—or the model of shallower but broader statutes like the Help America Vote Act.

Each of these analyses takes as its primary focus the impact of one of the three principal federal election statutes: BCRA, HAVA, and the VRA. We have compiled the papers in this one volume, however, because we recognize that campaign finance, election administration, and voting rights are intimately interrelated. Each addresses one aspect of the democratic process; each seeks to ensure that a vote that is cast is also meaningful. And it is crucial to understand that effective reform will require concerted strategic action on all fronts.

Likewise, several key themes cut across each of the three principal statutes, and reappear in many of the pages that follow:

1. **Federalism**. What is the appropriate role for the federal government in regulating election activity, and how much leeway should be left to the states? At what point should uniformity trump states' abilities to experiment? Is there a difference depending on the scale of the election: that is, should the rules governing presidential elections be more uniform across state lines than Congressional elections or elections for the State Assembly? Is there a difference depending on the value being regulated?

2. **Enforcement**. What are the appropriate enforcement mechanisms for the rights and regulations governing elections? Is enforcement best handled by federal or state agencies? Private actors? Opposing political parties? Funding incentives? And given the incentive to manipulate the rules of the contest for partisan gain, is there a means to ensure that the rules are refereed in nonpartisan fashion? If not, is

a bipartisan or multipartisan referee structure preferable, so that opposing interests are at least balanced?

3. **Role of the courts**. Courts have played a substantial role in regulating the broad guarantees of the Voting Rights Act and the far more specific guarantees of federal campaign finance law, and courts have only now begun to interpret and construe HAVA. What is the appropriate role of the courts in limiting or expanding the procedural guarantees regulating elections? Is the answer different if the judges making the decisions are elected? Are there particular procedural guarantees not provided by statute that courts should nevertheless protect as part of the inherent constitutional structure of a democracy?

4. **Political calculation**. To what extent is electoral politics itself responsible for these election regulations? Do the regulatory statutes reflect partisan calculation? Incumbency protection? Responsiveness to a motivated constituency? Leadership based on other factors? To what extent does electoral politics make further regulation either desirable or likely? Are these proper subjects for an initiative or referendum process?

5. **Symbolic equality**. Is there a value in ensuring symbolic procedural equality, even if actual equality is effectively impossible to achieve? Does the quest for symbolic procedural equality engender its own harms? Its own benefits? Is symbolic equality of process inherently better served for some values than for others? Are there currently procedural values for which symbolic equality is not considered important?

6. **Substantive guarantees**. Are there additional desirable regulations for the conduct of elections that are not currently reflected in existing law? Are they prophylactic, or do they address problems and deficiencies already apparent in the system? If the latter, are the problems uniform throughout the country, or geographically focused? Do they appear only in particular sorts of election contests, or under particular circumstances? What protections are necessary to ensure that the people have faith in the process?

The papers that follow provide many intriguing perspectives and insights on these questions.

Advocates, scholars, and practitioners all agree that we cannot yet guarantee that every eligible citizen will be able to cast a meaningful vote for a responsive representative, and have that vote counted. Beyond that, the field of debate is rich: there are many competing priorities and different policies, and even some dispute whether such a guarantee is a worthy goal. Yet even if perfection is unattainable, there are many means to make the election process more reliable, more responsive, and more fair. All of the proposals have very real consequences. And all will affect the character of the American democratic process, and the faith that we share in its potential.

Stepping Out of the Federal Shadow: Campaign Finance Law in the States

Richard Briffault
Columbia Law School;
Princeton University

INTRODUCTION

Campaign finance regulation is a critical issue in election law reform. Public debate has focused on the rise of soft money and issue advocacy; the protracted battle in Congress over whether and how to regulate these practices, culminating in the adoption of the Bipartisan Campaign Reform Act of 2002 (BCRA); and the subsequent constitutional litigation that resulted in the Supreme Court's 2003 decision in *McConnell v. FEC.*[1] The prominent role played by so-called 527 committees in the 2004 presidential election and the ongoing struggle in the current Congress over whether and how to restrict their activities have generated considerable attention. The problems with the presidential election public funding system[2] and the shortcomings of the Federal Election Commission are also central to contemporary discussions of campaign finance law. All these issues, however, concern federal campaign finance regulation. But federal campaign finance law is limited to federal elections, federal officeholders, and national political party committees. It largely ignores the state and local contests which constitute the overwhelming majority of American elections.

Those state and local elections are regulated by state—and sometimes local—laws.

Indeed, states have long regulated the financing of state and local election campaigns. The earliest state campaign finance laws predate comparable federal laws by some decades. Today every state has its own campaign finance law which addresses candidates, parties, and political committees in state and local elections. In several areas state legislatures and local governments have been particularly innovative, going well beyond Congress in developing new types of contribution restrictions or exploring mechanisms for providing public financial support to candidates or political parties. In several areas, such as judicial elections or ballot proposition elections, state law is the only relevant law since these elections do not even occur at the federal level.

This paper provides a sketch of state campaign finance law. The topic is an enormous one. There is tremendous state-to-state variation as well as considerable complexity within most states. The field is also constantly changing, with many states modifying old laws, enacting new laws, or implementing new regulations each year. As a result, the paper can provide only the briefest snapshot of how things stood in late 2005–early 2006, indicating only the principal themes and issues rather than providing a detailed analysis.

Part II provides an overview of the four main techniques of campaign finance regulation —reporting and disclosure requirements; contribution restrictions; expenditure restrictions; and public funding for candidates or parties. It considers how the states have utilized these techniques, with more detail concerning the states of the "Princeton region"—New Jersey, New York, and Pennsylvania. Beyond the greater local interest, these states nicely illustrate the variety of state campaign finance laws.

Part III looks at the impact of federal law on state and local campaign finance law. Federal law can affect state and local campaign finance law in three ways. First, some federal laws, such as section 527 of the Internal Revenue Code and BCRA, directly regulate some state campaign actors. Second, federal constitutional law shapes and constrains all levels of campaign finance regulation—federal, state, and local. Finally, federal laws also provide something of a model for state and local laws. Sometimes that model suggests possible roads that state and local law might follow; sometimes the federal "model" indicates some of the pitfalls of regulation or suggests routes to avoid.

Part IV concludes by considering some of the trends in and challenges for state and local campaign finance law. I will give particular attention to three issues—state innovations in contribution regulation, the increased state and local interest in public funding, and potential changes in federal constitutional law that could affect state regulation.

STATE CAMPAIGN FINANCE LAW: IN BRIEF

CAMPAIGN FINANCE REGULATORY TECHNIQUES

American campaign finance law has long relied on four types of regulatory techniques —reporting and disclosure; contribution restrictions; expenditure restrictions; and public subsidies to candidates and/or political parties.

Reporting and disclosure rules are the most basic form of campaign finance regulation. They obligate candidates and other organizations, such as political parties and political action committees, which raise and spend money in connection with election campaigns to reveal the sources of funds and amounts provided for contributions over a threshold amount and to report expenditures of campaign funds over a threshold level. Reporting requirements directly serve the interest in informed voter decision-making by enabling the voters to learn which individuals, organizations, and interests are providing financial backing to particular candidates or political committees. The voters can then take that information into account in deciding which candidates to vote for or in appraising the campaign messages of political committees. In addition, the prospect of disclosure may discourage some individuals or interests from making, and some candidates or committees from receiving, particularly large contributions. To that extent, disclosure can promote some of the interests served by contribution restrictions.

Contribution restrictions can take two forms: (i) limits on the amount of money a donor can give to a candidate or a political organization for electoral purposes; and (ii) prohibitions on donations from particular sources. Contribution restrictions are intended to restrict the potential for "corruption" that emerges when candidates and officeholders receive and, thus, may be grateful for, large donations, or when their official decisions are influenced by the need to secure large contributions for their next election. The Supreme Court has also indicated that by controlling the "appearance of corruption" contribution restrictions promote public confidence in government.

Expenditure restrictions can also either limit the amounts a candidate or political organization can spend on election campaigns or flatly prohibit certain actors from making any expenditures. Spending limits have been justified on multiple grounds—to discourage evasion of contribution limits, to limit the fundraising arms race that can arise when spending is unlimited, to equalize the spending of competing candidates, to control the influence of wealthy independent spenders. The Supreme Court in 1976 in *Buckley v. Valeo*[3] held expenditure limits on candidates and independent committees unconstitutional under the First Amendment, and the Court subsequently invalidated limits on party spending as well. As I will discuss in more detail below, the Supreme Court is currently considering a case, *Randall v. Sorrell,* which presents the question of whether spending limits may be constitutional, and thus could reopen Buckley—although at this point that seems unlikely.

Despite Buckley, two types of spending limits survive. The Court has upheld prohibitions on election spending by business corporations and unions,[4] and has also upheld "voluntary" spending limits that candidates agree to as a condition for receiving public funding.[5]

Public subsidies can take a variety of forms, including tax breaks for individuals to provide an incentive to make campaign contributions, or government-funded media that transmit campaign messages to the voters, such as ballot pamphlets or free mailings. More commonly, discussion of public funding focuses on cash grants to qualifying candidates or parties to defray some of the costs of campaigning. Many such public subsidy programs require the candidate who receives the funds to agree to accept a limit on his or her total campaign expenditures.

STATE REPORTING AND DISCLOSURE REQUIREMENTS

The states have long required some campaign actors to disclose their financial activities. The first American disclosure law was adopted by a state—New York—in 1890, or two decades before the first federal campaign disclosure requirement. Indeed, Colorado, Michigan, Massachusetts, California, Missouri, and Kansas all had some disclosure requirement in place before Congress passed the Publicity Act in 1910.[6] Today, all states require some level of disclosure from candidates, political parties, and political committees of the amount and source of contributions and of the amount and purposes of expenditures.

State laws, however, vary considerably with respect to such questions as the financial thresholds that trigger the duty to report;

the particular contributions and expenditures that need to be reported; the degree of detail required in disclosures, and the frequency with which reports are due, particularly in the pre-election period. There is also some variation in the extent to which the disclosure requirement applies to non-candidate, non-party actors.

In Pennsylvania a candidate (or a candidate's campaign committee) must file public reports if he or she receives contributions or make expenditures in excess of $250.[7] All contributions over $50, and all expenditures, must be itemized. With respect to contributions under $250, only the name and address of the donor need be reported; for contributions in excess of $250, the occupation and employer—or principal place of business if the donor is self-employed—must be reported as well. A political committee which receives contributions in excess of $250 must also report contributions and expenditures. So, too, a person other than a candidate or political committee who spends more than $100 in a calendar year on independent expenditures expressly advocating the election or defeat of a candidate or ballot question must report the same information as candidates and political committees.

Candidates are required to file pre-election reports six weeks before an election, and candidates, political committees, and independent spenders which have received contributions or made expenditures for purposes of influencing an election must file 10 days before the election. Candidates and political committees active in an election must also file a post-election report, as well as an annual report. In addition, a candidate who receives a contribution of $500 or more—or a person who makes an independent expenditure of $500 or more—after filing the last pre-election report must report this large late contribution/expenditure within 24 hours.[8] An additional requirement applies to a business entity that has been awarded a non-bid contract by the commonwealth or a political subdivision within the preceding year. The firm must, by February 15, report the name of any officer, director, partner, owner—or member of the immediate family of any of these people—whose campaign contributions exceeded $1,000 in the aggregate in the preceding year, and the name of any employee—or member of an employee's immediate family—who made a campaign contribution in excess of $1,000 in the preceding year.[9]

New York's reporting and disclosure requirements are fairly similar to Pennsylvania's. Any candidate who receives or spends more than $50 per year or $1,000 in an election cycle must file. So, too, a political committee that spends more than $1,000 in an election cycle and a committee that raises or spends $100 or more in support of or in opposition to a ballot proposition must file. Expenditures of $50 or more and contributions of $100 or more must be itemized—although the information required concerning donors is limited to name and address and does not include the business affiliation Pennsylvania requires of larger donors.

All candidates and committees active in elections must file two pre-election reports—32 days before and 11 days before—as well as one post-election report and two semi-annual reports. As in Pennsylvania, any large contribution received after the last pre-election report must be reported within 24 hours, although New York's reporting threshold is $1,000 and, unlike Pennsylvania, New York does not require special reporting of large last-minute independent expenditures. Nor does New York require special reporting by large government contractors.

New Jersey has by far the most extensive reporting requirements in the tri-state area and one of the most comprehensive reporting requirements in the country. New Jersey requires campaign disclosures from candidates, persons engaged in "pre-candidacy activity," recall and recall defense committees, continuing political committees, legislative leadership committees, political party committees, and governmental affairs agents (formerly known as lobbyists and legislative agents).[10] Under certain circumstances, citizen groups or other grassroots movements, write-in candidates and school board candidates, and individuals and groups making independent expenditures must also file.[11] In general, candidates must file two pre-election reports—29 and 11 days before the election—and a 20-day post-election report (with primaries, runoffs, and general elections treated as separate elections). Certain PACs, continuing political committees, legislative leadership, and party committees must make quarterly filings. As in other states, New Jersey also has a special 48-hour reporting requirement for large (above $1,000) contributions and expenditures made after the last pre-election report. Moreover, recent legal changes now require more detailed disclo-sure—contributor's occupation and employer as well as name and address—for contributions over $300.

In addition, under recently enacted legislation, starting in 2006, "professional campaign fundraisers" are required to register and file reports with the Election Law Enforcement Commission ("ELEC"). So, too, the state recently adopted a "pay-to-play disclosure" requirement for certain business entities. The new law requires that prior to entering into a contract with a government entity that is worth more than $17,500 and is not publicly advertised, a business entity must disclose to that government entity certain contributions made during the past year. A business entity with public contracts of $50,000 or more in a calendar year must file an annual statement with the ELEC reporting its contracts and certain contributions.[12]

STATE CONTRIBUTION RESTRICTIONS
As with reporting and disclosure requirements, states have long restricted campaign contributions—although until the post-Watergate era state contribution restrictions were aimed more at certain sources of donations, particularly corporations, rather than at limiting the amounts of campaign gifts.[13] Today, all but five states impose some limit on campaign contributions.[14]

The most popular form of contribution restriction concerns corporate financial activity. Twenty-two states ban corporate campaign contributions altogether while 23 more limit the amounts corporations may contribute.

As at the federal level, some states that ban corporate contributions permit corporations to sponsor separate, segregated funds—or PACs—which can solicit contributions from corporate officers, directors, and shareholders and use those funds to engage in electoral activity. Many states, although less than the number restricting corporations, also limit union campaign contributions or limit union campaign participation to PAC funds contributed by union members.

Thirty-seven states place limits on contributions by individuals to candidates. These limits range from $130 on contributions per election to a legislative candidate in Montana to $50,100 to a New York gubernatorial candidate for the primary and general election together. The average individual contribution limit across the 37 states is $6,800 for a gubernatorial candidate (primary and general election together) and $3,136 to a legislative candidate (same).[15]

Thirty-six states impose monetary limits on donations by political action committees (PACs) to candidates. Limits on PAC contributions are usually similar to, and are often the same as, the limits on individual contributions. However, some states impose different limits on PACs or differentiate among different types of PACs. In Arizona, for example, a PAC may qualify as a "super PAC" if it receives contributions from 500 or more individuals in amounts of $10 or more in a year. The contribution limit on such a "super PAC" is much higher than on a regular PAC.[16] Some states also limit the aggregate amount a candidate can receive from all PACs—in Arizona the aggregate PAC

cap is $75,624 for a gubernatorial candidate and $7,568 for a legislative candidate[17]—or limit the percentage of total campaign contributions that can come from PACs.[18] Rhode Island—limits the total amount a PAC can give to all recipients in a year.[19]

A little more than half the states place some limit on political party contributions to candidates. These limits tend to be significantly higher than the limits on individual or PAC contributions. Twenty-three states limit contributions to state political parties from most or all sources, including individuals, PACs, corporations and unions, and national party committees. These monetary limits often apply only to contributions to parties for election or candidate-support purposes, or states set different limits for candidate-related and party organizational/party building activities. An additional 14 states limit or ban contributions to parties by corporations and/or unions but do not restrict donations to parties from other sources. Fifteen states impose some restrictions on donations by national party committees to state party committees or on the purposes for which state parties can use funds provided by the national parties.

A common state-level contribution limitation without a federal analogue is the restriction on giving or receiving campaign contributions during the legislative session, or comparable restrictions on donations by lobbyists. Twenty-eight states place some restrictions—including an outright ban—on campaign contributions to state legislators during the legislative session. In 11 states, the restriction applies only to lobbyists and PACs; the other states restrict contributions to state candidates from all sources during the legislative session.[20]

Local governments have also been active in regulating campaign contributions in local elections. A recent survey by the National Civic League found that 115 city and county governments in 18 states and the District of Columbia have adopted their own contribution limitations.[21] A number of local governments specifically prohibit firms with local government contracts above a threshold amount from making campaign contributions to local candidates.[22] For example, Westminster, Colorado, amended its city charter to include a stringent conflict of interests rule that precludes any city councillor from both voting and participating in debate on any issue or matter coming before the council "involving a benefit" to any person who donated $100 or more to the councillor's campaign.[23] Contributions above the conflict-of-interest threshold fell by 50 percent from the election before the adoption of the charter amendment to the election after.[24]

Pennsylvania, New York, and New Jersey nicely illustrate the range of state contribution limitations. Pennsylvania has a minimally restrictive law. Pennsylvania prohibits corporations from making contributions, but otherwise does not limit either the sources or the amounts of campaign contributions.

New York imposes dollar limits on the size of donations to candidates for all offices, but it does not prohibit donations from any particular source. The dollar limits range from a low of $3,400 for candidates in the primary and general elections for the state assembly (the limit applies separately for each election) to $5,400 for state senate primaries and $8,500 for the state senate general election, to $16,200 for statewide primary elections and $33,900 for statewide general elections.[25] These limits are quite high both in comparison to other states and in comparison to limits on donations to federal candidates, which are currently $2,100 from an individual to a federal candidate per election. A recent study by Common Cause/NY found that 55 percent of the dollar value of individual contributions over the last three election cycles has been in amounts above the $2,100 federal ceiling.[26]

New York also limits the aggregate calendar year donations of individuals and corporations. The aggregate cap on individual donations is $150,000 in a calendar year—compared with the $101,400 limit on individual donations in connection with federal elections over a two-year election cycle. Corporations may make contributions, but they are subject to a $5,000 per calendar year contribution cap. However, each affiliated or subsidiary corporation, if a separate legal entity, has its own limit.

New York limits donations to political party committees, but these limits are both quite high and very porous. An individual can give up to $84,400 to a state party committee in a calendar year; the federal limit on donations to a national party committee is $26,700 per year. Moreover, New York's limits do not apply to donations to parties that support "ordinary activities which are not for the express purpose of promoting the candidacy of specific candidates."[27] There are no limits on donations to parties by either individuals or corporations for such "housekeeping activities." According to a *New York Times* story last year, large donations "pour through" this "gap."[28] The Common Cause/NY Report found that over the last seven years New York State's political parties have raised $47 million for their housekeeping accounts.[29]

New York law also limits individual donations in local elections. In general, the limit is five cents per registered voter in the candidate's party in the jurisdiction in a primary and five cents per registered voter in the jurisdiction in the general election, with a minimum cap of $1,000 and a maximum cap of $50,000 in each election. For New York City, state law sets the minimum cap in the primary for citywide offices at $5,400 and the maximum cap at $16,200; in a general election the contribution cap is $33,900.[30] New York City, however, has adopted much lower contribution limits for local elections. Initially, these limits applied only to candidates who elected to participate in New York City's public funding program (described more fully below). In 2004, however, the City extended its limits on contributions to all candidates for municipal office. The limits range from $4,950 to candidates for citywide office to $2,750 to candidates for the City Council—however, candidates not participating in the City's public funding program can contribute unlimited amounts to their own campaigns.[31] Unlike New York State, New York City also prohibits corporate contributions to municipal candidates.

New Jersey appears to have the tightest and most intricate set of state limits in the tri-state region. Individuals, corporations, unions, and associations are each subject to the following limits: $2,600 to a candidate per election; $7,200 to a political committee per election; $7,200 to a continuing political committee per year; $25,000 to a legislative leadership committee or state political party committee per year; $37,000 to a county political party committee per year; and $7,200 to a municipal political party committee per year.[32] State law gives considerable attention to committee-to-committee—and especially party committee-to-party committee—transfers. The state specifically limits donations by national political party committees, candidate committees, political committees, and continuing political committees to candidates, political committees, continuing political committees, legislative leadership, state party, county party, and municipal party committees.[33] The state also recently enacted restrictions on "pay-to-play" contributions, forbidding no-bid government contractors with state, county, or municipal contracts in excess of $17,500 from making campaign contributions to candidates and political parties at the same level of government as the contract during the year before and during a contract.

EXPENDITURE LIMITATIONS

States have long sought to restrict campaign expenditures. The earliest expenditure restrictions were adopted at the start of the 20th century, and by 1932, 39 states had enacted some expenditure caps, although state laws differed as to whether they applied to independent committees as well as candidates, and to primaries as well as general election.[34] With the Buckley decision, state and federal campaign spending limitations are now unconstitutional—with the two exceptions previously mentioned: prohibitions on spending by corporations or unions, and spending limits imposed as a condition for public funding. The states that limit corporate and union campaign contributions also generally limit corporate and union campaign expenditures.

Buckley to the contrary notwithstanding there has been continuing interest in expenditure limitation at the state and local level. Albuquerque, New Mexico, enacted spending limits for candidates for local office in 1974 and, amazingly enough, despite Buckley those limits remained on the books and were apparently enforced through 1995. The limits were temporarily enjoined in 1997, amended and restored in 1999, but ultimately enjoined in the 2001 mayoral election and finally struck down in 2004. During the final litigation over the limits, the federal district court found on the record that for more than two decades the Albuquerque spending limits had promoted competitive elections, increased citizen confidence in government, led to high voter turnout, reduced the role of large donors, created opportunities for lower-income and lower-middle-income candidates, and generally improved the quality of electoral campaigns without limiting the ability of candidates to campaign effectively.[35] But the court concluded that it was "constrained to find" the expenditure limits unconstitutional,[36] and the Tenth Circuit affirmed.[37]

Cincinnati, Ohio, also adopted spending limits on city council candidates notwithstanding Buckley. That 1995 action appears to have been motivated in part by a desire to challenge Buckley.[38] In the constitutional litigation that followed, the city presented evidence that wealthy donors dominated the financing of city elections, and that the overwhelming majority of local residents believed that large contributors wield undue influence over the local political system.[39] The Sixth Circuit, however, held that Buckley "foreclose[d]… as a matter of law"[40] most of the city's arguments and invalidated the ordinance.

Some localities have sought to limit campaign spending consistent with Buckley.[41] Several communities—including Richland, Washington, and Alta, Utah—have adopted voluntary spending limits with teeth. In Richland, a local ordinance asks candidates to abide by maximum expenditure limitations, and directs the city clerk to monitor spending levels, and publish in the local newspaper an advertisement indicating who is in compliance and who is not.[42] Alta, similarly, directs the city clerk to publicize which candidates have agreed to comply with voluntary limits and which have not.

One state has also sought to impose spending limits notwithstanding Buckley. The Vermont Campaign Finance Act of 1997[43] imposes expenditure limits on candidates for state office. In 2004, after years of litigation, in *Landell v. Sorrell,* a divided panel of the United States Court of Appeals for the Second Circuit upheld the limits on the theory that they addressed the threat of corruption by reducing candidates' dependence on "bundlers" to assemble the contributions needed to fund unlimited expenditures and that they protected the time of candidates and officeholders from the demands of fundraising.[44] Subsequently, the Supreme Court agreed to hear challenges to the spending limits—as well as to other features of the Vermont law including its relatively low contribution limits—and oral argument took place before the Court in the case now known as *Randall v. Sorrell* at the end of February 2006.

PUBLIC FUNDING

Probably the most important campaign finance role that states and local governments have played in recent years has been their experimentation with various forms of public funding. Indeed, as with the other forms of campaign finance regulation, the states have been pioneers. The first candidate public funding program in the United States was enacted at the state level when Colorado in 1909 voted to grant each political party funds equal to 25 centers per vote cast for the party's candidate for governor at the preceding general election. The law, however, was struck down by the state supreme court before it could be put into effect, and was formally repealed several years later.[45]

In Buckley, the Supreme Court upheld the constitutionality of public funding in presidential elections and today 24 states have some form of public funding for at least some state elections.[46] These vary considerably in form and scope. Eight states—Arkansas, Hawaii, Minnesota, North Carolina, Ohio, Oklahoma, Oregon, and Virginia—provide tax credits or deductions for small ($25–$100) contributions to candidates or political parties. Twenty-one states—including some of the tax incentive states—provide cash grants to candidates or political parties. Of those states, seven limit their grants to political parties; these grants tend to be relatively small. The remaining states make grants—usually funded by a tax checkoff or surcharge—to some qualifying candidates in exchange for the candidate's acceptance of contribution and/or spending limitations. Again, many of these grants are relatively small, are tied to relatively low spending limits, or are provided only to candidates for a small number of offices, sometimes only candidates for governor. These have not had much of an impact on elections in these states. Some states also provide candidates with in-kind assistance in getting their messages out by publishing and distributing to the electorate ballot pamphlets that include statements provided by the candidates.

In terms of providing cash assistance to candidates, probably the most significant state public funding laws are those in Minnesota, Maine, and Arizona. The Minnesota law, first enacted in 1974, is one of the few older public funding laws that make substantial matching grants to qualifying candidates for state legislative offices as to candidates for statewide office and to the state committees of political parties for multicandidate expenditures. In the 2002 state legislative elections, a little under half of all candidate campaign spending in Minnesota consisted of public funds.[47] Unlike legislative elections in most states, nearly all Minnesota state legislative elections are contested, and in 2004 over half of its state house incumbents faced competitive challengers.[48]

Maine and Arizona adopted public funding more recently—in 1996 and 1998 respectively. Unlike Minnesota's matching grant approach, Maine and Arizona follow the so-called "clean money" model in which candidates who collect a threshold number (the number varies according to the office sought) of $5 contributions in "seed money" then receive a state grant which pays the full costs of the primary and general elections up to the state-set spending limit. Candidates are required to abide by a spending and to forego private contributions other than the seed money. Participation is voluntary but participation rates appear to be rising. In the 2002 state legislative elections, 53.8 percent of candidate campaign funds in Arizona and 70.5 percent of candidate campaign funds in Maine consisted of Clean Money grants.[49] Both Arizona and Maine have witnessed increases in both contested and competitive state legislative races.[50] Vermont has adopted a Clean Money program limited to gubernatorial and lieutenant governor candidates. Massachusetts voters passed a clean money law in 1998, but due to legislative refusal to fund the program it as never implemented and was ultimately repealed in 2003. In December 2005, Connecticut adopted a clean money-style public funding program—as well as a host of other campaign reforms—which will apply to elections starting in 2007.

With state judicial elections increasingly the subject of high-spending campaigns, in 2002 North Carolina became the first state to offer full public financing for judicial candidates. Following the "clean money" model, candidates raising enough "seed" money from small con-tributors qualify for grants, and extra money is available for candidates who are outspent by self-financed opponents or targeted by independent committees. In 2004, there were 10 candidates for two seats on the North Carolina Supreme Court; seven accepted public funding, and public funds accounted for 63 percent of the total spent. Moreover, the share of campaign money attributable to law-yers dropped sharply while small contributions increased significantly.[51]

Local governments have also been active in providing public funds to candidates for local offices. Sixteen cities or counties have adopted public funding programs, and 12 of those programs are currently operating.[52] Public funding programs are currently in place in cities large—New York City, Los Angeles, San Francisco—midsize—Austin, Texas; Portland, Oregon;[53] Tucson, Arizona—and small, Cary, North Carolina; and Petaluma, California. The New York, Los Angeles, and Tucson programs have been considered particularly success-ful.[54] Tucson's system has been in operation the longest—since 1985—while the New York and Los Angeles systems date back to 1988 and 1990 respectively. In all three systems, public matching funds are provided to qualifying candidates who agree to comply with spending limits and abide by various administrative requirements. In Tucson, New York, and Los Angeles, public funds are avail-able for candidates for all municipal offices, and both the public match and the spending limit have been sufficiently attractive to candidates that in recent years most serious candidates have chosen to participate.[55] Studies have found that these programs have reduced candidates' dependence on large private donations and increased the role of small donors;[56] expanded the ability of women, people of color, and grass-roots candidates to run for office;[57] and have generally contributed to more competitive municipal elections.[58]

These cities and the other communities using public funding have experimented in interesting ways with how to determine which candidates qualify for public funds, how much to give candidates, how to distribute the funds, and how to finance and administer their programs.[59] Thus, Los Angeles has demonstrated the benefits of a public financing trust fund—adopted as a charter amendment—in assuring a "consistent and reliable" source of funding."[60] Tucson has shown that administration of the program by the city clerk, rather than a separate ethics commission or campaign finance board, can be an effective and professional way of implementing public funding.[61] And New York has indicated that public grants plus spending limits need not be a pro-incumbent device, as some critics of public funding have suggested.[62] By amending its law in 1998 to provide an unprecedented $4-to-$1 match for individual donations of $250 or less from New York City residents, the city council not only democratized campaign funding but also contributed to the increased competitiveness of city council elections.[63] And several of the cities that provide public funding—including Austin and San Francisco as well as Los Angeles and New York—have sought to use public funds to improve the quality of municipal election campaigns by requiring candidates who participate in the public funding program to participate in public debates.[64] At the state level, only Arizona and New Jersey also attach debate requirements to public funding.

The various city and county public funding programs have had to address a central challenge to all public funding programs—the ability of nonparticipating candidates, including wealthy, self-funded office seekers, and independent committees to engage in unlimited spending. Certainly, Michael Bloomberg's expenditure of $73 million of his personal fortune in his quest for the New York mayoralty in 2001 and over $80 million in 2005 indicates the limits of any voluntary funding and limits system.[65] To deal with the challenge posed by high-spending nonparticipants, Austin, Los Angeles, Oakland, and San Francisco eliminate the spending limit in any electoral contest when independent expenditures designed to influence that race exceed a specified amount.[66] New York eliminates the spending limit when a participating candidate faces a nonparticipating opponent who receives contributions or makes expenditures in excess of 50 percent of the spending limit, and it also increases the public match. As a result of the amendments enacted in 2004 the match rate was raised from 5-to-1 to 6-to-1. Potentially more significantly, the law now permits a participating candidate facing a high-spending nonparticipating opponent to receive a public grant of up to 125 percent of the spending limit.[67]

States have also addressed the impact of spending by nonparticipating candidates or independent committees on publicly funded candidates. In seven states, if a nonparticipating candidate exceeds the expenditure limit for a publicly funded candidate, the state either provides a participating candidate with more money, or raises the spending limit. Similarly, six states deal with independent expenditures against a participating candidate by either providing the targeted participating candidate with more matching funds or counting the independent spending against the spending limit of the participating candidate who is benefited by the spending.[68]

In the tri-state area, New Jersey is the only state with a public funding program. Since 1974, the state has made matching grants available to candidates for governor. A candidate who collects $300,000 in contributions of $3,000 or less is eligible for matching grants, but must accept a spending ceiling of $4,400,000 for the primary and $9,600,000 for the general election. In the 2005 gubernatorial election, neither major party candidate accepted public funding. Instead, each spent well above the spending ceilings—with Democrat Jon Corzine spending $39 million and Republican Douglas Forrester spending $12 million in the Republican primary and $19 million in the general election.[69] In 2004, New Jersey also voted to create a pilot legislative public funding program by providing public funds on a "clean money" two candidates in two state legislative districts in the 2005 general election. A nine-member commission is to review the program with an eye to its possible expansion to primary and general elections in 2007. After 2007, the ELEC will then report on the feasibility of making the program permanent.[70]

As previously noted, although no state in the tri-state area has a full-fledged public funding, New York City has made public funding available to qualifying and participating candidates for city-wide office, borough president, and city council—in primary, runoff, and general elections—since 1989. As most recently revised, the program particularly rewards small contributions by providing a 4-to-1 public match for each dollar a New York City resident gives, up to $250, to a participating candidate. In 2005, the program provided up to $3.15 million in public funds to a mayoral candidate in each of the primary and general elections, with the candidate subject to a $5.728 million cap for each election. The comparable amounts for a city council candidate were $82,500, and $150,000. As previously indicated, for a candidate facing a well-financed nonparticipating opponent, qualifying contributions are matched at a 6-to-1 rate up to $7.16 million for a mayoral candidate, and $187,500 for a council candidate.

FEDERAL CAMPAIGN FINANCE LAW AND STATE/LOCAL REGULATION

FEDERAL REGULATION OF STATE AND LOCAL ACTORS

Although federal campaign finance law regulates elections for federal office, federal law can affect state and local officials, candidates, parties, and political committees.

One federal law that directly implicates state and local politics is the Internal Revenue Code. In order for contributions to political committees not to be treated as income taxable to the recipient—or as gifts taxable to the donor—Congress in 1975 created Section 527 expressly for political organizations and provided that contributions to Section 527 organizations to pay for expenditures to influence or attempt to influence federal, state, or local elections are tax-exempt. As initially enacted, Section 527 asked relatively little of the organizations to which it applied. It included no requirements concerning the reporting or disclosure of the officers and directors of the organization or of its contributions or expenditures. In the late 1990s, Section 527 organizations active in federal elections became more controversial, and in 2000 Congress amended Section 527 to impose new reporting and disclosure rules, requiring the organizations to register and report the names and addresses of their officers, directors, and principal employees to the IRS, as well as to periodically report the names and addresses of contributors or $200 or more per year and the amounts of their donations, and the amounts, dates, and purposes of expenditures of $500 or more per year. As originally enacted, the new 527 requirements applied to organizations active in state and local elections as well as to federal or mixed federal-state-local committees. In 2002, Congress amended the law to exempt from IRS disclosure requirements 527 organizations engaged solely in state and local electoral activity that report and disclose their contributions and expenditures under a qualifying state law regime.[71] However, for any state or local political committee that operates in a state without a comparable disclosure rule, the Internal Revenue Code applies. Moreover, with Congress currently debating new contribution and expenditure restrictions for 527s, it remains a possibility that any new laws will apply to political committees engaged primarily (albeit not exclusively) in state and local elections.[72]

More significant federal regulation of state and local actors can be found in BCRA. As part of its effort to drive soft money—that is, money that does not comply with the dollar contribution limitations and source prohibitions of federal campaign law—out of federal elections, Congress regulated contributions to and expenditures by state and local parties. As the Supreme Court observed, "given the close ties between federal candidates and state party committees, BCRA's restrictions on national committee activity would rapidly become ineffective if state and local committees remained available as a conduit for soft-money donations."[73] Specifically, Congress defined four categories of "federal election activity" which, when undertaken by state and local parties, can be financed only with money that complies with federal law. These "federal election activities" are: (i) voter registration activity within 120 days before a regularly scheduled election for federal office; (ii) voter identification, get-out-the-vote and "generic" campaign activity in connection with an election; (iii) "public communications" that promote or attack a candidate for federal office; and (iv) the services of any state committee employee who spends more than 25 percent of his or her compensated time on federal election activities. In other words, if a state party wants to spend money promoting its entire ticket in an upcoming general election in which both federal and state candidates are on the ballot, all the money it uses to pay for that activity must comply with federal law (even though state law might permit larger individual contributions than federal law would allow, or state law would permit corporate or union contributions where federal law forbids them).[74]

BCRA makes a complicated exception to the general requirement that state parties comply with federal law when they engage in federal election activity. Under the so-called Levin Amendment, state and local parties can accept individual contributions above the federal ceiling up to $10,000 (if that is consistent with state law) for voter registration, voter identification drives, get-out-the-vote and generic campaign activities that support both federal and nonfederal candidates so long as the activities so funded do not specifically refer to a federal candidate, and so long as the funds are raised entirely by the state or local committee that spends them and are not transferred from the national party or from another state.[75]

State and local parties are also prohibited from donating soft money to or soliciting soft funds for tax-exempt organizations.[76] This, too, was seen as a means of preventing evasion of the exclusion of soft money from federal elections. Finally, BCRA includes a provision aimed directly at state and local officeholders and candidates. Like state and local parties, they are prohibited from spending soft funds to pay for public communications that promote or support, or attack or oppose, a clearly identified candidate for federal office.[77]

In short, the thrust of BCRA's restrictions is to require state and local candidates, officeholders, and parties either (i) to abide by federal campaign finance law when they support federal candidates or a ticket composed of federal and state/local candidates or when they engage in election-related activities in connection with an election in which federal candidates are on the ballot, or (ii) if possible, to sharply separate their electioneering for nonfederal candidates from their electioneering for federal candidates.

It appears that BCRA had a significant impact on state parties in 2004—the first presidential election to which it applied. National party transfers to state and local parties dropped sharply between 2000 and 2004, and on balance state parties had smaller budgets in 2004 than in 2000. But for many state parties the loss of national party soft money was at least partly offset by increases from other sources. BCRA's increase in the hard money contribution limits enabled the parties to raise more in hard money. So, too, corporate and union contributions to state parties increased in the states where they are permitted. Some state parties received more money from other political committees or from candidates. And some state party organizations—particularly, state legislative campaign committees—which had not received national party soft money transfers in the past were largely unaffected by BCRA.[78]

Studies have found that state parties responded to BCRA by changing their spending patterns. In general, they spent much less on media, particularly on issue ads, and put less money in their federal accounts.[79] Instead, they spent a higher fraction of their funds on state campaign activities and in supporting state candidates and local party committees. Indeed, "[d]espite the significant reduction in their budgets, state parties actually increased their support to candidates and local party committees in 2004, compared with the 2000 presidential election cycle."[80]

The pattern of state party fundraising and spending in the first post-BCRA election suggests that the fears of some BCRA critics that the anti-soft money provisions would cripple state parties financially were significantly overstated. To be sure, in 2004 state parties received considerably less money from the national party committees. But the evidence suggests that the money sent by the national parties before BCRA was effectively controlled by the national parties and was used to advance the national parties' agendas, particularly in promoting the party's presidential candidate. In effect, the state parties were tools of the national party, and could not use money from the national parties for state/local purposes. State parties got less national party money in 2004, but the money they raised was more fully theirs, and was more likely to be deployed for state and local electoral purposes. The capacity of state and local parties to support state and local candidates appears to have been strengthened, or at least not to have been impaired.

On the other hand, BCRA does promote a greater financial separation of the national parties from state and local parties, and, potentially, of candidates for federal office from their state and local ticketmates. It is not clear if that is a good thing.

Yet, as the development of soft money in the decades before BCRA suggests, in a federal system, with two sets of elections and two sets of election rules operating simultaneously, in order for federal election law to regulate federal elections effectively, either federal law must apply to state elections and state electoral actors, or there must be an institutional separation of federal from state/local election participants. Federal campaign finance law does not generally apply to state/local elections. But with BCRA on the books there is both greater application of federal law to state/local parties and candidates than hitherto and some structural incentives to separate federal from state/local election activity. (Or at least, all this appears to be the case based on the one post-BCRA federal election so far conducted).

FEDERAL CONSTITUTIONAL
CONSTRAINTS ON STATE AND LOCAL
CAMPAIGN FINANCE LAW

Regardless of the reach of federal statutory law, federal constitutional law shapes and constrains state and local regulation of state and local campaign finances. *Buckley v. Valeo* held that campaign contributions and expenditures are activities protected by the First Amendment, and in subsequent cases the Court applied the First Amendment to state and local campaign finance laws. Thus, state and local governments, like the federal government, are prohibited from limiting campaign expenditures by candidates or independent political committees, and state and local contribution restrictions and disclosure requirements are also subject to constitutional review. In fact, the constitution applies to state and local electoral practices that have no federal counterpart, such as judicial elections or ballot propositions.

Indeed, the Court recently emphasized that the First Amendment applies to judicial campaign speech,[81] and it has been particularly aggressive in applying the constitutional protection of campaign finance activity to ballot propositions. Although the Court has consistently upheld dollar restrictions on contributions to candidates, it invalidated dollar restrictions on contributions to ballot proposition committees. Restrictions on contributions to candidates were upheld on the theory that they reduced the danger of the corruption of officeholders, but since contributions to ballot proposition committees presented no threat of candidate/officeholder corruption, the Court struck them down.[82] So, too, while the Court upheld the ban on corporate spending in connection with a candidate election, it struck down a state's prohibition on corporate spending concerning a ballot proposition.[83]

Of course, not all campaign finance doctrine serves to preclude regulation. Some constitutional decisions support regulation. The Court has generally upheld disclosure requirements; limits on individual, PAC, and party contributions to and coordinated expenditures with candidates; restrictions on corporate and union campaign finance activity in candidate elections; and the provision of public funding to candidates, including requirements that candidates accept spending limits as a condition for public funding—provided that the candidate's acceptance of funding-plus-limits is voluntary.

Moreover, changes in doctrine can expand or contract the space available for state and local campaign finance regulation. For example, the 2000 decision in *Nixon v. Shrink Missouri Government PAC*[84] adopted a more deferential approach to contribution restrictions, with

the Court approving a state's decision to lower its contribution limits on a relatively slim empirical showing. So, too, the Court has been increasingly willing to accept restrictions on practices that may not themselves present a danger of corruption in order to prevent campaign actors from evading restrictions that do prevent corruption.[85] Thus, *McConnell v. FEC* upheld BCRA's extensive regulation of national party finances, including the financing party activities not related to federal theories, on precisely such an anti-circumvention theory. Presumably the same rationale would support greater state regulation of state party finances.

McConnell's validation of BCRA's electioneering communication not only widened the scope of federal disclosure law and of the federal restriction on corporate and union campaign spending but also provides states and local governments to similarly expand the scope of their campaign finance laws. Prior to McConnell, the Court had limited the regulable campaign finance practices of non-candidate individuals, committees, and organizations to contributions and expenditures that expressly advocated the election or defeat of clearly identified candidate. The express advocacy requirement exempted from regulation campaign expenditures that effectively promoted or opposed a candidate but avoided the so-called "magic words" of express advocacy. In finding constitutional Congress's broader definition of regulable "electioneering communication" the Court also implicitly gave the green light to more state regulation of electioneering activity that technically avoids express advocacy—as federal and state courts have since recognized.[86] Thus, states that limit their disclosure requirements to political committees engaged only in the express advocacy of the election or defeat of candidates could presumably expand disclosure to pick up committees that support or oppose candidates without using the magic words of express advocacy.

FEDERAL CAMPAIGN FINANCE LAW AS "MODEL"

Although the first state campaign finance regulations predated federal law, most contemporary state campaign finance laws, like the Federal Election Campaign Act, were enacted in the aftermath of—and in response to—the Watergate scandal. Today, state campaign finance laws generally follow the basic federal template with respect to reporting and disclosure and contribution restrictions. So, too, the earlier state public funding systems tended to emulate the matching grant format of the presidential primary public funding system. More recently, Congressional regulation of soft money and issue advocacy under BCRA—once validated by the Supreme Court in McConnell—has provided a model for states seeking regulate these practices at the state level.

Of course, another way to think about the federal "model" is that it provides a model of rules or practices to avoid. Federal law has been problematic in a number of areas; I will give brief attention to just three.

Contribution Limits: First, for nearly three decades—from 1974 through 2002—federal limits on contributions by individuals and PACs to candidates, by individuals to PACs and political parties, and on aggregate annual individual donations remained constant. In other words, they were steadily eroded by inflation so that by 2002 they had been effectively lowered by two-thirds. The steady de facto drop in the contribution ceiling no doubt contributed both to the growing pressures of fundraising and to the increased interest of donors and candidates alike in finding money outside the scope of federal restrictions. It was not until BCRA's enactment that Congress raised the limits on individual and party contributions and provided that they would thereafter be indexed to increases in the cost of living. If the purpose of contribution limits is to address the threat of undue influence of large donors without denying candidates the funds they need to campaign, then some regulation revision of the limits in light of changes in campaign costs is essential. Indeed, many states, including New York and New Jersey, have long provided for the automatic indexing of contribution limits or regularly revise those limits in light of inflation.

So, too, federal law oddly imposes the same maximum contribution limit on individual and PAC donations to candidates for the House of Representatives, the Senate, and President despite the enormous differences in the size of the constituencies for these offices and in the campaign treasuries needed to mount a vigorous electoral effect in each case. It seems implausible that an arguably corrupting donation to a candidate for the House would be just as corrupting to a presidential candidate amassing 50 to 100 times the funds as his or her House counterpart. Indeed, many states with contribution limits—including New York—vary the limit in light of the size of the electorate for the office sought.

Public Funding: The federal presidential public funding program suffers from a number of shortcomings, of which the most important (and linked) are inadequate levels of grants to candidates and unduly low spending ceilings. The tight spending ceilings contributed directly to the explosive growth of soft money in the 1990s. More recently, an increasing number of significant presidential candidates have chosen to opt out of presidential primary public funding. In 2000, George W. Bush became the first major party presidential nominee to opt out of public funding since its inception in 1976, and in 2004 for the first time since Watergate both major party nominees had foregone public funding in the primary phase of the election. There is currently considerable speculation that some of the major aspirants for 2008 might forego public funding in the general election as well.

Indeed, one—perhaps unintended—consequence of BCRA is to make public funding even less attractive to primary candidates. BCRA, as noted, doubled and indexed the limit on hard money donations to federal candidates, but did not increase either the level at which hard money contributions would be matched with public dollars ($500 since 1976) or the match ratio. As a result, it is now much more attractive to fund a presidential primary campaign with private, hard dollars.

The presidential experience indicates that states considering the adoption of public funding ought to be sure that the state provides adequate funding and permits spending consistent with the needs of a contemporary, hotly contested campaign. The purpose of public funding should be not to cut the level of campaign spending but to reduce the dependence of candidates on large private donors and to provide challengers with the funding necessary to enable them to run competitive races. Congress might want to look to some subnational examples—such as New York City's 4-to-1 match for smaller contributions—in revising the funding of presidential candidates.

So, too, federal law does not consider the impact of nonparticipating (and, thus, unlimited) candidates on candidates who choose public funds with spending limits. The prospect of being wildly outspent by an opponent may discourage a candidate from accepting spending limits. Some states and localities have addressed this possibility by either providing a participating candidate (who has a nonparticipating opponent) with more funds than otherwise, lifting the spending ceiling, or both. Again, here the states and localities may be something of a model for Congress.

Administration and Enforcement: Campaign finance regulation requires fair and effective administration and enforcement but the Federal Election Commission has long been subject to criticism from journalists, academics, public interest groups, and election lawyers. Indeed, it has been dubbed a "toothless tiger" and a "wobbly watchdog" that has "neither the will nor the means to deter wanton violators."[87] The FEC catches few election law violations; fails to penalize most of those it catches; and imposes penalties that are so small, and come so long after the election, that they do not have a meaningful deterrent effect.[88] The FEC's problems result from a combination of structural, political, and legal factors that appear to reflect a congressional desire to make the commission ineffective.

The structure and procedures for the administration and enforcement of campaign finance laws are profoundly difficult questions. We need an agency capable of taking vigorous and decisive action—of acting in "real time" to prevent campaign finance violations during the election in which they are occurring and of punishing and deterring lawbreakers. Yet, we also need an agency that is fair, not controlled by one party or officeholder, and subject to constraints that prevent it from abusing its mandate and intervening in elections—and potentially displacing the democratic process—when such intervention is not warranted. Moreover, the election finance agency is charged with the delicate task of regulating the very elected officials who have the authority to appoint and confirm its members, control its budget, and determine its legal powers. Elected officials are aware of just how crucial agency determinations can be for their electoral futures. Thus, vigorous activity can result in a loss of legal authority and fiscal resources. Some measures are needed to make the agency at least partially independent of the political process; yet the agency, like all other arms of government, must ultimately be accountable to the political process.

It is not clear that any jurisdiction has resolved this conundrum, and state electoral agencies may be as ineffective as the federal or unduly partisan.[89] But with 50 state campaign finance regulators and a number of significant local agencies at work, there may be models of successful campaign finance administration worthy of closer study. Certainly, New York City's Campaign Finance Board is highly regarded. Other agencies like New Jersey's Election Law Enforcement Commission appear to take a highly professional approach. Campaign finance administration is one area where the diverse state and local experiences are worthy of close consideration.

CONCLUSION: TRENDS AND CHALLENGES FOR THE FUTURE

CONTRIBUTION RESTRICTIONS

Part II's overview of state contribution restrictions indicates some interesting developments, particularly in the regulation of pay-to-play contributions by government contractors or by lobbyists. These restrictions fit nicely with the central purpose of contribution limitations—controlling the dangers of corruption and the appearance of corruption. Both pay-to-play and lobbyist limitations target donors whose goals are likely to be access to government officials and influencing the provision of government benefits rather than broader political, ideological, or electoral goals. And both types of limitations would tend to promote more competitive elections.

On the first point, scholars sometimes distinguish between contributions made for "electoral" purposes—e.g., to help the recipient win office—and those made for "legislative" or "access" or "influence" purposes, that is, to make it more likely that they will have access to elected officials. For the first type of contribution, the donor is using the donation (and the candidate) to advance ideological goals, really cares who wins, and may not be seeking anything from the recipient (other than the satisfaction of having an elected official who favors the policies the donor likes). For the second type of contribution, the donor is using the donation to advance more material goals, does not care who wins (the donor may be giving to both candidates), and is looking for something in return. The case for First Amendment protection seems stronger in the first situation; the corruption and appearance of corruption dangers seem stronger.

While it would be difficult to draw a hard and fast distinction between the two types of contributors—some may seek to advance both ideological and material goals—government contractors and lobbyists (particularly lobbyists making contributions to legislators in the legislative session) would appear to epitomize "access" contributors. Tight restrictions on these donors would advance the goals of anti-corruption goals of campaign finance regulation with limited impact on speech.

So, too, contractors and lobbyists give the lion's share of their donations to incumbents. After all, the incumbents are currently in position to provide the contracts, laws, and benefits that contractors and lobbyists are seeking. Their donations, thus, reinforce the pro-incumbent bias of the private campaign finance system. Restricting donations by individuals and groups that are almost inevitably pro-incumbent (regardless of party or ideological) could advance the goal of more competitive elections.

PUBLIC FUNDING

The most promising recent development in state and local campaign finance law has been the growing interest in public funding. As already noted, Minnesota, Arizona, and Maine have significant state-wide public funding programs in place, North Carolina recently provided for public funding for judicial elections, and Connecticut just adopted a "clean money" system for all state elections which will take effect later this decade. So, too, a number of large cities, including New York, Los Angeles, and San Francisco have some form of public funding in place for municipal elections, with Portland, Oregon, most recently joining that group.

Public funding provides a means of vindicating the principle goals of campaign finance reform—constraining the influence of large donors and interest groups, promoting competitive elections, alleviating the burdens of fundraising—without limiting and indeed expanding the resources available for campaign communications. Moreover, the core elements of public funding—that is, the provision of public funds with the requirement of a spending ceiling for publicly funded candidates—long ago received the Supreme Court's constitutional imprimatur. Public funding should be an important focus for campaign finance reformers at the state and local level.

To be sure, public funding raises a host of legal and policy issues. Under Buckley, a state or locality cannot mandate that candidates take public funding (with conditions). The decision to accept public funding must be voluntary. Of course, states can to some extent manipulate campaign finance law to induce candidate participation. For example, a state may set a higher contribution ceiling for a publicly funded candidate than for candidates who decline public funding.[90] So, too, states can eliminate some of the disincentives to participation by providing participating candidates facing nonparticipating high-spending opponents with additional funds or by releasing them from the spending ceilings.[91] The most difficult constitutional question that has arisen so far concerns what a state may do when a participating candidate is targeted by independent expenditures. Courts have divided over the constitutionality of state laws that provide participating candidates with additional public funds.[92] Presumably a statute that simply raised the spending limit for such a candidate would be constitutional.

Public funding also poses a number of policy questions—who should receive funding, how much, on what basis, subject to what spending limit? Should all qualifying candidates receive the same public grant, or should the amount of public funding differ for major party as opposed to minor party nominees? Should public funding aim to fully replace private funding, as in "clean money" systems, or be provided as a match to private grants (with the assumption that some significant fraction of total campaign money will remain private)?[93] States have shown growing interest in the clean money version, although New York City's four-to-one matching grant program demonstrates that matching funds can provide most of the benefits of public money while leaving room for significant private participation.

The key point for all programs is that they provide enough money to support effective, well-funded campaigns. Campaign finance reformers too often conflate unequal campaign war chests or "strings-attached" money with the asserted "evil" of money itself. But there is nothing wrong with high levels of campaign spending. Indeed, campaign spending is essential if candidates are to get out their ideas and positions, and if voters are to be informed and mobilized. Candidates, parties, and voters need well-funded campaigns. Campaign money is a problem only when it is unequally available or comes with obligations to donors. The goal of campaign finance reform—and of public funding—should be to assure that candidates have enough money to fund competitive elections without being dependent on private donors.

To be sure, public funding is no panacea. Under current constitutional law, elections cannot be fully publicly funded. Candidates cannot be forced into public funding, and spending by wealthy candidates and well-funded interest groups cannot be limited. Even the best public funding systems cannot control the spending of Douglas Forrester, Jon Corzine, or Michael Bloomberg. Still, even in those settings, public funding—if provided at adequate levels—can make it possible for non-wealthy candidates can get their message out without dependence on private donors.

Moreover, there may be some benefits in continuing to provide some room for private money in a campaign finance system. Public funding matching systems usually provide minor parties and independents with less money than their major party counterparts, and even in a clean money system where all qualifying candidates receive the same grant, political newcomers might prefer to take advantage of the greater spending available if they rely on private contributors in order to get their messages out. So, too, privately funded independent committees can play an important role in electoral communication and voter mobilization.

Still, public funding, if provided in realistic amounts, can play an important role in freeing candidates from a dependence on large donors, and in enabling candidates without wealthy supporters to mount competitive campaigns.

FEDERAL CONSTITUTIONAL DOCTRINE
In recent years, the Supreme Court has been relatively deferential to campaign finance regulation, at both the federal and subnational levels. In the four campaign finance cases it decided between 2000 and 2003, the Court took a pro-regulatory position each time.[94] In so doing, the Court reduced its already low standard of review for contribution restrictions; upheld tighter spending and contribution limits for corporations, unions, and political parties; repeatedly endorsed the "anti-circumvention" justification for limiting practices not necessarily corrupting in order to prevent evasion of anti-corruption rules; and, generally, signaled both a greater sympathy for campaign finance regulation and a greater deference to the political branches in the determination of what campaign finance practices require restriction. Indeed, when the Court agreed to take the

Vermont spending limits case, many commentators concluded that it was not out of the question that the Court would use the case to revisit and relax Buckley's ban on spending limits.

The recent changes in the composition of the Court—particularly the replacement of Justice O'Connor by Justice Alito—as well as the Court's most recent actions, suggest that the Court's support for regulation may have peaked and a change in trajectory may be imminent. In January 2006, the Court, for the first time in a decade, decided in favor of a challenge to campaign finance regulation, when it held in *Wisconsin Right to Life, Inc. v. FEC*[95] that the McConnell decision did not preclude an "as applied" challenge to BCRA's ban on corporate electioneering communications. A fairly minor decision in itself—the Court did not hold that BCRA does not apply but only that McConnell did not resolve the question—WRTL may be a straw in the wind, indicative of changes to come. A month later, the oral argument in the Vermont spending limits case indicated not only that the Court is unlikely to alter Buckley's invalidation of spending limits, but that many of the justices were skeptical of Vermont's low contribution limits and sympathetic to the speech concerns implicated by campaign finance regulation. Conceivably, the Court in Randall could either stiffen its standard of review of contribution restrictions or apply the current standard less deferentially by requiring states to provide greater proof that a particular restriction is required by anti-corruption concerns.

Another area in which the Court's doctrine could change concerns the prohibition on corporate and union campaign activity. In McConnell, the four justices who dissented from the Court's invalidation of BCRA's extension of the corporate and union bans to electioneering communications focused not on electioneering communications but on the corporate and union bans more generally. They would have invalidated the general bans on corporate and union campaign expenditures. Justice O'Connor was part of the majority that found the corporate and union prohibitions constitutional. Her replacement by Justice Alito could transform the Court's approach to this longstanding element of campaign finance law. Such a decision would result in the invalidation of laws in roughly two dozen states.

At this point it is, of course, premature to conclude that any changes are in the offing. The WRTL decision was entirely consistent with existing law. A decision in the Randall case striking down the spending limits but upholding the contribution limits would be consistent with existing doctrine, too. The Court's invalidation of Vermont's contribution limits would be a more substantial action, although its significance would be shaped by the Court's actual reasoning.

Of course, even if the court strikes down the Vermont contribution limits, many state limits are likely to be unaffected. Vermont's limits, by most measures, are the lowest in the country.

New York's, by contrast, are among the highest. Even New Jersey's limits on individual donations are higher than the federal levels, and Pennsylvania has no dollar limits at all. So long as the Court adheres to Buckley's basic idea that contributions can be limited, it would seem that New York could lower its limits significantly, and Pennsylvania could adopt limits, without running afoul of the constitution. So, too, many of the recent state initiatives in the area of contributions—anti-pay-to-play rules, restrictions on contributions during the legislative session and/or by lobbyists—are more clearly targeted on activities likely to be seen as raising the dangers of corruption and the appearance of corruption and are more likely to pass constitutional muster.

State and local campaign finance regulation inevitably operates within a policy space constrained by federal constitutional law. Right now, federal constitutional law gives states and localities considerable room for regulatory initiatives—in terms of disclosure requirements, contribution restrictions, very tight limits on corporations and unions, and public funding with spending limits. The only significant regulatory tool flatly prohibited is mandatory spending limitation. Certainly many states could undertake far more extensive regulatory measures than they have. However, with a changing Court currently considering an important case, constitutional doctrine—and the regulatory possibilities available to states and localities—may be subject to change.

References

1. 540 U.S. 93 (2003).

2. See, e.g., Michael J. Malbin, A Public Funding System in Jeopardy: Lessons from the Presidential Nomination Contest of 2004, 5 *Elec. L. J.* 2 (2006).

3. 424 U.S. 1 (1976)

4. *Austin v. Michigan Chamber of Commerce,* 494 U.S. 652 (1990) (corporations); *McConnell v. FEC, supra,* (corporations and unions).

5. Buckley, *supra,* 424 U.S. at 57 n. 65.

6. Louise Overacker, *Money in Elections* 291–94 (1932).

7. 25 P.S. § 1626.

8. 25 P.S. § 3248.

9. 25 P.S. § 3260a.

10. New Jersey Election Law Enforcement Commission, General Overview of Filing Requirements, www.elec.state.nj.us/ForCandidates/overview.htm.

11. *Id.*

12. New Jersey Election Law Enforcement Commission, "Pay-to-Play" Fact Sheet.

13. See Overacker, *Money in Elections, supra,* at 303–05 (as of 1932, 34 states prohibited contributions from corporations but only two states limited contribution amounts); Alexander Heard, *The Costs of Democracy* 130, 347 (as of 1959 about 30 states barred corporate contributions but only four limited contribution amounts).

14. See National Conference of State Legislatures, Campaign Finance, www.ncsl.org/programs/legman/about/campfin.htm. The five states that place no limits on campaign contributions are Illinois, New Mexico, Oregon, Utah, and Virginia.

15. See National Conference of State Legislatures, Contribution Limits, www.ncsl.org/programs/legman/about/ContribLimits.htm.

16. *Id.* Arkansas, California, Colorado, Louisiana, and Michigan have similar provisions.

17. Louisiana, Massachusetts, Minnesota, Montana, Nebraska, and Wisconsin also impose ceilings on aggregate PAC donations to a candidate. *Id.*

18. In Kentucky, most candidates cannot accept PAC contributions which in the aggregate exceed 50 percent of total contributions, or $10,000, whichever is greater, in an election cycle. Tennessee has a similar law.

19. *Id.*

20. National Conference of State Legislatures, Limits on Contributions during the Legislative Session, www.ncsl.org/programs/legman/about/duringsessionchart.htm. (Oct. 24, 2003).

21. See Nat'l Civic League, Local Campaign Fin. Reform (Feb. 2002), www.ncl.org/npp/lcf/inventory.html. Roughly two-thirds of the cities and counties that adopted campaign finance measures are in California. Other states where multiple local governments have been active in campaign finance reform include Colorado, Ohio, Washington, Maryland, Florida, Illinois, North Carolina, and Utah.

22. See Jia-Rui Chong, "Court Gives Campaign Finance Laws a Green Light," *Los Angeles Times,* May 21, 2005 (upholding Santa Monica, Pasadena, and Claremont "pay-to-play" prohibitions).

23. See *id.* The recusal requirement does not apply where the benefit to the donor is "merely incidental to an issue or question involving the common public good." The Westminster charter amendment, which was adopted in 1996, bears a close resemblance to the "recusal alternative" to contribution limits proposed by Professor John Copeland Nagle a few years later. See John Copeland Nagel, "The Recusal Alternative to Campaign Finance Legislation," 37 *Harv. J. Legis.* 69 (2000).

24. See Nat'l Civic League, Addendum To Local Campaign Fin. Reform: Additional Case Studies 45–47 (2001), www.ncl.org/npp/lcfr/lcfr_addendum.pdf.

25. 9 N.Y.C.R.R. 6214.0.

26. See *The $2,100 Club: What New York State Political Campaigns Cost, How Much Those Costs Are Rising, and Who's Footing the Bill,* A Common Cause/NY Report (March 2006), at 3.

27. N.Y. Elec. L. § 14–124 (3).

28. Michael Cooper, "Political Donations Pour Through Gap in New York Laws," *New York Times*, Feb. 17, 2005, at A1.

29. $2100 Club, *supra*, at 29.

30. 9 N.Y.C.R.R. 6214.0.

31. New York City Campaign Finance Board, Contribution Limits, Spending Limits, and Public Funds Requirements 2005 Citywide Elections, www.nyccfb.info/program_law/program_infro/program_2005_inf.htm. The ability of a candidate to contribute an unlimited amount to his or her own campaign is protected by *Buckley v. Valeo*.

32. New Jersey Election Law Enforcement Commission, Contribution Limits Chart, www.elec.state.nj.us/ForCandidates/elec_limits.html.

33. *Id.*

34. Overacker, *Money in Elections, supra*, at 308–12.

35. *Homans v. City of Albuquerque*, 160 F.Supp.2d 1266 (D. N.M. 2001), 217 F.Supp.2d 1200 (D.N.M. 2002).

36. *Id.* at 1206.

37. *Homans v. City of Albuquerque*, 366 F.3d 900 (10th Cir. 2004).

38. *Kruse v. City of Cincinnati*, 142 F.3d 907, 910 (6th Cir. 1998).

39. *Id.* at 911.

40. *Id.* at 915. One member of the Kruse panel, however, took issue with the panel's reasoning and raised the suggestion that spending limitations could also be justified by "the interest in preserving faith in democracy." *Id.* at 919 (Cohn, D.J., concurring).

41. Pitkin County, Colorado, also challenged Buckley when, in 1996, a voter initiative amended its charter to impose a spending limit in local elections. When the constitutionality of the provision was challenged on the eve of the 2000 elections, the county attorney, concerned about the measure's constitutionality, declined to enforce it. See Nat'l Civic League, Addendum To Local Campaign Fin. Reform: Additional Case Studies 14–15 (2001), www.ncl.org/npp/lcfr/lcfr_addendum.pdf.

42. Nat'l Civic League, Local Campaign Fin. Reform: Case Studies, Innovative and Model Legislation, (2005), www.ncl.org/npp/lcfr/lcfr_first_ed_ summary.html.

43. *Vt. Stat. Ann. Tit.* 17, § § 2801–2883 (2004).

44. *Landell v. Sorrell*, 382 F.3d 91 (2d Cir. 2004).

45. Overacker, *supra*, at 318.

46. See Center for Governmental Studies, State Public Financing Laws 2005.

47. Kenneth R. Mayer, *Timothy Werner, Amanda Williams, Do Public Funding Programs Enhance Electoral Competition?* (March 2005) at 21.

48. *Id.* at 18–19.

49. *Id.* at 21.

50. *Id.* For more information on the Arizona and Maine programs, see The Reform Institute, Enhancing Values: Practical Campaign Reforms for States 5–26, www.reforminstitute.org, Clean Elections Institute, Reclaiming Democracy in Arizona: How Clean Elections have expanded the universe of campaign contributors, www.azclean.org, Raymond LaRaja & Matthew Saradjian, *Clean Elections: An Evaluation of Public Funding for Maine Legislative Contests* (Center for Public Policy and Administration, April 2004). For a more critical evaluation, see John Samples, ed., *Welfare for Politicians? Taxpayer Financing of Campaigns* 31–106 (2005).

51. Institute on Money in *State Politics, State Elections Overview* 2004 (December 2005) at 13–14.

52. See Paul Ryan, Beyond BCRA: Cutting-Edge Campaign Finance Reform at the Local Government Level, 92 *Nat'l Civ. Rev.* 3, 4 (2003). Of the four programs no longer in operation, three were terminated as the result of state-level voter initiatives, two in Washington state and one in California. There is a good argument that the California measure was terminated erroneously by a state court. Sacramento County had adopted public funding in 1986. In 1988, California voters passed Proposition 73, which banned the payment of public funds to candidates. In 1990, an intermediate California appellate court held that this preempted the Sacramento public funding system. County of *Sacramento v. Fair Political Practices Comm'n.*, 271 Cal. Rptr. 802 (Cal. Ct. App. 1990). However, two years later, in a case in which Proposition 73 was used to challenge Los Angeles' public funding system, the California Supreme Court upheld the Los Angeles public funding program and labeled the Sacramento

decision—which was possibly distinguishable because it involved a county and not a home rule city—"highly questionable." *Johnson v. Bradley*, 841 P.2d 990, 1001 (Cal. 1992). The fourth defunct public funding program, in Cincinnati Ohio, was terminated by a local ballot measure. See Center For Governmental Stud., Public Financing Laws In Local Jurisdictions 5 n.1 (2005) available at www.cgs.org/publications/docs/PublicFinancingLaws2005.pdf.

53. As of this writing, Portland is the most recent major city to have adopted public funding. In May 2005, the city council passed an ordinance creating a voluntary public funding system for city auditor, city commissioner, and mayor. The first election to be held with public funding is the May 2006 primary. See Publicly Financed Campaigns in Portland—Ordinance and Report, available at www.portlandonline.com/auditor/index.cfm?c=37740.

54. See Paul Ryan, Center for Governmental Stud., A Statute of Liberty: How New York City's Campaign Finance Law Is Changing the Face of Local Elections 15 (2003), www.cgs.org/publications/docs/ nycreport.pdf (referring to the New York City law as a "model for the nation"). See also Paul Ryan, Center for Governmental Stud., Eleven Years of Reform: Many Successes—More to Be Done, Campaign Financing in the City of Los Angeles (2001), available at www.cgs.org/publications/docs/lacamp_fin.pdf [hereinafter Ryan, Eleven Years]; Paul Ryan, Center for Governmental Stud., Political Reform That Works: Public Campaign Financing Blooms in Tucson (2003), available at www.cgs.org/publications/ docs/Political_Reform_That_Works.pdf [hereinafter Ryan, Public Financing Blooms].

55. See Ryan, *A Statute of Liberty*, at 21–23 (candidate participation rate was 79 percent in New York City in 2001 elections); Ryan, Eleven Years, at 18–19 (serious candidate participation in Los Angeles was 70 percent in 2001); Ryan, *Public Financing Blooms*, at 9–11 (100 percent participation rate in Tucson program in 2001 and 2003 elections).

56. See Ryan, *A Statute of Liberty*, at 15–18; Ryan, Eleven Years, at 21–23, 26–28.

57. See Ryan, *A Statute of Liberty*, at 18–21; Ryan, Eleven Years, at 23–24.

58. See Ryan, *Public Financing Blooms*, at 19–21.

59. See Ryan, *Beyond BCRA*, at 7–11.

60. New York's law provides another model for a program funding mechanism "equally well insulated from political pressures." See Ryan, *Beyond BCRA*, at 28; Ryan, *Eleven Years*, at 25.

61. See Ryan, *Public Financing Blooms*, at 16. On the other hand, New York's Campaign Finance Board suggests than an independent administrative body can also do a very successful job. See Ryan, *supra* note 1, at 31–34.

62. See Bradley A. Smith, *Unfree Speech: The Folly of Campaign Finance Reform* 98–102 (2001).

63. See Ryan, *Beyond BCRA*, at 15–18.

64. See Ryan, *Beyond BCRA*, at 11–12.

65. To be sure, Bloomberg's opponent, Mark Green, spent $16.2 million (including $4.5 million in public funds) in the same election, which was more money than any successful candidate for New York mayor had ever spent, other than Bloomberg.

66. Ryan, *Beyond BCRA*, at 11.

67. The law appears to have had little impact on Mayor Bloomberg's campaign spending. In 2005, he spent $84 million—or $10 million more than in 2001—on his successful reelection campaign. See Jim Rutenberg, "Bloomberg Spent $84 Million To Remain Mayor, a Record," *New York Times*, Jan. 14, 2006, at B2. Even with the City's generous matching program, Bloomberg's 2005 general election opponent, Fernando Ferrer, raised only $5.3 million in private contributions and received just $3.9 million in public financing. Ferrer's total spending was just $9.1 million. Public funding accounted for approximately 42 percent of Ferrer's total funding. See Sam Roberts, "Offers of Coal for the Mayor's Newcastle," *New York Times*, Dec. 16, 2005, at B4.

68. Center for Governmental Studies, State Public Financing Laws 2005 at 17–18.

69. Forrester's principal primary opponent, Bret Schundler, did participate in the public funding program. He spent $2.2 million, including $1.5 million in public funds. In the 2001 election, three candidates, including the two major party nominees in the general election, received public funding and accepted spending limits in both the primary and general elections.

70. New Jersey Election Law Enforcement Commission, 2004 Annual Report, at 10.

71. See 26 U.S.C. § 527(e)(5), (j)(5)(C).

72. See Richard Briffault, The 527 Problem . . . and the Buckley Problem, 73 *G.W. L. Rev.* 1701, 1731–32 (2005) (noting that certain pending proposals to regulate 527s would affect organizations primarily focused on state and local elections).

73. *McConnell v. FEC,* 540 U.S. 93, 161 (2003).

74. BCRA explicitly excludes public communications that refer solely to nonfederal candidates; contributions to nonfederal candidates; and the cost of grassroots campaign materials like bumper stickers that refer only to state candidates.

75. 2 U.S.C. § 441i(b)(2).

76. 2 U.S.C. § 441i(d).

77. 2 U.S.C. § 441i(f). Exempted from the restriction are communications made in connection with an election for state or local office which refer only to the state or local candidate or officeholder making the expenditure or to any other candidate for the same state or local office. 2 U.S.C. § 441i(f)(2).

78. See *The Institute on Money in State Politics, Shifting Gears: State Party Strategies Post-BCRA* (Sept. 2005) at 7–12.

79. *Id.* at 12–13.

80. Denise Roth Barber, *Declining Fortunes: State Party Finances,* 2004 (The Institute on Money in State Politics, Sept. 2005) at 15.

81. See *Republican Party of Minnesota v. White,* 536 U.S. 765 (2002). See also *Suster v. Marshall,* 149 F.3d 523 (6th Cir. 1998) (invalidating judicial canon limiting spending in judicial elections).

82. *Citizens Against Rent Control v. City of Berkeley,* 454 U.S. 290 (1981).

83. Compare *First National Bank of Boston v. Bellotti,* 435 U.S. 765 (1978) with *Austin v. Michigan Chamber of Commerce,* 494 U.S. 8/24/2006. 652 (1990). The Court has also invalidated laws prohibiting the payment of people who carry the petitions and solicit the signatures necessary to place a proposition on a ballot. See *Meyer v. Grant,* 486 U.S. 414 (1988).

84. 528 U.S. 377 (2000).

85. See, e.g., *FEC v. Colorado Republican Federal Campaign Committee* (Colorado Republican II), 533 U.S. 431 (2001) (limits on party expenditures coordinated with a candidate justified by need to prevent donors from using parties as conduits for large donations to candidates).

86. See, e.g., *Alaska Right to Life Comm. v. Miles,* __ F.3d __ (9th Cir., Mar. 22, 2006).

87. Richard Briffault, "The Future of Reform: Campaign Finance After the Bipartisan Campaign Reform Act of 2002," 34 *Ariz. St. L.L.* 1179, 1209 (2002).

88. Association of the Bar of the City of New York, *Dollars and Democracy: A Blueprint for Campaign Finance Reform* 75 (2000). See also Brooks Jackson, *Broken Promise: Why the Federal Election Commission Failed* (1990); Project FEC, *No Bark, No Bite, No Point: The Case for Closing the Federal Election Commission and Establishing a New System for Enforcing the Nation's Campaign Finance Laws* (2002).

89. For a critical evaluation of state campaign finance administration and enforcement, see Michael J. Malbin and Thomas L. Gais, *The Day After Reform: Sobering Campaign Finance Lessons from the American States* (1998).

90. See, e.g., *Wilkinson v. Jones,* 876 F.Supp. 916 (W.D. Ky. 1995).

91. See, e.g., *Gable v. Patton,* 142 F.3d 950 (6th Cir. 1998); *Rosenstiel v. Rodriguez,* 101 F.3d 1544 (8th Cir. 1996),

92. *Compare Day v. Holahan,* 34 F.3d 1356 (8th Cir. 1994) with *Daggett v. Commission on Governmental Ethics,* 205 F.3d 445 (1st Cir. 2000).

93. More radically, funding could be effectuated through vouchers provided to voters, who then give the public funds to the candidates of their choice. Voucher plans have drawn some academic support, see, e.g., Bruce Ackerman & Ian Ayres, *Voting with Dollars: A New Paradigm for Campaign Finance* (2002), but no jurisdiction has enacted such a plan.

94. See *Nixon v. Shrink Missouri Gov't PAC,* 528 U.S. 377 (2000); *FEC v. Colorado Republican Federal Campaign Comm.,* 533 U.S. 431 (2001): *McConnell v. FEC,* 540 U.S. 93 (2003); *FEC v. Beaumont,* 539 U.S. 146 (2003).

95. 126 S.Ct. 1016 (2006).

On the Renewal of Section 5 of the VRA: Why Congress Failed Voters of Color

Guy-Uriel E. Charles
University of Minnesota Law
School

Luis Fuentes-Rohwer
Indiana University–Bloomington

The United States Congress has recently renewed Section 5 of the Voting Rights Act (the VRA), one of the most successful civil rights provisions ever enacted. Prompted by the civil rights community, an overwhelmingly bipartisan Congress has passed the Fannie Lou Hamer, Rosa Parks, and Coretta Scott King Voting Rights Act Reauthorization and Amendments Act of 2006 (the Reauthorization Act), and the president has signed it. While one would think that passage of the Renewal Act ought to be a cause for rejoicing, such a reaction would be misguided. Unlike passage of the Voting Rights Act of 1965, which gave rise to the original Section 5, this voting rights bill is high on politics and low on substance. The Reauthorization Act will not do much, if anything at all, to improve the lives of voters of color and does not hold anywhere near the transformative promise that shadowed the original enactment of Section 5 and its subsequent renewals.

Leaving aside the extension of the language assistance requirements and the provision for federal election observers—real contributions that should not be too controversial if considered on their merits—the Reauthorization Act has three goals. First, it reauthorizes the preclearance requirement for covered jurisdictions for the next 25 years. Second, it reverses the Supreme Court's decision in *Reno v. Bossier Parish* (Bossier II),[1] which held that the Department of Justice (DOJ) must approve a redistricting plan that was discriminatory but did not make voters of color worse off. Third, it rejects the Court's contextual approach in *Georgia v. Ashcroft,*[2] where the Court concluded that jurisdictions covered by Section 5 may trade a safe district—a district in which voters are virtually guaranteed the chance to elect the candidate of their choice—for influence or coalition districts—districts in which voters of color may influence the outcome or by coalescing with like-minded voters determine the outcome of an election. Assuming that the amendment accomplishes its stated objectives, none of these aims will substantially improve the positions of voters of color in the political process. In fact, an honest assessment of the renewal amendment might find a scant difference between renewal and allowing Section 5 to sunset.

Perhaps it is unfair to compare the renewal amendment to the original enactment of Section 5. Section 5 was promulgated at a time when voters of color in many parts of the country—specifically African-American voters in the South—were treated as second-class citizens. Much was expected of Section 5 and the provision did not disappoint. In the jurisdictions covered by Section 5, that provision is primarily responsible for the dramatic improvement in voting protections for voters of color. To expect the Reauthorization Act to hold similar promise for dramatically transforming the electoral landscape is perversely unreasonable.

Notwithstanding this caveat on the realistic upper bounds of expectations for a renewed Section 5, Congress' latest effort is deeply disappointing. Congress and the civil rights community have persisted on preserving Section 5 in its current form, for the next 25 years, without critically assessing the needs of voters in the contemporary electoral context. As we argue in this chapter, the primary objection to preserving Section 5 in its current from is that Section 5's extant preclearance mechanism is incapable of responding to the problems that voters of color face in the 21st century. Indeed, the fatal problem with a reactive (and dare we say politically motivated) extension of Section 5 is that Section 5's preclearance mechanism is no longer doing the work it once did. Instead of taking a forward-looking approach and thinking about voting rights challenges for the new millennium, Congress so far appears to be mired in the challenges of the last.

Take the State of New York where three counties—Bronx, King, and New York—are covered by Section 5. For approximately the three and half decades that those counties have been covered, the DOJ has written 18 total objection letters to submission requests from those three counties. The last objection letter was written in 1999. This means that for the last five years, the DOJ has not objected to a single submission from New York. For the last decade the DOJ has objected to only one submission from New York. Given these facts, what is the point of renewing the VRA without assessing the modern voting rights needs of voters from Bronx, King, and New York counties?

As we will show in this paper, New York's experience is typical with respect to the contemporary relevance of the current VRA regulatory framework. Part I of this chapter details the statutory architecture of Section 5 and offers a short contextual history of the events that gave rise to the VRA. Part II shows the almost instantaneous effects that accompanied passage of the Act. Part III demonstrates how few objections are interposed by the DOJ. Part IV argues that the Renewal Act will not do much to ferret out objectionable submissions through the preclearance process.

I.

In its second report, published in 1961, the U.S. Commission for Civil Rights reported that "more persons than ever before are exercising more fully their rights as citizens of the United States."[3] This was welcomed news, as "[t]he gap between the promise of liberty and its

TABLE 1

VAP percentages in states initially covered by VRA

	1965 White	1965 Black	Gap
Alabama	69.2	19.3	49.9
Georgia	62.6	27.4	35.2
Louisiana	80.5	31.6	48.9
Mississippi	69.9	6.7	63.2
North Carolina	96.8	46.8	50.0
South Carolina	75.7	37.3	38.4
Virginia	61.1	38.3	22.8
Average	73.7	29.3	44.0

Sources: U.S. Commission on Civil Rights, Voting (1961); U.S. Commission on Civil Rights, Political Participation (1968).

fulfillment is narrower today than it has ever been."[4] But as the commission made clear, when it came to race, "a gap remain[ed], wide and deep, and the demand to close it is more urgent than ever."[5]

And quite a gap it was. Table 1 provides an estimate of registration percentages between white and black voters in the initial states covered by the VRA the year the VRA was enacted. As Table 1 shows, the average white registration rate in Alabama, Georgia, Louisiana, Mississippi, North Carolina, South Carolina, and Virginia was 73.7 percent. The average registration rate for black voters was 29.3 percent. On average, the registration gap between blacks and whites for the states in question before the enactment of the VRA was 44 percent.

The reasons for this large gap are well-documented. State and local officials, especially in the South, used multiple devices to disenfranchise voters of color. These devices included outright violence, intimidation, and economic reprisals. They also included poll taxes, literacy tests, white primaries, residency requirements, vote dilution, ballot stuffing, and severe racial gerrymandering.[6]

Prior to enacting the VRA, Congress had thrice within the previous 10 years attempted to address the problem of racial discrimination in voting. These attempts had failed largely because Congress had "adopted the alternative of litigation" as a strategy for dealing with racial discrimination in the political process.[7] This strategy was ineffectual for at least two reasons. First, the pace of litigation was "tortuous [and] often ineffective."[8] Second, the worst-offending jurisdictions were consistently unwilling to comply with statutory mandates and judicial decrees, choosing instead to meet attempts at reform by Congress and the courts with "evasion, obstruction, delay, and disrespect."[9]

The VRA must be understood against the backdrop of Congress' previously unsuccessful effort at ridding the political process of racial discrimination. In the words of then-Attorney General Katzenbach, what was needed was "a systematic, automatic method to deal with discriminatory tests, with discriminatory testers, and with discriminatory threats."[10] The VRA was designed to remedy the failings of Congress' previous efforts by making it harder for recalcitrant state and local officials to stay one step ahead of the regulatory frameworks then attempting to shape their behavior.

Indeed, this backdrop of systemic and pervasive discrimination framed the Supreme Court's response when South Carolina challenged the constitutionality of the VRA in *South Carolina v. Katzenbach*.[11] The Court stated that the "constitutional propriety of the Voting Rights Act of 1965 must be judged with reference to the historical experience which it reflects."[12] This experience reflected an encounter with "an insidious and pervasive evil which had been perpetuated in certain parts of our country through unremitting and ingenious defiance of the Constitution."[13] Thus, though the Court remarked that in promulgating certain statutory provisions of the VRA "Congress exercised its authority under the Fifteenth Amendment in an inventive"[14] and even an "uncommon"[15] way, it concluded that "exceptional conditions can justify legislative measures not otherwise appropriate."[16] In light of the pervasive history of discrimination in the exercise of the franchise, the Court agreed with Congress that the VRA was necessary to effectuate the commands of the Fifteenth Amendment.

The VRA accomplished this task in two general ways. First, it targeted the jurisdictions with the worst track records of racial discrimination in the electoral process. Section 4(e) of the VRA, which determined the jurisdictions that would be covered by the Act, provided that the Act would apply to any jurisdiction that had implemented a test or device with respect to voting (i.e., a literacy test) and had failed to register 50 percent of its voters on November 1, 1964, or whose turnout for the 1964 presidential election failed to reach 50 percent. Under this coverage formula, Alabama, Georgia, Louisiana, Mississippi, South Carolina, Virginia, and 26 counties in North Carolina came under the coverage of the Act.

Once jurisdictions came under the purview of the Act, they were subject to its special, temporary provisions. These included the appointment of federal registrars and poll observers; the elimination of literacy tests; and the one provision that, while subject to little debate during the 1965 hearings, soon became the focal point of the Act: the preclearance requirement of Section 5.

Under Section 5 of the Act, a covered jurisdiction must preclear with the attorney general any new "voting qualification or prerequisite to voting, or standard, practice, or procedure with respect to voting."[17] The covered jurisdiction may also seek a declaratory judgment that its proposed changes are not discriminatory from the United States District Court for the District of Columbia. Preclearance would serve as a rebuttable presumption of sorts, as the submitting jurisdictions had to persuade either the DOJ or the D.C. District Court that the submitted changes "do[ ] not have the purpose and will not have the effect of denying

Registration gap between black and white voters

	1965	1967	1970–71	1982
Alabama	49.9	38.0	23.6	22.2
Georgia	35.2	27.7	2.8	14.9
Louisiana	48.9	34.2	20.9	3.4
Mississippi	63.2	31.7	9.4	14.8
North Carolina	50.0	31.7	15.9	21.9
South Carolina	38.4	30.5	3.2	1.7
Virginia	22.8	7.8	7.2	4.7
Average Gap	44.0	28.8	11.2	11.9

Sources: U.S. Commission on Civil Rights, The Voting Rights Act: Ten Years After (1975).

or abridging the right to vote on account of race or color."[18] By barring implementation of any voting changes prior to preclearance, Section 5 transferred the constitutional inquiry in time and placed the burden on the covered jurisdictions to prove that their proposed changes did not violate the 15th Amendment.

The Court's expansive understanding of the purpose and scope of the VRA displayed in *South Carolina v. Katzenbach* continued in *Allen v. State Board of Elections*.[19] In Allen, the Court maintained that in promulgating Section 5, Congress intended "to give the Act the broadest possible scope."[20] Consequently, "any state enactment which altered the election law of a covered State in even a minor way" would be subject to preclearance under Section 5.[21]

II.

As seen in Table 2, the effects of the VRA were almost immediate. The average registration gap between black and white voters in the states initially covered by the VRA narrowed considerably—from 44 percent to 28.8 percent—a scant two years after the Act took

effect. This downward trend continued for the next two censuses, to a low of 11.2 percent in 1971 and 11.9 percent in 1982. These dramatic results demonstrated that Congress had finally targeted the root of the problem with the right method. Undoubtedly, "the Voting Rights Act transformed the basis of the southern electoral system, inasmuch as it was the vehicle for destroying the institutional barriers to black registration."[22] The registration gap continued to narrow to the point where observers could reasonably conclude that by 1988 blacks and whites "registered in near equal proportions relative to their voting-age populations."[23]

As successful as the VRA has been in facilitating the registration of eligible voters of color, it has also been successful in enabling voters of color in covered jurisdictions to elect candidates of color. The point of registration and voting, of course, is for voters ultimately to elect the candidates of their choice and to have a say in the policies that directly affect their lives.[24] From that perspective, the rise in the number of African-American legislators in

TABLE 3
Percentage of black elected officials in the South, 1970–85

Year	% Black Pop.	U.S. Congress	State Senate	State House
1970	20.4	0.0	1.3 (6)	1.9 (26)
1975	20.4	2.8 (3)	2.4 (11)	6.2 (83)
1980	19.6	1.8 (2)	3.1 (14)	8.3 (110)
1985	19.6	1.7 (2)	7.2 (33)	10.8 (143)

the South tells a story of clear progress due to the VRA.

As Table 3 illustrates, the percentage of black elected officials in the South rose dramatically, particularly in state houses, from 1970 to 1985. In 1970 only 1.3 percent of all sate senators in the South were black. By 1985 that number was 7.2 percent. Similarly, in 1970 only 1.9 percent of state housemembers were black; by 1985 that number was 10 percent.

By contrast, compare the number of elected officials in states outside of the South, as presented in Table 4. When one examines both the raw numbers and the percentages of black elected officials in relation to the existing black population, one can see that the South compares quite favorably to the non-South.

In fact, when one compares the number of black elected local officials, the South outperforms the non-South. As illustrated by Table 5, by 1985 almost 6 percent of county and city council officials in the South were black compared to about 1 percent in the non-South.

This data points to the conclusion that the Voting Rights Act has had a clear and direct impact in the vast improvement in Southern black office holding. As Grofman and Handley conclude in an important study, "[t]he primary reason for the disproportionate increase in southern black officeholding… is the Voting Rights Act."[28]

III.

To understand the impact that the Renewal Act is likely to have on the electoral prospects of voters of color in covered jurisdictions, it is important to assess how the Department of Justice (DOJ), the primary entity responsible for administering Section 5, has understood objectionable submissions under Section 5.

TABLE 4
Percentage of black elected officials in the non-South, 1970–85

Year	% Black Pop.	U.S. Congress	State Senate	State House
1970	7.7	2.7 (9)	1.6 (25)	2.6 (40)
1975	7.7	4.0 (13)	2.7 (42)	3.3 (75)
1980	8.5	4.0 (13)	2.9 (44)	3.3 (84)
1985	8.5	5.3 (17)	3.2 (49)	3.8 (159)

TABLE 5
Percentage of black elected local officials, 1970–85

Year	County Councils South	City Councils South	County Councils Non-South	City Councils Non-South
1970	0.6 (24)	1.2 (263)	0.3 (40)	0.4 (289)
1975	4.2 (192)	2.6 (605)	0.7 (75)	0.8 (621)
1980	6.8 (310)	4.4 (1,043)	0.8 (84)	1.0 (756)
1985	5.9 (425)	5.6 (1,330)	1.0 (109)	1.1 (850)

For purposes of this chapter, we have gathered objection letters for the original jurisdictions covered by the Voting Rights Act of 1965. These jurisdictions are Alabama, Georgia, Louisiana, Mississippi, significant parts of North Carolina, South Carolina, and Virginia. In addition to these original jurisdictions, we have also added Texas to our analysis, which became a covered jurisdiction in 1975. By almost all accounts, the VRA was designed to address racial discrimination in voting rampant in those eight states.[29]

Table 6 depicts the number of objections interposed by the DOJ to submissions for preclearance by the covered jurisdictions by decade. The most striking observation from the table is the paucity of objections interposed by the DOJ after the 1990s. In fact, the number of objections interposed by the DOJ from 2000–04 is more comparable to the number of objections interposed from 1965–70 than in any other time period. Table 6 presents very clearly why we do not view renewal of Section 5 in its current form as beneficial to voters of color: the DOJ does not object to many submissions under Section 5.

To best appreciate how few submissions are objectionable, Table 7 presents the number of submissions for covered jurisdictions, the number of objection letters written by the DOJ, and the percentage of submissions that the DOJ found objectionable. As the table demonstrates, from 1970–79, there were few submissions that were not objectionable. The DOJ wrote more objection letters than there were submissions by covered jurisdictions.[30] But the rate of objections declined sharply thereafter.

Some of this decline is to be expected. There were very few submissions between 1965 and 1979 because covered jurisdictions were mostly refusing to cooperate and sometimes were unsure as to what changes ought to be submitted for preclearance. Moreover, as indicated by the rate of objections between 1965 and 1979, almost all of the early submissions were discriminatory and in reaction to the then-newly enacted VRA. Thus, this early period was characterized by few submissions but a high rate of objections.

The middle period, between 1980 and the mid 1990s is characterized by a similar number of objections but a tremendous spike in the number of submissions. For example, between 1980 and 1990 covered jurisdictions submitted over 33,000 proposed changes for preclear-

TABLE 6
Number of objections

Decade	Number of objections
1965–69	10
1970–79	334
1980–89	360
1990s	342
2000–05	32
Total	1,068

ance by the DOJ. As a practical matter the DOJ could not object to even a substantial number of these changes as most of them were undoubtedly insignificant. Consequently, as a mathematical matter the rate of preclearance had to decrease even though the number of objections increased slightly in this middle period. Thus, the preclearance mechanism is amply justifiable in both the early and middle periods.

The problem is justifying the current preclearance mechanism for what we are calling the late period, from 1996–2005, and especially from 2000–05. As Table 7 shows, from 2000–05, the DOJ precleared 99.03 percent of proposed submissions. This is a very telling figure, as these are preclearance rates of submissions from the jurisdictions for which Section 5 was precisely designed.

Table 7 clearly indicates that Section 5 has not been an efficient regulatory tool for the last 25 years. This is not to say that preclearance was not necessary for the last 25 years. It certainly was; between 1980 and 2000, the DOJ prevented hundreds of discriminatory proposed changes from going into effect. This is also not to say that Congress should have allowed Section 5 to sunset. Rather, and as we argue below, Congress should have retooled Section 5 so that the provision would be responsive to the electoral problems that voters of color face in the 21st century.

IV.

The question then is whether there is reason to believe that the Renewal Act will increase the number of objections interposed by the DOJ. There are two leading explanations for the decline in Section 5's effectiveness. One explanation, the one that undergirds the Renewal Act, is that Section 5's effectiveness is undermined by Supreme Court interpretations of the VRA that have been too restrictive. An alternative explanation, and the one we shall propound, is that Section 5's regulatory mechanism is outmoded.

Table 8 shows the types of submissions from covered jurisdictions that the DOJ found

Table 7
Objections and submissions by decade, 1970–2005

Year	Submissions	Objections	Percentage
1970–79	221	334	1.5
1980–89	33,435	360	1.0
1990–99	152,931	342	.2
2000–05	44,161	32	.07

TABLE 8

Types of objectionable submissions by decade, 1970–2005

Type of Objectionable Submission	Decade				
	1970–79	1980–89	1990–99	2000–05	Total
Voting systems	335	149	110	13	607
Redistricting	59	142	176	20	397
Procedures	111	101	58	2	272
Government structure	43	62	74	4	183
Boundaries	42	36	26	3	107
Total	590	490	444	42	1,438

objectionable. We examined all of the objection letters from the covered jurisdictions between 1965 and 2004. From these objection letters we noted all of the characteristics of a proposed change that the DOJ viewed negatively in the objection letter. We catalogued these negative characteristics into five categories: voting systems, redistricting, elections procedures, government structure, and boundary changes.[32] When the DOJ objected to a proposed change because the submission involving the use of single-member or at-large districts, numbered posts, staggered terms, or majority vote requirements, we categorized those objections as objections to voting systems. Election procedure objections included objections to polling place changes, changes in voter registration requirements, and changes in candidate registration requirements. Government structure refers to submissions that sought to change offices from elective to appointive, increase or decrease the number of seats on boards, councils, or commissions, and changes involving judgeships. Boundary changes primarily include annexations and de-annexations, school district, city and county boundary changes.

Three observations are worth noting from the data in Table 8. First, over half of the objectionable submissions that caught the DOJ's eye between 1970 and 1979 were to proposed changes involving voting systems. Once voters of color were able to register, particularly with the help of the federal examiners provided by the VRA, Congress anticipated that covered jurisdictions would attempt to manipulate electoral structures to minimize the electoral impact of voters of color. As Table 8 shows, Section 5 was instrumental in keeping many of those manipulations from going into effect.

To the extent that the number and types of objections reflected attempts by covered jurisdictions to undermine the voting rights of voters of color, one can understand why Section 5 has been tremendously successful. These are precisely the types of structural changes for which Congress designed the preclearance requirement. The DOJ made it very clear that there are certain types of structural changes—particularly those involving voting system changes—that it would not approve.

An early objection letter, dated March 20, 1972, from the United States Assistant Attorney

General David Norman to Alabama's Assistant Attorney General Leslie Hall is illustrative. Alabama submitted for preclearance proposed changes that would alter the method of electing county commissioners from single-member to at-large districts and would change the threshold of electability from plurality vote to majority vote. The DOJ objected to the submission. The DOJ explained:

> Where as here a county with a majority white population has within it an election district within which a majority of the population is black, the change from election by districts to an at-large method of election necessarily has the effect of diluting that black voting strength, especially when a majority of the votes cast is required for election to an office.[33]

From the DOJ's perspective, given the demographic factors, this type of change was almost per se discriminatory. From 1970–79 the second highest number of objections was for submissions containing changes to election procedures. Consider here a letter from Assistant Attorney General Stanley Pottinger to the city attorney of Martinsville, Virginia, objecting to the City's proposed precinct consolidations:

> We have carefully considered the submitted changes and supporting materials as well as information received from private citizens. The total of the information available to us reveals strongly opposing views as to the effect of the change involved. As we understand the City's position, the consolidations will result in economic savings to the City since the reduction in number of polling places will require fewer voting machines and fewer persons to man polling places on election day. Opponents maintain that generally the consolidations of precincts and accompanying reduction in polling places will result in added inconvenience to voters in their exercise of the franchise but,

> more particularly, will impose an inordinate burden upon black voters in precincts 1 and 6. We have been told that the number of blacks who vote will be diminished by this consolidation since many blacks vote during the early morning hours and after work and the longer lines resulting form consolidation will discourage them from voting. We also understand that a large percentage of black voters in the past have gotten to the polls without the necessity of transportation but that the substantial increase in distance of more than a mile, plus the existence of a main thoroughfare which would bisect the consolidate precinct, would make walking to the polls, as in the past, a significant but apparently unnecessary hardship for many persons in that precinct.

> …While we have weighed carefully all the information before us, we cannot conclude that the consolidation of precincts 1 and 6 will not have the effect of denying or abridging the right to vote on account of race or color. Consequently, on behalf of the Attorney General I must interpose and objection to the consolidation of those two precincts.[34]

Second, Table 8 also depicts the prevalence of objectionable redistricting submissions. Starting in 1980 objections to redistricting submissions constituted the majority of objectionable submissions from the covered jurisdictions. In fact, as Table 8 shows, more than half of the objection letters written by the DOJ from 2000–04 involved redistricting submissions. The DOJ examined redistricting submissions for the impact that they would have on black voters in covered jurisdictions. Consider as an example an objection letter from Assistant Attorney General Jerris Leonard refusing to preclear the reapportionment of a county in Mississippi. Mr. Leonard explained the objection on the ground that:

The available demographic information shows that the Negro majority in the existing District 3 has been changed to a white majority in the proposed District 3. Our study also has persuaded me that there are alternative means of redistricting which would probably not have this effect. Therefore, we cannot conclude that this redistricting plan has no racial purpose or effect.[35]

Lastly, Table 8 reinforces the observation noted in Table 6 that the DOJ is currently objecting to very few submissions by covered jurisdictions. When one examines the types of proposed changes to which the DOJ objected, one can begin to see at least one significant reason for the decline in objections.

Section 5 was designed for a world in which elected officials in covered jurisdictions would maneuver electoral structures to discriminate routinely and intentionally against voters of color. The operating assumption of Section 5's regulatory scheme is that state officials in covered jurisdictions could not be trusted because their interactions with voters of color more often than not would result in or be motivated by discrimination. Under those assumptions, the regulatory regime should define broadly submissions that are subject to preclearance and should set a fairly high bar for approving those submissions.

From 1965 until 1980 those assumptions were unerringly correct; state officials were intent on discriminating against voters of color in covered jurisdictions. And perhaps more importantly, the tools of their trade were known to the regulators. Following the enactment of the VRA, Section 5 review picked up a slew of discriminatory structural changes: single-member districts changed to at-large; plurality vote requirements changed to majority vote with a run-off; anti-singleshot provisions were enacted, etc. Section 5 review also caught evident procedural changes: polling places consolidated or moved; registration requirement changes, residency requirement changes, etc. This is why the DOJ, in the first full decade of Section 5's implementation, objected to virtually all of the substantive proposed changes by covered jurisdictions on the ground that they either had the purpose or the effect of minimizing the electoral prospects of voters of color.

Additionally, because state officials could be trusted only to disenfranchise voters of color, as evidenced by *Allen v. State Board of Elections,* we saw a regulatory regime that defined the scope of Section 5 as broadly as possible and set a fairly high bar for preclearance. Consider here an objection letter from Acting Assistant Attorney General David Norman to an attorney representing the Merion County Board of Supervisors in Columbia Mississippi. This letter referenced a proposal to change the Board of Supervisor's district lines. Mr. Norman wrote:

> I have carefully examined the data you and the Marion County officials have furnished, as well as information gathered by my staff. I understand the complexities involved in drafting a reapportionment plan and the difficulties in developing accurate population statistics. However, because of conflicts between population figures reported by the Bureau of the Census and those compiled by the county, I am unable, based on the presently available facts, to resolve questions I have concerning the effect of the new districts. In view of this, I am compelled at this time to object on behalf of the Attorney General to the redistricting submission.[36]

At some point, the assumption that the modal submission from covered jurisdictions would be discriminatory in purpose or effect became untenable as a factual matter. Significantly, changes from single-member to at-large districts, which were the types of changes to which the DOJ objected frequently, virtually disappeared over time. This was because most jurisdictions ceased using at-large election systems as a voting structure. And so, in moving forward, the preclearance process became ineffectual in addressing the types of problems that it was designed to address. More importantly, it was not retooled to pick up the post-civil rights electoral problems that plagued voters of color.

Certainly by 2005, when 99.9 percent of all submissions from covered jurisdictions were precleared by the DOJ, one cannot say that even a substantial minority of proposed changes submitted to the DOJ were discriminatory. The DOJ was receiving significantly more of all types of submissions for preclearance each decade,[37] but it was objecting to essentially the same amount of requests (though significantly different and lower percentages) in the 70s, 80s, and 90s. A slight exception here, as shown by Table 9, is redistricting submissions. The DOJ's preclearance rate for redistricting submissions remained exactly the same for three decades. But even with redistricting submissions, by 2000 the rate of preclearance had plummeted, consistent with the other categories.

The problem is that while the assumptions that supported the promulgation of Section 5 changed, Congress failed to change the scope and reach of Section 5. This task was ultimately left to the Court, who was not as reticent and in fact too eager but ill-equipped to the task. As we noted earlier, the Supreme Court's early cases on the VRA reflected a robust understanding of congressional power to enact the Act and a broad understanding of its substantive provisions. In addition to *Katzenbach v. Morgan* and *Allen v. State Board,* other notable cases in this vein include *Dougherty County Board of Education v. White,*[38] where the Court held that the Dougherty County Board of Education must preclear a rule requiring board members who run for elective office to take an unpaid leave of absence.

By 1975, however, it was clear that the Court had started to chart a new course. The shift was signaled by two cases in the 1970s and it was completed by two cases this decade. The first case was *City of Richmond, Virginia v. United States.*[39] *City of Richmond* addressed the City of Richmond's annexation of an adjoining predominantly white territory that changed the city's racial make-up as a predominantly black city pre-annexation—52 percent black—to a predominantly white one post-annexation—58 percent white. The black population in Richmond was growing to the point that black voters would constitute a majority of the city's voting age population and would soon control the city council. Prior to annexation black voters constituted 44.8 percent of the city's voting age population; after annexation they constituted only 37.3 percent.[40] The Court held that the annexation did not violate Section 5's effects prong because the post-annexation electoral system fairly apportioned political power between whites and blacks.[41]

The majority's decision was met with howls of protest by Justice Brennan in dissent. Justice Brennan remarked that "such a significant dilution of black voting strength" could not be "remedied, for Section 5 purposes, simply by allocating to blacks a reasonably proportionate share of voting power within the postannexation community."[42] To the majority's contention that the VRA was not meant to hold covered jurisdictions captive when annexation would reduce the percentage of black voters, Justice Brennan demurred. He retorted:

> Congress was certainly aware of the hardships and inconveniences which Section 5 and other portions of the Act could impose upon covered states and localities; but in passing the Act in its final form, Congress unmistakably declared that those hardships are outweighed by the need to ensure effective protection for black voting rights.[43]

City of Richmond is not necessarily distinctive because of its outcome. Though the majority and dissenters would have decided the case differently, it is not clear that the DOJ would have agreed with the dissenters. In fact, the best available evidence is that the DOJ probably would have sided with the majority. In its objection letter responding to Richmond's proposed annexation and in another objection letter written a couple months earlier responding to a similar proposal, the DOJ took the position later adopted by the *City of Richmond* majority that a post-annexation reduction in the black population was per se dilutive and in violation of Section 5 but only where the annexing territory used an at-large election system. Thus, the violation could be cured by a post-annexation adoption of single-member districts that fairly apportioned political power between black and white citizens.

City of Richmond was notable because it signaled an early, clearly premature, and sufficiently perceptible recognition that a majority of the Court was uncomfortable with the assumptions underlying Section 5. Even in the face of racial bloc voting, evidence of discriminatory purpose, and the fact that we were dealing with Virginia in the early 1970s, the Court was unwilling to accept the position that it certainly would have accepted a decade earlier, that annexation under those circumstances was undoubtedly violative of Section 5. As the dissent lamented:

> [The] decision seriously weakens the protection so emphatically accorded by the Act. Municipal politicians who are fearful of losing their political control to emerging black voting majorities are today placed on notice that their control can be made secure as long as they can find concentrations of white citizens into which to expand their municipal boundaries.[44]

The dissent was clearly right. The majority's interpretation did weaken the Act. Moreover, the majority's opinion was deeply unsatisfactory, especially given the factual context of the case. But the dissent had no answer for the majority's legitimate worry that adopting the dissent's position would lead to no annexations in covered jurisdictions unless the annexation maintained the pre-annexation division of political power between the races. It was no answer—at least no answer that the majority was willing to accept 10 years after the passage of the VRA—to say that the VRA imposed "hardships" and "inconveniences" upon covered jurisdictions.

Year	Submissions	Objections	Percentage
1970–79	993	59	5.9
1980–89	2,835	142	5.0
1990–99	3,456	176	5.0
2000–05	2,936	20	.68

The majority was not willing to travel that road because it recognized that the underlying assumptions had changed. There were legitimate reasons why covered jurisdictions might opt for annexing adjacent territories in circumstances that reduced black political power. One could no longer assume that the modal submission was discriminatory.

This is precisely where guidance from Congress would have been helpful. What types of trade-offs should be made in these circumstances? Perhaps annexations should be treated differently under the VRA so that black voters do not lose political power at the very moment that they are on the verge of gaining it. But Congress was nowhere to be found.

City of Richmond was followed a year later by the landmark case of *Beer v. United States*.[45] *Beer* involved a reapportionment plan for City of New Orleans city council. The plan contained five single-member districts and two at-large seats. At the time that the plan was enacted, 55 percent of the population was white and 45 percent black. The plan created one district in which the majority of registered voters were black and two districts in which the total majority of voters were black. No African American had ever been elected to the city council. The district court, in a wonderful contextual opinion by Judge Spotswood Robinson,[46] concluded that the plan violated Section 5 because the plan did not facilitate the representation of African-American voters in proportion to their numbers.

The Supreme Court reversed. The Court held that "the purpose of Section 5 has always been to insure that no voting-procedure changes would be made that would lead to a retrogression in the position of racial minorities with respect to their effective exercise of the electoral franchise."[47] The Court ruled that because the redistricting plan improved the positions of African-American voters—they were virtually guaranteed to elect their preferred candidate in one district, where before they had none—the plan was not retrogressive. Thus, under the Court's interpretation of Section 5, because voters of color were so discriminated in New Orleans that they did not get any representation under previous plans, the fact that they got some this time around was sufficient to satisfy Section 5's preclearance requirement.

Beer reduced the barrier to preclearance substantially, at least for redistricting submissions. Again, as in *City of Richmond*, the Court opted for an outcome that minimized black political power even in the face of compelling facts that could have led in the other direction. Once again, Congressional guidance could have been useful. Maybe reapportionments should not be within the purview of covered jurisdictions. Or maybe Congress could have required neutral commissions (in the same way that Congress moved Section 5 preclearance suits to the District Court for the District of Columbia). The point is that Congress could have required something. And yet, once again, Congress was not anywhere in sight.

Beer stood for almost 30 years until the Court decided *Georgia v. Ashcroft*.[48] At issue in the case was whether Georgia, a covered jurisdiction, was permitted by Section 5 to reduce the percentage of black voters in three senate districts from 60.58 percent, 55.43 percent, and 62.45 percent to 50.31 percent, 50.66 percent, and 50.80 percent, respectively. The district court concluded that the reduction was retrogressive because it reduced the opportunity of African-American voters in those districts to elect candidates of their choice.

The Court disagreed. The Court noted that a reduction in the opportunity to elect is neither the sole nor determinative factor in determining retrogression. Rather, retrogression is determined by the totality of all applicable circumstances "such as the ability of minority voters to elect their candidate of choice, the extent of the minority group's opportunity to participate in the political process, and the feasibility of creating nonretrogressive plans."[49]

Georgia v. Ashcroft is as right a voting rights case as we have seen from the Supreme Court in a long time. And it is right for a number of reasons, not least of which is because Georgia fatally undermined the Court's decision in *Beer*. *Beer* imposed both a floor and a ceiling on the electoral prospects of voters of color and did so in a way that is completely contrary to the aims of the VRA. Under *Beer*, as long as a jurisdiction did not make voters of color worse-off, the jurisdiction did not violate Section 5. That standard might be fine depending upon the baseline, but under *Beer* the baseline could be 1965. Thus, a correct interpretation of *Beer* is that Section 5 did not require progress or improvement; it just did not permit retrogression—as if one could retrogress from zero. That view of the VRA cannot be right; if the VRA and Section 5 had only one aim, certainly progress was that aim.

In contrast to *Beer*, the underlying premise of *Georgia* is that Section 5 must be sufficiently flexible to allow for progress. Where voters of color are inefficiently grouped—as say in an overly safe district 60 percent black voting age population district—the state may reduce the number of voters of color in the overly safe district and spread them to other districts so as to allow them to aggregate with like-minded others or simply influence the outcome. Of course whether that strategy is worth pursuing depends upon contextual factors for which risk is a function of the denouement of real-world circumstances. This is not quite "a sea of imponderables."[50] Some of the factors, such as the extent of racial bloc voting and white cross-over voting, are sufficiently ponderable. *Georgia* was rightly decided because it provided "a solution that accommodates imponderables and does not demand precision where the nature of the subject can yield only approximations."[51] Thus, the Court deemphasized the focus on electing a candidate of choice or at least made it more nuanced and contextual.

The difficult issue presented in *Georgia* is assessing whether state actors are moving voters of color around so as to enhance their electoral prospects or whether they are moving them around so as to diminish their electoral prospects. All of the justices agreed that in light of changed circumstances, in particular some appreciable decrease in racial bloc voting in covered jurisdictions, some moving around could be warranted. Depending upon the factual circumstances, for example, a 60 percent black district could be vote dilution by packing. What divided the Court was determining how to assess the appropriate level of risk.

Once again, this is an area where tremendous trade-offs are being made and an area that could benefit from Congressional guidance. This time Congress did provide a response, but it was pitiful and retrograde. In the Renewal Act, Congress sought to overturn the Court's judgment in *Georgia* and return the Section 5 inquiry to *Beer's* mechanical and restrictive retrogression standard. The Renewal Act provides that any voting qualification that has the purpose or effect of diminishing the ability of voters of color to "elect their preferred candidates of choice" violates Section 5.

It is of course ironic that Congress and the civil rights community clamored to resurrect an opinion—*Beer*—that had long been viewed as inimical to the voting rights of color. Leaving

that issue aside, the problem is precisely how one determines who the candidate of choice is. Is the candidate of choice the candidate who emerges after the creation of a majority-minority district where one can be created? Suppose that one cannot be created. Is the state obligated to create coalition districts and would the candidate of choice be the product of that coalition? What happens when white voters coalesce with enough voters of color to produce a Denise Majette over the preference of the majority of black voters who wanted a Cynthia McKinney?

The issue is that the "candidate of choice" is an endogenous contextual variable that can best be evaluated by, well, examining the totality of the circumstances on the ground. Congress did not provide any guidance on that very difficult but key question. As an aside, this is precisely the reason that the Court in *Georgia v. Ashcroft* used John Lewis as a proxy for determining the best interest of voters of color. Indeed, there is no reason to believe that in interpreting the language that purportedly reversed *Georgia v. Ashcroft*, the Court might end up in the same place with another *Georgia v. Ashcroft*—looking at the facts on the ground, the totality of circumstances, and using the preferences of leaders of color as proxies for divining the best interest of communities of color.

Granted, in assessing the outcome in *Georgia v. Ashcroft*, Congress and the civil rights community were distracted by the fact that the right approach in *Georgia* came from the Court's conservatives. These were the conservatives that penned the most obnoxious voting rights decision of this decade, *Bossier II*. In *Bossier II*,

the Court held that even though a redistricting plan was enacted with a discriminatory
purpose, but because it was not retrogressive, it did not violate Section 5. *Bossier II* is a
bad opinion in the line of *Beer*, from which it
springs. But correcting *Bossier II* does nothing
to address the modal problems faced by voters of color. While intentional discrimination
is bad and some of that still exists, it is not the
modal concern.

CONCLUSION

The Voting Rights Act of 1965 played a central
role in the difficult and longstanding fight
against racial discrimination in voting. The
preclearance provision was a key component
of this new and radical statutory regime. It
was also effective, as seen by the numbers of
objections entered by the DOJ against jurisdictions covered under the Act. With changed
context and circumstances, however, we have
witnessed a dramatic drop in the number of
objections, especially since the year 2000. This
evidence counseled against a mechanical reauthorization of the expiring provisions. Yet that
is exactly what Congress has done.

Perhaps more perversely, Congress failed to
remove jurisdictions such as New York and
New Hampshire where objections by the
DOJ have been virtually nonexistent. Congress failed to explore whether such regional
distinctions militate against a mechanical
reauthorization process. After all, what is the
purpose of requiring New York to submit
proposed changes for the next 25 years when
there are jurisdictions, such as Ohio, and other
concerns, such as ballot design, that ought to
compel Congressional attention? Rather than
look to the future and the needs of voters
of color in the 21st century, Congress took
us back to a time when the Court began to
interpret the preclearance requirement narrowly and against the intent of Congress. And
rather than adapting the statute to current
needs, we instead got more of the same, even
in the face of very strong evidence that the
same is simply not working. In this instance,
by renewing Section 5 without an assessment
of the contemporary needs of voters of color,
Congress failed voters of color.

References

1. 528 U.S. 320 (2000).

2. 539 U.S. 461 (2003).

3. U.S. Commission on Civil Rights, Voting 1 (1961).

4. *Id.*

5. *Id.* (Only 26 counties were initially covered by the VRA.

6. *Id.* at 5.

7. 1965 House Hearings at 5

8. *Id.* at 9

9. *Id.* at 5.

10. *Id.*

11. 383 US. 301 (1966).

12. *Id.* at 308.

13. *Id.* at 309.

14. *Id.* at 327.

15. *Id.* at 334.

16. *Id.*

17. 42 U.S.C. § 1973c (2000).

18. *Id.*

19. 393 U.S. 544 (1969).

20. *Id.* at 566–76.

21. *Id.* at 565.

22. See James E. Alt, "The Impact of the Voting Rights Act on Black and White Voter Registration in the South," in *Quiet Revolution In the South: The Impact of the Voting Rights Act, 1965–90,* at 351, 372 (Chandler Davidson and Bernard Grofman eds., 1994).

23. *Id.* at 366.

24. As Martin Luther King Jr. while speaking at a rally in Selma, Alabama, "If Negroes could vote, there would be no Jim Clarks, there would be no oppressive poverty directed against Negroes, our children would not be crippled by segregated schools, and the whole community might live together in harmony." Dr. King, in Selma, Urges Voter March, *New York Times,* Feb. 1, 1965, at 16, quoted in David J. Garrow, *Protest at Selma: Martin Luther King Jr., and the Voting Rights Act of 1965,* at 47 (1965).

25. Lisa Handley and Bernard Grofman, "The Impact of the Voting Rights Act on Minority Representation: Black Officeholding in Southern State Legislatures and Congressional Delegations," in *Quiet Revolution, supra* note, at 345 (table 11.1).

26. *Id.* at 345 (table 11.1).

27. *Id.* at 345 (table 11.1).

28. *Id.* at 335.

29. These eight states will be referred to henceforth as the covered jurisdictions.

30. The submission data were received in aggregate form from the Department of Justice Submission Tracking and Processing System. The statistic for the objection letters come from our dataset, which contains every objection letter written by the DOJ for the period and states in question. The submission data do not appear to be one hundred percent accurate. For example, we have objection letters for the State of Alabama from 1965–69 that reference submissions by that state. However, the aggregate submission numbers that we received from the DOJ does not note any submissions for Alabama for the 1960s. As we have no method of verifying the number of submissions that the DOJ receives, we have no choice but to rely on the numbers that they have given us.

31. This number represents the total number of objection letters, including objection letters to resubmissions and requests for new information.

32. Redistricting measures are boundary changes, but because of the number of objection letters involving redistricting, we decided that redistricting should be its own category.

33. Letter on file with authors.

34. Letter on file with authors.

35. Letter on file with authors.

36. Letter on file with authors.

37. See www.usdoj.gov/crt/voting/sec_5/changes.htm.

38. 439 U.S. 32 (1978).

39. 422 U.S. 358 (1975).

40. *Id.* at 386–87.

41. *Id.* at 378.

42. *Id.* at 387.

43. *Id.*

44. *Id.*

45. 425 U.S. 130 (1976).

46. Judge Robinson's approach was later vindicated in *Georgia v. Ashcroft.*

47. Beer, 425 U.S. at 141.

48. 539 U.S. 461 (2003).

49. *Id.* at 479.

50. *Vieth v. Jubelirer,* 541 U.S. 267, 290 (2004).

51. *Public Service Commission of Utah v. United States,* 356 U.S. 421, 463 (1958).

* Editor's note: Professor Charles' co-author, Luis Fuentes-Rohwer, did not assist in writing the initial draft of the paper that was presented at the time of the conference.

The Future of Voting Rights Policy: From Anti-Discrimination to the Right to Vote

Richard H. Pildes
New York University School
of Law

INTRODUCTION

To many Americans, it comes as a surprise to learn how little national legislation exists to regulate and protect the election process, including even elections for national offices, such as the Presidency, Senate, and House. If there are any doubts about that, recall that resolution of the disputed presidential election of 2000 turned primarily, in the first instance, on matters of Florida law and decisions of the Florida courts, and ultimately, on the United States Supreme Court's interpretation of the vague generalities of the Equal Protection Clause of the Constitution.[1] With the most powerful elective office in the world at stake, observers in other democracies watched in stunned disbelief as American lawyers and commentators went scurrying to the statute books of Florida—even to the election administration regulations of individual counties—to understand the laws and processes for the design of ballots, the standards for what counted as a valid vote, and the institutional mechanisms by which election disputes involving such issues were to be resolved. We are still in the early stages of reverse engineering ourselves out of the pathological decentral-ization of American elections, even national elections, that is a path-dependent product of America's unique political history—including, ironically, the fact that American democracy was established over 200 years ago and has endured since.

The most significant legislative initiatives to bring national consistency and uniformity to American elections, since the short-lived post-Civil War era of Reconstruction, have been the 1965 Voting Rights Act (VRA) and its amendments,[2] the 1993 National Voter Regis-tration Act (NVRA),[3] and, in response to the 2000 election, the 2002 Help America Vote Act (HAVA).[4] But, though not widely appreci-ated, these statutes embody radically different philosophies about when and why national oversight of elections is needed. The original VRA, enacted in 1965, reflected an anti-discrimination approach to national protection of voting rights. The VRA did not protect the right to vote as such; instead, it protected vot-ing rights in two more selective and narrowly targeted ways.

First, the Act was limited to prohibiting racially discriminatory voting practices. The few other moments in American history at which Congress had also acted to protect voting rights, during Reconstruction, all had a similar structure, as does the Fifteenth Amendment to the Constitution, which was the source of authority under which Congress acted when it legislated on voting rights.[5] Thus, the statutes Congress enacted did not protect the right to vote as such, but instead were largely limited to one potential reason the votes of some Americans might be denied or abridged: race. Second, the Act selectively singled out particular jurisdictions for uniquely aggressive federal oversight—jurisdictions that had a long history of racially discriminatory voting practices.[6] Thus, the philosophy that animated national legislation in the VRA, and in those few federal statutes that protected the right to vote before the 1990s, was that federal oversight was uniquely justified not to secure the right to vote itself, but to protect against racially discriminatory manipulation of the vote.

The legislation of more recent years, NVRA and HAVA, embody an entirely distinct philosophy and approach (for simplicity, I will call this alternative model the "HAVA model," but the same points could be made about the NVRA). In the wake of the 2000 election nightmare, Congress enacted the first piece of major national legislation structured to protect the act of voting itself. HAVA's right to cast a provisional ballot, its requirement of statewide registration databases, and its financial incentives for improved voting technology, apply uniformly nationwide and are not selectively targeted to protect only against racial discrimination in voting. HAVA, Congress' most recent enactment in this arena, like the NVRA a decade earlier, reflects a shift in national voting-rights legislation from an anti-discrimination to a substantive right-to-vote model. The question I want to focus on is whether HAVA or the VRA should be the model for the future of national voting-rights legislation.

That question is particularly urgent because Congress will soon reconsider the VRA itself. Portions of the VRA automatically expire in 2007, unless Congress reauthorizes them.[7] An important part of the future of voting rights is therefore now: this sunset provision will necessarily put voting rights on the national policymaking and public agenda soon, a process that has begun already. Congress last revisited the VRA in 1982, nearly 25 years ago. In this essay, my primary aim is to suggest that, when Congress revisits the VRA now, it should not remain conceptually locked within the VRA model of voting-rights protection but instead consider building on the more recent model, in expanded and more aggressive forms, of statutes like HAVA and the NVRA. The coming renewal debate over the VRA thus provides an ideal opportunity for the future of voting-rights policy to become organized around a model that better fits the voting-rights problems of today. I then want to explain why that will not, in fact, happen.[8]

THE PAST

The Voting Rights Act (VRA) is a sacred symbol of American democracy. The Act, the most effective civil rights statute enacted in the United States,[9] was the last significant stage in the nearly universal formal inclusion of all adult citizens in American democracy. Yet precisely because the VRA is an icon of American democracy, discussion over whether to renew or modify, let alone to move away from the model of the VRA for enforcing voting rights, will not be easy or unfreighted. Given the status and practical effects of the Act, discussion of changes in the Act will create understandable anxieties that hard-fought rights will be whittled away. That risk is all the greater for the VRA, for "The Voting Rights Act" represents and means dramatically different things to different audiences; when discussion of "the Act" takes place, different minds conjure up distinct features of "the Act." Yet, like many major laws, "the Act" is comprised of varied provisions, some enacted at different times than others, some justified by distinct policy aims from others.

It is important to begin, therefore, with clarity about what is—and what is not—at stake in discussion over renewing or modifying "the VRA." As noted above, the philosophy of the Act involves narrow and selective targeting of voting practices in two ways: first, by geographically singling out particular states and local governments for unique federal oversight;[10] second, by singling out minority voting rights, as opposed to voting rights in general, for unique federal protection.[11] These two different targeting approaches were built into the original VRA in 1965 and continue in the basic structure of the Act today.

The original Act was the most aggressive assertion of federal power over voting issues since the Civil War and Reconstruction. The 1965 Act enabled the attorney general to send federal examiners to take over the voter-registration process in areas that had resisted recognizing the voting rights of black citizens for the entire 20th century.[12] In addition, for states and local governments that

had a history of racially discriminatory voting practices, the Act directly suspended the use of various "tests and devices" as prerequisites to registration and voting.[13] And in the central provision of the 1965 Act—a provision that is the focus of the coming public debate—the Act directly put (and continues to put) the election systems in certain parts of the country under what is, essentially, a form of federal receivership.[14] The part of the Act that does so is known as Section 5.

Section 5, initially enacted for five years, was designed to be limited in time and geographic scope. These limitations reflected the law's extraordinary structure and justification, a structure unique in the arsenal of federal civil rights policy. Congress banned areas of the country that had used racially discriminatory voting practices from putting into effect any new provision or change that affects voting, no matter how large (redesigning election districts) or small (keeping polls open one hour later), until the town, county, or state seeking to make the change secures permission from the federal government to do so.[15] The structure of Section 5 thus expresses an exceptionally proactive regulatory philosophy: it puts the burden on the local jurisdiction to submit its proposed change to the federal government and to demonstrate to federal officials or judges that the change will not violate the VRA. Until precleared, no change in voting practices can be made. Section 5 thus embodies strong skepticism about the parts of the country which it singles out. In areas under this special "coverage" framework, any change in voting is, in essence, presumed to be suspect until the jurisdiction convinces the federal government the change will not impair minority voting rights.

This unique structure of Section 5 directly reflects its historical justification. In 1965, Congress confronted a long experience of Southern jurisdictions that had continually crafted new devices to restrict minority voting whenever courts had declared illegal some barrier to voting. Fearing that this cat-and-mouse game would continue, Congress created the targeted structure of Section 5: certain states and localities were put under special "coverage;"[16] they could not implement any change with respect to voting until the federal government had pre-cleared the change (either through the United States Department of Justice (DOJ) or a specially designated three-judge federal court in Washington, D.C);[17] and, reflecting Congress' suspicion, the jurisdictions would bear the burden of proving that their proposed changes were consistent with the VRA.[18] Section 5 and its "preclearance review" process applied, and continues to apply today, only to selected areas of the country (nine states as a whole and selected counties in five others).[19]

The Act's other central provision, Section 2,[20] applies nationwide without geographic distinction. The selective targeting feature of this part of the Act is that it singles out minority voting rights for uniform national protection. Section 2 is a permanent, nationwide ban on voting practices that deny or abridge minority voting rights.[21] In the early years of the Act, this provision was of limited importance, but after Congress substantially strengthened it in 1982, when Congress last revisited the VRA,

Section 2 became a major tool in race-based legal challenges to election structures.[22] The VRA thus reflects Congress' position that there are two distinct voting-rights problems that require distinct solutions: proactive federal oversight for certain regions, based on their history, and a more general nationwide set of rules selectively targeted at election structures and voting practices that disadvantage minority voters.[23]

The part of "the Act" due to expire in 2007 unless renewed is the geographical targeting embodied in Section 5 (as well as certain provisions affecting ballot materials for language minorities, though none of my comments in this essay, for reasons explained later, apply to these language-assistance provisions in "Section 203").[24] Though frequently said in short-hand form that "the Voting Rights Act" will expire unless reauthorized, this short-hand is misleading, creates unjustified fears, and hinders appropriate policy discussion. The VRA itself does not expire, nor do the crucial provisions in Section 2. These are permanent: they will continue to impose uniform, nationwide bans on discriminatory voting practices. In contrast, the Congresses that enacted and amended the VRA over the last 40 years recognized that Section 5 and its unique elements should remain responsive to ever-changing circumstances. Thus, when first enacted in 1965, Section 5 was designed to last five years; Congress extended this for another five years in 1970; then for another seven years; and in 1982, for another 25 years, until 2007. That brings us to the question of the moment, which is whether the selective targeting approach of Section 5 remains appropriate today. I want to raise questions about that and suggest instead that an approach modeled on statutes like HAVA and the NVRA might be more appropriate for the voting-rights problems of today—and more effective for minority voters themselves.

THE PRESENT

In singling out certain areas for unique federal oversight, Section 5 of the VRA rests on the philosophy that national policy can identify, in advance, areas of the country in which voting rights problems (that is, minority voting rights problems) are considerably more likely to arise systematically than in other areas. In addition, Section 5 locates the threat in changes to existing voting rules and practices; it is only these changes, rather than the status quo baseline practices, that the federal government must approve in advance in certain areas.[25] At the time of the 1965 Act, these narrow targeting features made sense and were exceedingly easy to apply: the Act was aimed centrally at the states of the Old Confederacy, which had systematically denied black citizens (and poor whites) the vote for decades, in part through changing voting rules and practices to frustrate federal oversight.[26]

But consider the kinds of voting issues that we face today. First, because policy no longer confronts the virtually complete, decades-long exclusion of black voters from political participation in certain states and counties, the voting-rights issues of the present are not as obviously unique or confined to any particular region of the country as when the VRA was first enacted.[27] Nor is it as easy to predict in advance of actual elections, through national legislation, where such problems are likely to emerge in elections over the coming years. Thus, continued reliance on a model that requires statutory identification in advance of where those problems are likely to arise is increasingly problematic. In addition, such a model will underenforce minority voting rights, for similar reasons. In the 2004 presidential election, for example, the most significant voting rights issues arose in the battleground state of Ohio.[28] Had the election turned instead on any other single state, issues similar to those in Ohio would likely have surfaced there as well. Yet in 1982, when Congress last addressed the structure of Section 5, there would have been no way to anticipate that these would be the states in which the voting rights controversies of today would arise. Similarly, in the 2000 presidential election, the voting controversies centered on Florida. Unlike Ohio, Florida was a state that the VRA did, to some extent, anticipate as a potential problem area based on the state's past history. Nonetheless Section 5 was of no relevance during the 2000 post-election legal disputes; indeed, Section 5 had not been able to anticipate that voting-rights conflicts would arise in the particular areas of Florida that they did. Section 5 reached only five counties in Florida[29]—not including those that spawned the major conflicts in 2000.[30] In the 2004 election cycle, the most intense post-election litigation over state and local elections took place over the governorships of Washington and Puerto Rico and the mayor's office in San Diego[31]—none of them places which the VRA's geographic targeting approach reaches.

Ohio, Florida, Washington, Puerto Rico, and San Diego do, however, share one feature—all had exceptionally competitive elections with small margins of victory in the relevant election. This reveals part of the problem with trying to tailor modern voting-rights protection to specific areas picked out by federal law in advance: the incentive to manipulate voting rights will be greatest today where elections are extremely competitive and small margins will determine winners and losers. Similarly, complaints and perceptions of large-scale deprivations of voting rights, including minority voting rights, are most likely to emerge in elections that turn out to be closely contested. But there is little way to base national regulation on ex ante predictions regarding where races for electoral votes, the Senate, the House, or state and local races are likely to be determined by small margins over the next generation. When the geographic targeting approach of Section 5 was adopted, there were distinct areas that systematically, election after election, denied minority voting rights, whether or not elections were competitive.

Second, the nature of voting-rights issues today also is less geographically concentrated in a distinct way than in the past. Consider the kinds of problems that have received the greatest attention in recent years. These include concerns about voting technology; lack of clear standards for what counts as a valid vote; ballot-design confusions; corrections to the provisional balloting system established in HAVA; long lines at polling places; partisan administration of election laws; sheer incompetence in election administration at the precinct level; burdensome voter-registration require-

ments, such as the need to re-register upon moving; and felon-disfranchisement laws.[32] These problems arise in many different parts of the country, sometimes only in some elections. It is difficult to conclude that they systematically and uniquely arise in particular areas that federal law can accurately pre-identify.

Take one of the largest emerging controversies today, whether voter identification should be required to combat so-called fraud, and if so, what forms of identification should be permitted. The most visible of these laws so far was enacted in Georgia. The federal district court eventually enjoined that law as a violation of the fundamental right to vote under the Constitution (after the DOJ had pre-cleared the law through the Section 5 process).[33] To some, that might confirm the need for continuing the geographical targeting approach of Section 5. Georgia was one of the states initially designed to be put under Section 5's federal receivership regime; it remains a specially targeted state today. But voter ID requirements are being adopted and considered in other states as well. Wisconsin and Indiana, for example, have recently adopted such laws.[34] And the national Carter-Baker Commission recommended a national voting ID requirement (over the vigorous dissent of some members).[35] To be sure, debates now taking place over voter ID requirements in several state legislatures have an overwhelming partisan dimension. But there is not an obvious geographic dimension to the issue, particularly not one that easily correlates with other voting-rights issues to suggest that certain states or areas are systematically infringing on voting rights.

Third, recall that current Section 5 selectively targets only changes in voting rules and practices. Yet here too, the problems of today differ, in critical ways, from those that generated this statutory structure over 40 years ago. Felon-disfranchisement laws, for example, are among the most significant barriers today to African-American suffrage, in terms of the number of otherwise eligible voters affected. But most of these laws are not recent enactments, nor do they reflect a recent change in state law. Issues arise with respect to these laws today precisely because many of them were enacted long ago, in eras of much lower incarceration rates, and have remained unchanged even as their effect has mushroomed with soaring felony-conviction rates. Yet because these are not recent "changes in state law," they are completely beyond the reach of Section 5. Nor could such laws be brought within the scope of Section 5 through modest amendments. For recall that the entire approach of Section 5 is premised on the assumption that federal oversight should be targeted most aggressively on changes in voting practices and rules.[36]

Similarly, when it comes to problems with voting technology, such as pre-scored punch-card ballots, or partisan election administration or incompetence, the problem is not that these are recent changes. Indeed, the problem is the opposite: it is preservation of the status quo— the failure to update old voting technology, the failure to create non-partisan election administration structures, the failure to train election officials properly—that is the problem. Far from being suspicious, change is precisely what we ought to want in these areas.

For these three reasons at least, the narrow targeting model of Section 5—its effort to single out particular areas and changes in voting rules—is less well suited to the voting rights problems of today than was the original Section 5 to the voting-rights problems of its day. Meanwhile, voting-rights activists and scholars are busily scrambling to find ways to establish that certain jurisdictions remain systematically guilty of infringing minority voting rights in ways that justify continuing Section 5 in essentially its current form.[37] Some of these efforts focus on the pattern of DOJ objections and related actions under Section 5; some focus on the pattern of court findings of VRA violations over the last 25 years under the general, nationwide anti-discrimination provisions of the Act; some efforts seek to combine, somewhat arbitrarily, a number of different proxies for identifying minority voting problems unique to certain states or localities. But these efforts to adapt Section 5 to today's circumstances reveal, ironically, the greater difficulties today in the project of singling out particular areas for unique federal oversight. Some major studies, for example, correctly note that racially-polarized voting continues to be documented in court cases; yet these same studies point out that, of the states for which this is true, half are covered and half are not under the current Section 5.[38] Similarly, studies identify over 100 cases since 1982 in which courts have found violations of the nationwide ban in Section 2 against discriminatory election structures and voting rules; yet, once again, these violations are not overwhelmingly concentrated in areas specially covered under Section 5, but instead occur throughout the nation.[39] In other words, there is less dramatic difference than in the past between the South (or those areas currently covered under Section 5), and other areas of the country with substantial minority populations.

That is partly because the type of problem central to the VRA today is different than in the past. Earlier, the primary issue was exclusion of minority voters from the polls; today, the vast majority of VRA cases and violations instead focus on the issue of vote dilution.[40] And to the extent vote dilution is a problem and the issue of the era, that issue arises in many (perhaps most) areas with significant minority populations, rather than overwhelmingly in any one discrete part of the country. Since 1990, for example, there are more court findings of Section 2 violations in New York or Pennsylvania than in South Carolina.[41]

This is not to say that it is impossible to identify jurisdictions that continue today to generate unique and recurring minority voting-rights problems. The more narrowly targeted the geographic focus of Section 5 becomes, the more likely that is to be true. By any measure, for example, the state of Mississippi continues to generate more of these problems than any other state. Similarly, if the focus of a renewed Section 5 shifts more from the state level to the county level, other than for a few states, such as Mississippi, it might become easier to selectively target in advance areas that systematically generate threats that support singling them out from other areas for the unique federal oversight of Section 5.[42] The more narrowly and precisely targeted Section 5 becomes, the more credibly national policy would be able to identify specific areas

of unique and systematic minority voting-rights problems. But if the geographic scope of a renewed Section 5 remains more or less as is, it will become increasingly difficult to account for the differences between areas covered and areas not. There are also serious questions about the constitutionality of a renewed Section 5 that cannot tie its geographic coverage to areas that have unique race-based voting-rights problems.[43] At the same time, a smaller geographic scope for national voting-rights legislation will not address the central voting problems of today; nor will it help us bring the greater centralization to national election processes that we would almost certainly adopt if we were creating our national elections today, rather than working within the structures inherited from so long ago.

The challenge is more fundamental than whether we can craft a new Section 5 with a more accurate formula for identifying "bad" jurisdictions, a formula that both makes policy sense and will support the statute's constitutionality. The real question is whether the model and philosophical basis of Section 5 continues to make policy sense today, in any but a limited number of jurisdictions. Should national voting-rights legislation continue to be based on the principle that we should or can figure out how to selectively target specific places that warrant unique federal oversight? I wonder, as a matter of policy, whether that is the best approach today (though as a matter of politics, I expect that to be the approach to which Congress adheres).

Based on what I have said thus far, some might conclude that the right answer is simply to expand Section 5 to apply nationwide. Such an expansion would recognize the futility of trying to specify ex ante through national law particular places that demand particularly aggressive federal oversight. But I do not believe that is a plausible or sensible policy response. Recall that Section 5 is a form of federal receivership; any change affecting voting cannot go into effect until examined and cleared by a federal actor. This unique, proactive form of exceptionally intensive federal oversight cannot, realistically, be extended to the entire country. The entire voting system of the United States cannot be put under federal receivership, absent a massive expansion in the federal bureaucracy that is not imaginable. And even if it could, doing so would still not address some of the critical problems mentioned above. In particular, it would not address the problem of federal voting-rights law being limited to changes—in local and state voting rules—a limit essential to the structure of Section 5 review remaining in its current form. Nationwide extension of Section 5 is neither wise policy nor a politically serious proposal.

THE FUTURE

That the philosophy of the VRA's Section 5 structure might not be as well suited to the nature and geographic distribution of voting problems today as in the past has led some commentators to conclude that Section 5 should be allowed to expire.[44] But I reach a different conclusion. We should not remain so locked into the Section 5 method of protecting voting rights as to fail to think beyond that model today. Instead, we might consider shifting the focus of policy debate from selec-

tive federal oversight of specific areas, tied to changes in voting practices, to greater emphasis on the need for additional federal legislation modeled on the form of the statutes of more recent years, such as HAVA and the NVRA. That is, federal oversight should, perhaps, move from attempting to be selectively targeted on specific jurisdictions to being of uniform national scope. At the same time, the focus should shift from a federal prophylactic against changes in voting rules to a direct, first-order focus on defining the appropriate baseline itself of proper election practices—precisely as HAVA does with respect to provisional ballots and the NVRA does with respect to voter registration. Because the concept of preclearance review itself was fundamentally tied to suspicion of changes to voting practices in particular jurisdictions, the preclearance process might be "traded," conceptually and/or politically, for greater first-order protection of the right to vote itself through national legislation establishing uniform voting standards. The preclearance process actually plays a relatively minor role these days in any event, even with the broad geographic scope of the current Section 5. In the 1996–2002 period, for example, the DOJ refused preclearance in about only 0.05 percent of the cases it reviews.[45] Although the first years after a new census and redistricting typically generate the greater number of DOJ objections, the number of these objections in the post-2000 years has been by far more than in comparable earlier periods.[46]

Despite the limited practical role of preclearance review, an enormous defense of it has been mounted already and will continue to be marshaled as the renewal process reaches center stage in Congress. But the renewal process presents an opportunity for rethinking what the model for federal voting-rights protection ought to be. Rather than mechanically reaffirming a model from earlier decades that is increasingly irrelevant and not designed for the voting problems of today, the renewal process could be used as a vehicle for moving voting-rights policy forward, not just in the details, but in the essential philosophy and structure of national policy. HAVA and the NVRA already represent major breakthroughs of this sort, though the NVRA is limited to registration issues and HAVA is limited to voting technology and provisional ballots. But HAVA constitutes a major recognition, in the wake of the 2000 election, that we need uniform, nationwide laws to structure at least certain aspects of the democratic electoral process. This is not to say that HAVA itself is perfect in all its details (indeed, far from it); but it is to say that statutes like HAVA and the NVRA provide a distinct model or form that national voting-rights legislation has taken in the last 15 years and might, in principle, best take in coming years.

Not all aspects of elections, of course, require national standards. National standards are most justified in the context of national elections. And certain administrative matters are best handled, at least for the foreseeable future, at the state level (though not at the level of individual counties). Voter registration databases are one example. Even when national oversight is justified, that oversight need not take the form of old-style, command-and-control legislation, in which the national government imposes one mandatory

substantive standard throughout the nation. National oversight can involve establishing goals and targets, while leaving states a great deal of flexibility in determining how best, in their circumstances, to reach those goals and targets. HAVA, in fact, works precisely this way with respect to voting technologies. HAVA sets standards of accuracy that voting systems must meet and offers financial incentives for states to do so, but HAVA does not require states to adopt one or another specific voting technology.

Issues like the forms of identification necessary and justified to protect against voter fraud, however, might best be resolved as a matter of national policy. There seems little need or justification for state variation in this area. Under the VRA (and the general model it embodies), the legality of different state ID requirements will turn on fortuities that have little to do with whether such requirements are needed and justified and in what circumstances. Under Section 5, the same ID requirement might be illegal in states covered by Section 5 but legal in others. Under the provision of the VRA that applies nationwide, Section 2, the same ID requirement could be illegal in states with significant minority populations but legal in others, even if in the latter such requirements unjustifiably disenfranchised the elderly, the poor, or others (as long as the ID did not do so on the basis of race or minority-language status). Through constitutional litigation, the federal courts might conclude that certain ID requirements violate the Constitution, as the district court recently concluded in the Georgia case. But the fact that constitutional rights and limits are implicated only confirms that this is one area in which national uniformity is appropriate. That uniformity should come through national legislation, rather than awaiting years of constitutional litigation in which individual state ID requirements are challenged one-by-one.

Though a more controversial example, the same might be thought true of whether felons and ex-felons should be eligible to vote or not. As the Supreme Court has recognized for 40 years, the right to vote is a fundamental constitutional right. The judgment of who is legally entitled to the right to vote (or who has disentitled themselves) therefore is similarly a matter of fundamental rights that should, in principle, be resolved uniformly throughout the nation, certainly for national elections. Given that these judgments have traditionally been made at the state level, state officials would surely resist strongly if Congress sought to legislate on the subject. And Congress, of course, would almost certainly like nothing to do with the issue. But none of that changes the fact that, as a matter of basic principle, the question of who is eligible to vote in the United States is a matter of fundamental constitutional status that, in national elections at least, ought to have a general, nation-wide answer. But the opportunity to use the VRA's renewal process as a moment to focus national policy debates on these issues requires a willingness to move discussion from the geographic focus of Section 5—debates over which areas ought and ought not to be covered—to a more general approach to voting rights.

At the outset, I noted that the VRA is nar-rowly and selectively targeted in two respects. The first is the geographic targeting central to Section 5, which is the main focus of this article and the focus of the congressional renewal process. The second is the minority-voting rights targeting central to the entire Act itself and to Section 2 in particular. I now want to raise some analogous questions for Section 2 that I have discussed at length for Section 5. I can only offer suggestive observations here, designed not to be definitive but to stimulate fresh thought on how best to protect voting rights going forward.

The main question is whether the selective focus of Section 2 on only minority voting rights—as opposed to voting rights per se—is the right or exclusive model for the future. Recall that just as HAVA and the NVRA are not geographically selective, they are not selective in this way as well. HAVA, for example, protects the right to cast a provisional ballot of all citizens in all jurisdictions.[47] Similarly, HAVA's measures on statewide registration databases and its financial incentives for improved voting technology apply nationwide without regard to determinations about whether approaches to registration and technology are racially discriminatory or not.[48] The question, then, is whether HAVA's redefinition of the problem from protection of minority voting rights to protection of voting rights as such represents the future of voting rights—and whether it should.

I will offer three brief reasons that the protection of voting rights—including minority voting rights—would be enhanced, at least in some respects, by such a shift. First, it is important

to bear in mind that Congress had historically limited national voting-rights protections
to the context of race (and later, other than
minority groups) not only because the problems were most severe in these areas, but
partly because constitutional understandings
and doctrine were thought to limit Congress'
power over voting issues to the prevention of
racially discriminatory voting practices.[49] But
since 1965, it has become much clearer that
Congress has constitutional power to directly
protect the right to vote itself. HAVA and the
NVRA are manifestations of this. Whatever
else the Supreme Court's decision in *Bush v.
Gore*[50] does, it further confirms this point:
the Constitution protects the right to vote
from being arbitrarily infringed, for any reason
at all, whether or not race is involved. The
Court now recognizes the right to vote as a
fundamental constitutional right in all general
elections, whether national, state, or local.[51]
Congress therefore has concomitant power,
for these elections, to legislate to protect the
right to vote as such. Simply because earlier
Congresses might have believed themselves
constitutionally limited to protecting voting
rights in the context of racial discrimination
is not a reason to remain locked into that
model today. Indeed, the Supreme Court of
today might well be more accepting of (and
deferential to) congressional power to protect
the right to vote as such than of congressional
power to single out regions of the country or
voting practices that disadvantage minorities,
without a discriminatory animus, for unique
voting-rights protection.

Second, in the context of modern politics, it
is often difficult to attempt to separate racial
considerations from partisan ones when voting
rights are at stake. In the voter ID controversies of the moment, for example, Republican
legislators are the initiators of efforts to
adopt ID requirements; Democratic legislators typically resist. Some charge that these
requirements are adopted for racial reasons.
But to those who believe these requirements
unjustified, are they being adopted for partisan or racial reasons? And should it matter,
assuming we could answer the question? The
same is true of national legislation that might,
for example, ban the intimidation of voters.
Would it be better (for minority voters, as
well as others) for such legislation to target
intimidation "based on race" or simply illegal
intimidation per se?

The VRA model of selectively focusing on
racially discriminatory voting practices requires
courts to determine whether race or partisan
politics is the cause (or the predominant
cause or, perhaps, a cause) for the adoption of
certain voting practices. But such an inquiry is
often intractable, for courts or other actors.
As long as black voters remain overwhelmingly Democratic, race and partisanship will
remain intertwined, perhaps inextricably so.
National legislation based on separating the
two elements will always, therefore, be problematic, at the least. This problem can lead
to underprotection of minority voting rights
themselves. The more difficult it is for courts
to separate racial from partisan or other
considerations, the greater the risk that courts
will reject voting-rights challenges on the
ground that partisan considerations, not racial
ones, account for the practice at issue. Perhaps
paradoxically, the more general the form of

voting-rights protection, the more minority voting rights will be effectively protected.

Third, and related, national legislation that differentially provides greater protection to minority voting rights than to voting rights per se creates unavoidable incentives to racialize conflicts over voting policies. Challenges and objections to voting policies based on national law must, in this model, be cast in racial terms, if those are the only terms national law recognizes as legally cognizable. Under the VRA model, voter ID requirements can only be challenged on the grounds that they are racially discriminatory. They cannot be challenged under the Act as unnecessary and unjustified restrictions on the right to vote itself (such provisions can be challenged in this form under the Constitution, which does provide general protection for the right to vote as a fundamental right). It is not clear that legislation which forces voting-rights claims to be cast in racial terms is desirable, just as it is not clear that doing so always provides the most effective protection for minority voters themselves.

Thus, there is some reason to believe that both the selective targeting features of the VRA model of voting rights—the singling out of certain places and of certain subcategories of voting rights for federal oversight and protection—represent the past of voting rights, but not the future. This is not to say that racially discriminatory voting practices are no longer a problem. But racially discriminatory voting practices are a subset of a more sweeping set of challenges to full and fair political participation in American democracy. The most effective way of providing legal

protection for voting rights, including minority voting rights, might increasingly be less through an anti-discrimination vision than through a vision focused directly on the substantive right to vote itself. To be sure, there are some voting-rights issues, that cannot be addressed through universal legislation that protects the right to vote, but only through legislation that singles out minority voting rights. The most prominent example is vote dilution; to the extent policy views this as a problem, it is unintelligible for law to attempt to protect all "groups" from having their voting power "diluted." Vote dilution can be regulated only if law singles out particular groups for such protective regulation. In addition, nothing I have said about "targeted" voting-rights legislation applies to the language-assistance provisions of Section 203, also currently up for renewal. Those provisions address an issue that, by definition, is only relevant to voters with unique language-assistance needs; these provisions ensure universal access to the ability to participate in voting at all.

Perhaps, to some extent then, national policy will need to reflect both visions: uniform national voting-rights protections as well as protections selectively targeted both geographically and on certain groups of voters. But at the least, voting-rights policy should not remain so embedded within the model of the past as to preclude looking beyond that model to consider whether different visions, such as those reflected in the NVRA and HAVA, ought to become more dominant as we move forward.

CONCLUSION

I have attempted to illuminate two distinct models of national voting-rights legislation. My aim is to provoke more self-conscious recognition that we have these two distinct models to choose from in defining the future of voting-rights policy, and that public discussion ought to grapple seriously with that choice at those few, exceptional moments at which national attention becomes focused on voting rights. Now I will explain why that will not happen.

In theory, the VRA itself, through Section 5, should provide an ideal mechanism for catalyzing a contemporary approach to voting rights legislation that reflects the current context in which these issues arise. Section 5, with its automatic sunset provision, was designed for exactly this purpose. As Section 5 expires, it forces Congress and the country to consider the changing circumstances in which voting-rights issues arise and affords the opportunity to tailor voting-rights law to these circumstances. But I do not expect Congress to engage virtually any of the kinds of questions raised here. There is simply no constituency to press these issues or to ask hard questions about what the future of voting rights ought to look like. Instead, there is every incentive for the critical actors to avoid these questions altogether.

Partisan politics, sometimes an effective vehicle for generating robust public debate, is unlikely to do so here. Republicans fear that raising any questions about the "the Voting Rights Act" will alienate Hispanic voters, a critical and up-for-grabs constituency for the Republican future.[52] Moreover, it is now generally rec-

ognized that Republicans benefit politically in the arena in which the VRA most significantly affects partisan power: political control of representative bodies.[53] The VRA's mandate to create safe minority election districts (when certain factors are present) has benefited the Republican Party at the expense of the Democratic Party, even as that mandate has also led to the election of many more minority legislators. For both reasons, Republicans have little political incentive to change the current status quo and much reason to endorse it. And for Democrats, this reality creates what might be viewed as a tragic choice; fewer safe minority districts might enhance the prospects of the Democratic Party, including its prospects to control political bodies such as the U.S. House, but at the cost of reducing the number of minority officeholders elected. Thus, there is too great a risk that raising questions about whether Section 5 of the VRA should continue in the form it has had since 1982 will be seen as an attack on a statute that is viewed as sacred by important constituencies in the Democratic Party.

Absent some side in Congress being willing to take the lead on this issue, one might look to outside leadership. The most likely candidate is the voting-rights community: the organizations, activists, scholars, community leaders, and others most actively involved in these issues over many years. If they were to suggest that the time is right to discuss "trading" some of the protections of the VRA for more aggressive, uniform national legislation, along the model of HAVA and the NVRA, the political and moral authority they wield would enable serious discussion of the future of voting rights. But this, too, is unlikely. Even were these groups to suggest such a trade, there is not likely to be any one with whom to trade. More concretely, those in control of Congress and the White House would have to indicate a willingness to consider more HAVA-like legislation in exchange for a more narrowly focused Section 5 of the VRA. But there is no indication that the political leadership in control of both Congress and the White House would be receptive to such a deal. In addition, the voting rights community, like many groups who have fought long and hard for political success, continues to operate largely within the ideological framework that dominated and succeeded in the past. Viewing themselves as on the defensive, voting rights advocates define victory as preservation of as much of the Section 5 structure and scope as possible.

Thus, a conspiracy of silence is likely to prevail among the critical actors. The likeliest result is that Congress will simply reauthorize Section 5, perhaps with modifications at the margins, but essentially in its present form. Difficult questions will be hushed over. The voting-rights community will proclaim victory, but this victory will be largely symbolic—the preservation of a past that is increasingly irrelevant and tangential to the main issues. Possibly, that is the only sort of victory available. The profound questions avoided, however, will surface only when the courts, to which Congress will likely abdicate these questions, are forced to judge whether Congress' silence compromises the constitutionality of a renewed Section 5. But the policymaking process will generate no serious discussion of whether the philosophy of Section 5 of the VRA continues to make sense today, more than 40 years after the Act's original creation, or, even more importantly, of what philosophy and approach to voting rights might now be more effective. And the day will be still further postponed at which the United States works itself out of a voting regime that remains excessively dependent, even for national elections, on the rules and institutions, not to mention the competence and whims of election officials, of the more than 3,000 counties in the oldest and one of the largest democracies in the world.

References

* Sudler Family Professor of Constitutional Law, New York University School of Law. Carnegie Scholar 2004. This article was originally presented at the *Wiley A. Branton-Howard Law Journal* Symposium, held at Howard University School of Law, Washington, D.C., on October 28, 2005. I was honored to be included in this tribute to a great and honorable man about whom I had heard so much from his close friend, and my boss from 1984–85, Justice Thurgood Marshall. A version was presented at a subsequent conference, "Making Every Vote Count," at Princeton University in April 2006, and I benefited greatly from the incisive and respectful comments of my commentators there, Frank Askin, Juan Cartagena, and Eddie Hailes. Finally, my greatest debt is to the distinguished contributors to the forthcoming book *The Future Of The Voting Rights Act* (David Epstein et. al. eds., 2006), for which I am one of the co-editors, and which is the most comprehensive contemporary analysis available of the past and future of the Voting Rights Act. Thanks also to Guy-Uriel Charles

and Richard Briffault for thoughts on earlier drafts and to Caitlin Bales for timely research assistance.

1. See *Bush v. Gore,* 531 U.S. 98 (2000).

2. Enacted as Pub. L. 89–110, 79 Stat. 437. Codified as amended at 42 U.S.C. §§ 1971, 1973 to 1973bb-1 (2000).

3. 42 U.S.C. § 1973gg (2000).

4. HAVA was enacted as Pub. L. No. 107-252, 116 Stat. 1666. In 1994, Congress also enacted the Uniformed and Overseas Citizens Absentee Voting Act, which required states to permit certain voters to participate in national elections by absentee ballots. 42 U.S.C. §§ 1973ff to 1973ff-6 (1994). This statute affects fewer voters than the NVRA or HAVA.

5. U.S. CONST. amend. XV, § 1. In several momentous cases during Reconstruction, the Supreme Court construed recently enacted national voting-rights laws as applying only to racially based denials of the vote, on the grounds that to read the statutes more broadly would call into question whether Congress had legislated beyond the limited authority that the Fifteenth Amendment grants to Congress. See, e.g., *United States v. Cruikshank,* 92 U.S. 542 (1876); *United States v. Reese,* 92 U.S. 214 (1876). In the last decade of the 19th century and the first of the 20th, Congress repealed approximately 94 percent of the voting laws it had enacted during Reconstruction. *Richard M. Valelly, The Two Reconstructions: The Struggle For Black Enfranchisement* ix (2004).

6. For elaboration on the structure of Section 5, see *South Carolina v. Katzenbach,* 383 U.S. 301 (1966), the principal decision upholding the constitutionality of the 1965 Act.

7. More specifically, in addition to Section 5, the provisions due to expire in 2007, absent congressional reauthorization, include Section 4, which contains the formula for determining which jurisdictions must comply with the geographically targeted provisions of the Act; Sections 6–9 and 13, which permit the Department of Justice to send federal examiners and observers to polling places in certain circumstances; and Section 203, which requires certain jurisdictions to provide language assistance to speakers of Spanish, Native American and Alaskan, and Asian languages. For simplicity, I will refer to all of these provisions as "Section 5," except where more specific distinctions between these expiring provisions requires greater specificity. The Voting Rights Act Amendments of 1982, Pub. L. No. 97–205, 96 Stat. 131, renewed Section 5 and these other provisions for 25 years, which is why they are due to expire in 2007 unless reauthorized.

8. Editor's Note: On July 27, 2006, President George W. Bush signed legislation reauthorizing the VRA without fundamentally rethinking its underlying philosophy or basic mechanisms.

9. For a summary of studies on the effectiveness of the Act, see Richard H. Pildes, "The Politics of Race," 108 *Harv. L. Rev.* 1359 (1995) (book review).

10. 42 U.S.C. § 1973c (2000).

11. *Id.* § 1973.

12. For discussion of this provision and empirical analysis of its effects, see James E. Alt, "The Impact of the Voting Rights Act on Black and White Voter Registration in the South," in *Quiet Revolution In the South: The Impact of the Voting Rights Act 1965–90,* at 351, 365–69 (Chandler Davidson and Bernard Grofman eds., 1994).

13. 42 U.S.C. § 1973a(b) (2000).

14. *Id.* § 1973.

15. For detailed discussion of the structure and justification of Section 5, see *South Carolina v. Katzenbach,* 383 U.S. 301 (1966), which upheld the constitutionality of this provision, and *Allen v. State Bd. of Elections,* 393 U.S. 544 (1969), which defined the scope of voting practices that Section 5 covers.

16. 42 U.S.C § 1973c (2000).

17. *Id.*

18. *Id.*

19. Coverage is determined by a formula specified in Section 4. 42 U.S.C. § 1973b(b) (2000). States currently covered as a whole are Alabama, Alaska, Arizona, Georgia, Louisiana, Mississippi, South Carolina, Texas, and Virginia. In addition, selected counties in California, Florida, New York, North Carolina, and South Dakota are covered. See App. to 28 C.F.R. Pt. 51; see also Department of Justice Web site, Section 5 Covered Jurisdictions, www.usdoj.gov/crt/voting/sec_5/covered.htm (last visited April 26, 2006).

20. 42 U.S.C. § 1973 (2000).

21. *Id.*

22. For discussion of the 1982 Amendments to Section 2, see the most important Supreme Court decision giving content to Section 2, *Thornburg v. Gingles,* 478 U.S. 30 (1986).

23. The difference between these two features of the Act is that the nationwide rule of Section 2 operates through the ordinary legal system, rather than the unusual "preclearance review" process; a voter must bring a lawsuit to challenge a voting practice, the practice can go into effect immediately unless a court enjoins it, and the voter bears the burden of proving that a law violates the Act (outside the areas reached by Section 5, there is no general presumption that state officials are acting illegally in regulating voting). Section 2 is therefore more costly, more time consuming, and substantively more difficult for those challenging a voting practice than is Section 5.

24. See *supra* note 8.

25. I am indebted to comments from Richard Briffault for emphasizing this point.

26. See generally *Quiet Revolution In the South: The Impact of the Voting Rights Act 1965–90* (Chandler Davidson and Bernard Grofman eds., 1994) (presenting the history of the original Voting Rights Act and detailed, empirical analysis of its effects).

27. With the exception of Native American voters, who face exclusionary barriers to voting resembling those of the pre-VRA world. See *Native Vote: American Indians, the Voting Rights Act, and the Right to Vote* (Jennifer Robinson et. al., forthcoming, Cambridge University Press, 2006).

28. See Daniel P. Tokaji, "Early Returns on Election Reform: Discretion, Disenfranchisement, and the Help America Vote Act," 73 *Geo. Wash. L. Rev.* 1206, 1220–39 (2005). I have also learned a great deal about these issues from Nate Persily's work, including his contribution to this symposium.

29. The five covered Florida counties were Collier, Hardee, Hendry, Hillsborough, and Monroe. See Section 5 Covered Jurisdictions, http://www.usdoj.gov/crt/voting/sec_5/covered.htm (last visited April 26, 2006).

30. *Bush v. Gore* arose from controversy surrounding recounts in Palm Beach, Miami-Dade, Broward,

Volusia, and Nassau counties, none of which are covered by Section 5. See 531 U.S. 98 (2000).

31. For details of these election disputes, see Samuel Issacharoff, Pamela S. Karlan, and Richard H. Pildes, *The Law of Democracy: Legal Structure of the Political Process* 199–205 (rev. 2d ed. Supp. 2005).

32. For excellent general discussion of these diverse issues, see Daniel P. Toakji, "The New Vote Denial: Where Election Reform Meets the Voting Rights Act," 57 *S.C. L. Rev.* 689 (2006).

33. See *Common Cause/Georgia v. Billups,* 406 F. Supp. 2d 1326 (N.D. Ga. 2005).

34. Wis. Stat. 5.02 (Supp. 2005); Ind. Code 3-5-2-40.5 (Supp. 2005). A federal district court upheld Indiana's new law against federal constitutional and voting rights challenges. See *Ind. Democratic Party v. Rokita,* No.1:05-cv-00634-SEB-VVS (S.D. Ind. filed Apr. 14, 2006).

35. Carter-Baker Commission, "Building Confidence In U.S. Elections: Report of the Commission on Federal Election Reform" 21 (2005).

36. The race-based structure of the VRA creates significant hurdles of its own to felon disfranchisement laws even under the nationwide provisions of Section 2. See, e.g., *Johnson v. Governor of Fla.,* 405 F.3d 1214 (11th Cir. 2005) (*en banc*) (holding that Section 2 of the VRA does not apply to felon-disenfranchisement laws at all, in the context of a challenge to a Florida constitutional provision that had been most recently re-enacted in 1968), cert. denied, 126 S. Ct. 650 (U.S. 2005). A panel of the Second Circuit similarly rejected a Section 2 challenge to New York's felon disfranchisement law, though the Second Circuit is currently reviewing *en banc* the panel's decision. *Muntaqim v. Coombe,* 366 F.3d 102 (2d. Cir. 2004), rehearing *en banc* granted, 396 F.3d 95 (2d. Cir. 2004). The Ninth Circuit has permitted a Section 2 challenge to Washington's felon disfranchisement law to proceed to trial, *Farrakhan v. Washington,* 338 F.3d 1009 (9th Cir. 2003), where the case remains pending.

37. See, e.g., Lawyer's Comm. "For Civil Rights Under Law, Nat'l Comm'n on the Voting Rights Act, Protecting Minority Voters: The Voting Rights Act at Work, 1982–2005" (Feb. 2006). It is noteworthy that this report provides extensive factual information on voting issues, but does not suggest what

that information should be interpreted to mean for any of the concrete policy issues concerning renewal of Section 5, such as which areas of the country should be under Section 5 today, for how long Section 5 ought to be renewed, and the like.

38. See *supra* note 37, *Lawyer Committee's Report,* at 95 and *id.,* at 95 n.308. This information applies to statewide redistricting plans, for which there are judicial findings of racially polarized voting since 1982 in 16 states.

39. *Id.* at 81-84.

40. *Id.* at 82–83.

41. Ellen Katz and the Voting Rights Initiative, Documenting Discrimination in Voting Under Section 2 of the Voting Rights Act, Voting Rights Initiative Database (2005), www.votingreport.org. Of course, much more information would have to be assessed before knowing what this fact reveals about race and politics in these states. I offer this finding only suggestively, as an illustration of the complexity in documenting state differences that were obvious on these issues in the past.

42. For the suggestion that an amended Section 5 should be targeted at counties rather than states, see Bernard Grofman and Thomas Brunell, Extending Section 5 of the Voting Rights Act: The Complex Interaction between Law and Politics, in *The Future of the Voting Rights Act, supra* note 1.

43. There are serious constitutional issues as well. The Supreme Court might hold a renewed Section 5 unconstitutional absent a close fit between the areas singled out and actual evidence of discriminatory voting practices that justify unique federal oversight of those areas. See *Nev. Dep't of Human Res. v. Hibbs,* 538 U.S. 721, 756 (2003) (Kennedy, J., dissenting); *United States v. Morrison,* 529 U.S. 598 (2000); *City of Boerne v. Flores,* 521 U.S. 507 (1997).

44. See, e.g., Abigail Thernstrom & Edward Blum, "Do the Right Thing," *Wall St. J.,* July 15, 2005, at A10; Abigail Thernstrom, "Emergency Exit," *New York Sun,* July 29–31, 2005, at 10.

45. Richard L. Hasen, Congressional Power to Renew the Preclearance Provisions of the Voting Rights Act After *Tennessee v. Lane,* 66 *Ohio St. L. J.* 177, 192 (2005). This reflects a dramatic decrease from comparable periods in earlier decades, such as the first four years after a new census and redistricting cycle. This sharp decline might be explained by jurisdictions having internalized the requirements of Section 5 and complying with them; jurisdictions complying because the shadow of the Section 5 process hangs over them; Supreme Court decisions during the 1990s that restricted the scope of the Act; less aggressive DOJ enforcement of the Act; and/or the fact that most of the "safe" African-American majority election districts that could be created in the country were created in the 1990s, often after DOJ objections to proposed plans, which left few new "safe" districts to be created in the 2000s and hence few DOJ objections to the failure to create such districts. Determining the precise causal role of any of these factors in isolation, or in combination, to the limited role of Section 5 in recent years requires more sophisticated analysis than has been available to date.

46. See *supra* note 37, *Lawyer Committee's Report,* at 80.

47. See Help America Vote Act, Pub. L. No. 107–252 § 302(a), 116 Stat. 1666 (2002).

48. *Id.* §§ 101–102, 303.

49. See *United States v. Reese,* 92 U.S. 214 (1876); *United States v. Cruikshank,* 92 U.S. 542 (1876).

50. 531 U.S. 98 (2000).

51. See, e.g., *Kramer v. Union Free School District* No. 15, 395 U.S. 621 (1969) (local elections); *Harper v. Virginia Bd. of Elections,* 383 U.S. 663 (1966) (state elections).

52. See David Lublin, *The Republican South: Democratization and Partisan Change* (2004).

53. *Id.*

Complying with the Help America Vote Act (HAVA): Variations Among the States

Sarah F. Liebschutz
State University of New York–
Brockport

Daniel J. Palazzolo
University of Richmond

The Help America Vote Act (HAVA) provided states with federal funds to upgrade their voting systems and improve election administration. To comply with the law, states had to develop implementation plans and meet established deadlines for voting safeguards (i.e., provisional voting and voter identification for first-time voters who register by mail), a statewide voter registration list, and voting system standards. Yet HAVA allowed states to implement the requirements in different ways, and they were expected to take advantage of that flexibility. As political scientist Robert Montjoy observed, HAVA's goal of providing uniform and nondiscriminatory standards for federal elections applies "within states, not across states."[1] This paper seeks to address a fundamental question: How did states with decentralized election systems adapt to a federal law that required greater state centralization and responsibility for election administration?

Our focus is on both the causes for the variations in state compliance with HAVA and the consequences of HAVA requirements for election administration, with particular emphasis on the experiences of New Jersey, New York, and Pennsylvania in implementing HAVA. We identify administrative, political, and policy-related reasons for variations in HAVA compliance in each state. We also consider the effects of HAVA on state and local government interactions, funding decisions, and policy innovation. We begin by reviewing HAVA compliance requirements, describing how states responded to those requirements, and comparing New Jersey, New York, and Pennsylvania with the national norms for compliance.

HAVA COMPLIANCE: VARIATIONS ACROSS THE STATES

HAVA is a "modified direct order" from the federal government to the state governments because it consists of a combination of incentives and requirements.[2] Incentive grants are provided under Title I of the act to support election administration and replace punch cards and lever machines with electronic voting machinery. HAVA also provided states with funds under Title II to meet requirements in Title III under specified deadlines:[3]

- January 1, 2004, for compliance by the states with provisional voting, voter identification, and voting information requirements (Section 302);
- January 1, 2004, with potential for a waiver to January 1, 2006, for compliance with computerized statewide voter registration list and voting information requirements (Section 303); and
- January 1, 2006, for compliance with voting systems requirements, including: preventing overvotes by allowing a voter to verify, correct, or change a ballot before a vote is cast; providing a permanent paper record that can be used in an audit; allowing the disabled to cast an independent and secret ballot; meeting the language minority requirements of the Voting Rights Act of 1965; ensuring that voting systems do not contain error rates that exceed Federal Election commission standards; and establishing a uniform definition of a vote (Section 301).[4]

Although all states were required to meet the deadlines under Title III, they operated on different schedules and differed in how they spent HAVA funds and how they implemented the requirements under Title III.[5]

With respect to voting safeguards, all but five states, including New Jersey, had provisional voting in place by the January 1, 2004, deadline.[6] New York allowed provisional voting before the 2000 presidential election and Pennsylvania adopted provisional voting legislation in 2002, prior to the passage of HAVA.[7] Ten states, including New Jersey and New York, failed to comply with HAVA's voter identification requirement by the deadline.[8] All states, however, met HAVA requirements for provisional voting and voter identification in time for the 2004 presidential election.

Compliance with statewide voter registration requirements under HAVA has been a greater challenge for many states. Forty-one states applied for a waiver of the January 1, 2004, deadline. By the January 1, 2006, deadline, at least 40 states had a statewide voter registration database compliant with HAVA, including Pennsylvania. Several others, including New Jersey, were nearing completion of a statewide database, while New York was far behind in complying with this requirement.[9]

Although we do not have reliable surveys on compliance with all of the voting system standards in Title III, in one of the most important areas of compliance—providing access for voters with disabilities—over one third of states had not provided at least one machine that would allow the disabled to cast an independent and secret ballot by January 1, 2006.[10] Many states that accepted federal funds to replace punch cards and lever machines did not meet the deadline. New Jersey has been relatively successful by comparison to other states. New York expects new machines to be certified by 2007, though it has not yet contracted with a vendor. Pennsylvania continues to operate with a medley of optical scan, DRE, lever, and hand-counted paper ballots. We take up the issue of voting machinery in greater detail in the case studies below.

States needed to complete an implementation plan to apply for any funds under HAVA, including estimates of how HAVA funds would be spent on various aspects of election reform. These initial estimates were often adjusted after the plans were submitted; for instance, New Jersey and Pennsylvania received more

TABLE 1

Allocations and Percentage of HAVA Funds by Major Category (in millions of dollars)*

Spending Category	New Jersey	New York	Pennsylvania**	National Ave.
Voting Equipment	$48.6 (58.0%)	$190.0 (86.0%)	$76.1 (61.0%)	$30.1 (57.2%)
Registration Database	$25.0 (30.0%)	$20.0 (9.0%)	$13.1 (10.0%)	$12.8 (23.3%)
Voter Education/Poll Worker Training	$4.0 (6.0%)	$10.0 (5.0%)	$7.2 (5.0%)	$4.1 (9.6%)
Provisional Voting	$1.0*** (1.0%)	0.0 (0.0%)	$.2 (<1.0%)	$.02 (4.3%)
Other****	$6.2 (7.0%)	$1.0 (<1.0%)	$26.5 (21.0%)	$.03 (5.5%)
Total	$88.8	$221.0	$123.2	$52.7

Sources: For New Jersey, HAVA Executive Summary, April 13, 2005; for Pennsylvania, Commonwealth of Pennsylvania State Plan As Amended, September 15, 2005, p. 35; for New York, New York State Board of Elections, May 24, 2006.
* Numbers may not add to 100 percent due to rounding.
** The Pennsylvania data—breakouts and total—reflect appropriations of federal funds for 2003 and 2004, and do not include additional Title II funs estimated at about $40 million for receipt in 2005.
*** The New Jersey HAVA State Plan allocated $1 million for provisional voting; a figure left out of the more recent executive summary.
**** Other expenses refer to office, transportation, salaries, and voter registration.

federal funds than anticipated by their original plans. As Table 1 indicates, states planned to spend a majority of HAVA funds on replacing and upgrading voting equipment. All three states expected to spend near the national average percentage of funds on replacing and upgrading voting equipment.

COMPARING NEW JERSEY, NEW YORK, AND PENNSYLVANIA

New Jersey, New York, and Pennsylvania have strikingly similar political and institutional characteristics. All three neighboring states have predominantly individualistic political cultures,[11] politically competitive electoral systems, professional state legislatures, and governors with strong institutional powers.[12] All three states score high on the dimensions of state aid to local government and direct state spending.[13] They also had similar election systems prior to the passage of HAVA. All three states had decentralized systems of elections, wherein the states provided no funds to localities for election costs, no training of election officials, and the localities purchased their own voting equipment, albeit with the approval of the state.[14] None of the three states required any form of voter identification prior to HAVA.[15] They differed, however, on other aspects. For instance, although at least some voters in all three states voted on lever machines prior to HAVA, New York led the way with lever machines in use statewide. New Jersey had largely moved to direct-recording electronic systems (DRE), and Pennsylvania voters cast ballots on a wide range of systems. New York and New Jersey had some form of provisional balloting, though only New York's policy was standard across the state. New Jersey and Pennsylvania had compilation registration databases that gave localities authority to make changes to voter rolls, whereas New York had no such database. Given the similarities and a few differences in election systems among the three states, we consider how each responded to HAVA's requirements and incentives.

PENNSYLVANIA AND HAVA: MOSTLY ON SCHEDULE

Pennsylvania is distinctive from New Jersey and New York for its accelerated timing of election reform and for its timely compliance with HAVA mandates. In the aftermath of the 2000 election, Republican Governor Tom Ridge established a Voting Mobilization Task Force via Executive Order, and the General Assembly created a Joint Select Committee to Examine Election Laws. Then, the Pennsylvania legislature (General Assembly) passed legislation to create a statewide voter registration database (Act 3 of 2002), provisional voting, and identification requirements (Act 2002–150) in advance of HAVA.[16]

These election reforms enacted by the legislature were "incremental," hastened by "fears of a 'Florida' election and the emerging realization of the weak capacity of existing election law" but limited by partisan divisions over reforms, such as voter identification, that could advantage or disadvantage Republicans or Democrats.[17] The voter identification issue resurfaced again in 2006, when the Republican-controlled General Assembly adopted legislation requiring all voters to present identi-fication at the polls—not just first-time voters as stipulated in HAVA. Democrat Governor Edward Rendell vetoed the bill, contending that it would place an onerous burden on urban voters.

Following enactment of HAVA, two implementation boards authorized in the 2002 Pennsylvania legislation were appointed—the Voting Standards Development Board and State Plan Advisory Board. Pennsylvania's HAVA Implementation Plan was adopted in 2003, with amendments filed with the Election Assistance Commission in 2004 and 2005. Pennsylvania complied with the HAVA January 1, 2004, deadline regarding provisional voting and voting information. The state requested and received waivers to January 1, 2006, of the January 1, 2004, deadlines for replacement of lever machines and punch card systems, and establishment of the statewide voter registration database. As of January 1, 2006, Pennsylvania had met the statewide database and voting systems mandates of the act. Nonetheless, Pennsylvania experienced complications in bringing the statewide database system on-line, timely selection and delivery of replacement voting machines, and voter identification requirements at the polling place.

SURE

Pennsylvania's Statewide Uniform Registry of Electors (SURE) was a long-sought response to discontent at both county and state levels for many years before HAVA.[18] Prior to the adoption of SURE, each of the state's 67 counties "administered its own voter registration records, and county officials had no means to crosscheck these records with the records of other counties."[19] SURE is the clearest evidence of greater centralization of election administration in Pennsylvania. Established in law in January 2002, nine months before HAVA, and developed by Accenture, SURE was fully operational by the January 1, 2006, deadline. The process, however, of developing and implementing this centralized voter registration database was not entirely smooth.

Initial reactions to SURE varied according to whether counties had "Chevrolet" or "Cadillac" voting systems.[20] Smaller and rural counties—with Chevrolets—were "grateful for a better voter registration system."[21] "We all used to do our own thing," the director of elections of Wayne County observed, "Now we feel more comfortable that other counties are doing as we are."[22] Larger counties, notably, Allegheny, Philadelphia, and Montgomery—with Cadillacs—had systems in place that were more sophisticated than SURE. Philadelphia, for example, with an electronic registration system which incorporated images of completed voter registration forms (with signatures) for its nearly one million voters, resisted linkage with SURE which did not include such images.[23]

The technical challenges of creating a statewide electronic voter database were not trivial. As Philadelphia officials anticipated, SURE was not initially capable of efficiently handling the electronic transfer of about one million registrations from Philadelphia without slowing down the entire state system. An unrealistically fast development timeframe of one and one-half years, under a 2002 state contract with Accenture during the administration of Governor Ridge, contributed greatly to start-up problems. An external, independent review initiated by Governor Rendell, Ridge's successor, led to a three-year renegotiated contract with Accenture and a "PA SURE-Go Forward Strategy" in 2005. There are still technical challenges, local and state officials agree, but the level of intergovernmental cooperation in problem-solving has improved. Philadelphia, finally overcoming "kicking and screaming about abandoning its old system," was the last county to join the SURE system in 2005.[24]

Under SURE, the role of the Pennsylvania Department of State has been enlarged, although the role of the counties remains substantial. The department now has responsibility for maintaining the database and for coordinating registration records with the departments of transportation and health. Counties continue to play key roles in the administration of elections, by registering new voters, using state-designed forms, maintaining local voter registration records, and retaining authority for modification of local records. Also they maintain the ability to print poll books—a function they consider crucial for the smooth running of elections.

VOTING SYSTEMS

HAVA's voting systems requirements also increased the role of state government, but maintained county discretion in the selection of voting systems.[25] In the November 2000 election, three types of voting methods were used in the state's 67 counties, with lever machines accounting for 65 percent, electronic voting systems, 34 percent, and paper ballots, less than 1 percent. HAVA mandates affected all 67 counties in the state, not only those who had to replace their lever machines, but also those with electronic systems (DREs, optical scans, and electronic punch cards) to ensure that they were accessible to individuals with disabilities.

The state government assumed authority under HAVA to certify compliant voting systems. It did not challenge the local option of counties to replace or upgrade their voting systems. Rather, the Department of State "encouraged" them, using reimbursement incentives to "procure a single HAVA compliant precinct count electronic voting system that can be used by all voters, including persons with disabilities, that provides full compliance with the voting system requirements of Federal and State laws."[26]

Pennsylvania permits, but does not require, a voter verifiable paper audit trail (VVPAT). The State Plan recognizes the points of difference between proponents and of opponents of VVPAT. Local elections officials interviewed for this chapter did not express a preference for VVPAT; rather, they expressed concerns about invasion of secrecy if a voter number were matched with the voter's choices.

MAY 2006 PRIMARY ELECTIONS

The May 16, 2006, primary elections were the first statewide test of compliance with HAVA's voting systems requirements. The process of replacing outmoded machines in time for the

primary in Pennsylvania's 67 counties could be characterized as "zig-zag."[27] The entire process was initially held up because of late formation at the federal level of the Election Assistance Commission and delays in certifying voting systems by the federal independent testing authority, and, as a consequence, by the states. Two other factors also contributed to delays—a legal challenge and the inability of a vendor to commit to delivering machines in time for the May primary elections. Plaintiffs in Westmoreland County argued in February 2006 in a Commonwealth (trial level) Court that the state constitution required voter approval before purchase of new machines; a position upheld by the judge. The ruling was overturned on March 3, 2006, by the Pennsylvania Supreme Court, the state's highest, which agreed with the position of the Department of State, namely, that federal law preempts state law.[28]

The May primary date created another obstacle for timely acquisition of replacement machines. Advanced Voting Systems (AVS) was not certified by the Pennsylvania Department of State until mid-February 2006. Ten counties with AVS contracts for delivery of machines within 90 days were informed on March 13, 2006, that the vendor "was doubtful of its ability to deliver the machines in time for the county to train poll workers and familiarize voters for the primary."[29] While seven of the 10 counties switched to other systems guaranteed for timely delivery, three small rural counties—Northampton, Lackawanna, and Wayne—remained with AVS. Although AVS subsequently delivered the machines two weeks before the primary and conducted three-day training sessions for poll workers, the truncated time frame was difficult for local officials. "I'm at the point where I'll just be glad when this election is over. Everything has fallen in our laps. All the stress … all the responsibility."[30] Bucks was the lone Pennsylvania county that failed to switch from lever to HAVA-compliant machines. After the vendor with which it contracted for delivery of 700 electronic voting machines, Electec Inc., a subsidiary of Danaher Corporation, indicated it could not deliver the machines, Bucks County commissioners "hastily crafted a plan to use only paper ballots." That plan was ruled unlikely to be HAVA-compliant by the state elections commissioner. In the end, Bucks County officials decided to risk the loss of $950,000 in HAVA funds by using lever machines.[31]

On the whole, the May primary with new HAVA-compliant voting systems went relatively smoothly in most Pennsylvania's counties. The director of elections of rural Wayne County noted the advantage of testing the new machines in a primary election. "Of all elections," she observed, "it was best to have a primary [with the new machines] because of fewer candidates and voters."[32] Officials in urban Allegheny County, which overlies Pittsburgh, concurred. Despite "glitches, particularly with getting the new electronic voting machines started" and longer time to count votes than in the past, they and their counterparts in other western Pennsylvania counties were relatively pleased with the adaptation of voters to the new systems.[33]

VOTER EDUCATION AND ELECTION WORKER TRAINING

While education of voters and training of election-day workers are county responsibilities, the role of the state government has been enlarged. Respectful of the statutory authority of the counties for these matters, yet anticipating potential confusion from the use of new voting technology, the Department of State developed an extensive voter education and outreach program and training sessions for elections officials. The Pennsylvania Plan stipulates a wide variety of educational activities, developed in consultation and with the support of county boards of elections that were mounted across the state beginning in 2004. Both state and local officials made clear that the purpose of all of these activities was for understanding the new voting systems and ensuring accessibility to them, not in generally extending the franchise.

REINFORCING CENTRALIZATION

The major effect of HAVA in Pennsylvania has been to reinforce a trend toward greater centralization in election administration. While the prerogatives of the counties in election administration remain strong, they have been diminished and those of the state government, strengthened. The trend toward centralization of elections was in place prior to HAVA. In part, it was attributable to the National Voter Registration Act (NVRA) of 1993, which increased the role of the state Motor Vehicles Department (DMV) in voter registration. The other centralizing influence was SURE, Pennsylvania's own initiative to address the problem of duplication of records under NVRA, which

involved central electronic processing of registration forms by the DMV, then transmittal
by paper to the counties. Until the NVRA and
SURE, the "Department's role was largely
ministerial, and it had little authority—except
through policy direction and assistance—over
the county boards of elections and registration
commissions."[34]

HAVA reinforced the centralization trend
by making states accountable for compliance. While Pennsylvania respected the
constitutional authority of counties to select
state-certified voting machines, at the same
time, it required them to share accountability. All 67 counties were required to submit
written county plans prior to disbursement of
HAVA funds by the Department of State; the
plans detailed intended uses of HAVA funds
and how the county would maintain current
levels of local funding for election administration. These contractual relationships, new
in the history of elections administration in
Pennsylvania, were explicitly intended "as a
means to determine a county's compliance
with HAVA."[35]

HAVA's effects have not been uniform across
Pennsylvania's counties. The state's influence
has been greatest on smaller, rural counties
regarding selection of replacement voting
machinery and accession to the SURE system.
Counties like Philadelphia, the state's largest, with its own pre-HAVA sophisticated
electronic voter registration database and
electronic voting machines (acquired in 2002
with its own funds, pursuant to a 1999 city
ballot initiative), did not welcome an enlarged
state government role. Nonetheless, HAVA,

under the direction of the state government,
trumped all of these local variations.

NEW JERSEY AND HAVA: DELAYED COMPLIANCE AND POLICY INNOVATION

Four general observations emerge from New
Jersey's efforts to implement HAVA. First,
New Jersey represents a case of delayed
compliance with HAVA requirements, and the
reasons for delay are different for each of the
three main areas of reform: voter safeguards,
statewide registration database, and voting
system standards. Second, HAVA provided
a stimulus for policy innovation, and those
innovations mainly have been directed toward
expanding voter access and participation.
Third, the degree of partisanship in election
policy varies by issue, and partisan differences
are greatest on issues dealing with voter access
and identification. Finally, HAVA and subsequent policy innovations that stem from HAVA
have forced state level policymakers and local
election officials to negotiate a tenuous balance between state responsibility and local
control over elections. Officials in the attorney
general's office and legislators have learned to
value the experience and expertise local election officials bring to the policy process, and
they have solicited their input,[36] but the lines
of authority in the attorney general's office
and its articulation of election administration
polices are not entirely clear to local officials.[37]

DELAYED COMPLIANCE

Compared with most states, the New Jersey
legislature acted swiftly in response to HAVA,
passing bipartisan bills (A3151 and S2348) in

June 2003 with compliance provisions for provisional balloting and voter identification.[38] The
legislation was enacted even before completion of the final report in August 2003 of the
HAVA state planning commission. But the bill
contained a controversial item; it required all
voters who registered after January 1, 2003,
and had not presented personal identification
(not just those who registered by mail for the
first time as required by HAVA) to provide
proof of identification at the polls. Though this
provision extended HAVA's voter identification requirement, legislators believed that it
created a more uniform approach to voters
who had registered for the first time. But,
at the urging of unions and other advocacy
groups who opposed a voter identification provision, Democratic Governor James
McGreevey vetoed the bill. After stripping
the bill of its voter identification language, the
Democrat Assembly majority approved the
bill, but the Senate, equally divided between
Democrats and Republicans, defeated the
measure along party lines.

This delay caused New Jersey to be one of
just 10 states to miss HAVA's deadline of January 1, 2004, for provisional voting and voter
identification.[39] After the 2003 elections, in
which Democrats gained a majority in the
Senate, both chambers passed in July 2004,
and the governor signed into law S701, a bill
that complied with HAVA voter identification
and provisional voting guidelines. The vote on
S701 reflected partisan divisions over voter
identification. In the Assembly, all Democrats
voted for the bill, while only two Republicans
voted in favor and 29 voted against; in the

Senate all Democrats voted in favor, while only
seven Republicans voted in favor and 10 voted
against.[40]

In 2005, the New Jersey legislature enacted
two additional pieces of legislation related
to HAVA compliance standards, both with
bipartisan support. A bill to improve poll place
accessibility for the disabled (A3392/S1387),
with input from Director of Elections Ramon
de la Cruz and local election officials, met
and exceeded the requirements of HAVA
and passed both chambers unanimously.[41] A
statewide registration database bill (A45/S28),
with input from the attorney general's office
and local government officials, also passed with
overwhelming support by the legislature with
one just one dissenting vote in the Assembly.

The development and implementation of the
statewide voter registration database (SVRS)
proved to be more difficult, revealing the
challenges of introducing a centralized system
in a state where local governments have traditionally run elections. The attorney general
was slow to act on what turned out to be an
enormous challenge: to coordinate the input
and efforts of local governing boards, election
officials, and various state agencies that would
eventually share data on a single system comprised of voter lists that had been developed
and maintained by the various 21 counties
across the state. When the attorney general
proposed a top-down centralized voter registration database, the New Jersey Association
of State Election Officials threatened to file a
lawsuit.[42]

Eventually, the attorney general appointed Michael Gallagher, formerly director of administration with the Motor Vehicle Commission, to direct the SVRS project. Local officials demonstrated to Gallagher and other staff in the attorney general's office that vendors proposing to build the SVRS did not have a back-up system and could not guarantee that information would be secure if the system failed.[43] Gallagher's solution was to allow local governments to keep their servers and maintain their voter lists. He also developed a communication plan consisting of system protocols, newsletters, weekly updates, and special bulletins.[44] Coordination among the various stakeholders also improved as a result of Joint Application Development (JAD) sessions, where the attorney general's staff, local election officials, and representatives of various state agencies involved in the project exchanged information and ideas and worked out compromises.[45] Gallagher maintains that the state could not have developed a system without input from local election officials.[46]

In spite of these improvements in the process, SVRS was not completed by the January 2006 deadline. The delay was partially a consequence of the scale of the project, which Gallagher describes as a "comprehensive electoral management system," with "real time architecture," that allows voter registration information entered by local officials to be checked instantaneously by records from various state agencies.[47] Progress also slipped as a result of programming problems. The SVRS was fully deployed in all 21 counties by May 15, 2006. Yet the counties brought on line last could not use the system during the June primaries, and

some individuals worry that it will take months to troubleshoot the complicated system. If the system succeeds, despite its delayed implementation, New Jersey officials contend it will be one of the most advanced voter registration databases in the nation.

VOTING SYSTEMS

New Jersey also lags behind many states in terms of making its voting systems HAVA compliant, and at least some of the problems stem from a lack of administrative support for voting machine certification. An inventory report of the attorney general in 2004 showed that virtually all of New Jersey's 21 counties needed to be either replaced or upgraded.[48] Under the HAVA plan, the state reimburses local governments for 75 percent of their costs of replacing voting machines. The plan also noted that the attorney general would need to "promulgate rules and regulations that comport with the latest technology of voting machines," and redefine the voting machine committee that examines machines for certification and charge the committee with addressing security issues and problems associated with access for disabled voters.[49] Several observers have noted that these steps have not been taken, creating delay in ordering voting machines.[50] Even counties with machines in place anticipate training and operational problems with the audio kits and software designed for disabled access machines.

Meanwhile, certification has been further complicated by a bill (A33) passed by the state legislature in 2005 requiring all machines to produce a voter-verified paper trail (VVAPT) of votes. Though the technology had not yet been fully developed when the bill passed, the state's estimated cost of implementing the new requirement was between $26.4 and $39 million, and the local cost was "unknown."[51] In addition to costs, issues about storing, operating, and maintaining the machines had not been resolved when the bill was signed into law.[52]

ELECTION EDUCATION AND VOTER OUTREACH

New Jersey contracted with the Center for Government Services at Rutgers University to develop a first-of-its-kind training course on election administration for election officials.[53] Professor Earnest Reock of the Center for Government Services involved experienced election experts in the development and instruction of a "Basic County Elections Administration."[54] Hundreds of election officials took the four-day course, which was offered in several locations throughout the state. Several counties have also involved students at local high schools to work at election-day polls.[55] These efforts are generally viewed positively by policymakers and administrators.

The most striking and controversial aspect of New Jersey's voter education program has been an extensive voter outreach program designed to increase voter registration and turnout. Attorney General Peter Harvey broadly interpreted the voter education provisions of HAVA, stating that one of HAVA's goals was to increase voter participation and turnout.[56] The point is stated in the HAVA state plan: "The fundamental goal of any electoral process, at any level of government, is

to have the largest number of qualified voters turnout to vote.... This is clearly one of the goals of HAVA, to engage as many qualified voters in exercising the franchise."[57] Actually, though HAVA does not preclude states from spending funds on voter outreach, it does not recommend that states use federal funds to promote participation. HAVA's voter education provisions are intended to support state efforts to provide voters with information about how to register and vote, and to ensure that every vote is counted. HAVA generally sought to strike a balance between access and ballot security often described as "making it easier to vote, but harder to cheat."[58] Harvey's voter outreach program was clearly focused on the first part of this statement.

In 2004, the attorney general's office launched its "BE POWERFUL, BE HEARD" voter education campaign, which was explicitly designed to encourage young people to vote.[59] Harvey contended: "We have to advertise voting and other civic responsibility the same way we advertise leisure activities and the same way we advertise beer. We need to get people excited about voting and explain to people why their vote matters."[60] The advertising campaign features celebrities in the entertainment and sports industries. The attorney general held a "Hip Hop" Summit, recruited the New York Giants, and devoted the Division of Elections home page to streaming videos from famous musicians, actors, and athletes.[61] According to one source, Harvey spent $2.7 million of the $3 million in HAVA funds planned for voter education on the advertising campaign.[62] The voter outreach campaign was the third-largest expense of the

$28.4 million New Jersey had spent up until 2006; $15 million was spent for new voting machines and the $9 million for the statewide voter registration system.

The attorney general's office attributes increases in voter registration and voter turn-out data, particularly among 18–24 year olds, in the 2004 election to the voter outreach campaign.[63] But the program clearly pushed the intention of HAVA's voter education provision toward the advocacy end of the spectrum and drew criticism from some observers of HAVA who believed the funds could have been used more constructively to educate young people about the election process.[64]

HAVA AND BEYOND: POLICY INNOVATION IN NEW JERSEY

New Jersey's voter outreach campaign, the statewide voter registration database (SVRS), legislation to improve disabled access to voting, and the voter verified paper audit trail (VVPAT), exemplify the innovative spirit of the state's efforts to exceed HAVA requirements. In 2005, the New Jersey legislature passed a bill (A35/S1133) to allow no-excuse absentee voting, yet another example of New Jersey's efforts to make it easier for people to vote. Consistent with previous roll calls dealing with voter access, the bill reflected partisan divisions.[65] Thus HAVA has been a stimulus for election law reform, and with the Democrats in charge, those reforms have clearly emphasized easing voting restrictions and encouraging voter access to the system.

NEW YORK AND HAVA: EVENTUAL REFORM

New York was the last state to bring its laws into compliance with HAVA. Governor Pataki's signature on July 12, 2005, of the Election Reform and Modernization Act, adopted unanimously by the state legislature on June 23, 2005, marked the end of a long and divisive political process. After failing to meet HAVA deadlines, on March 1, 2006, the United States Department of Justice filed suit against the New York State Board of Elections, alleging violations of the Help America Vote Act.

New York's troubles in complying with HAVA reflect what scholars refer to as "strategic delay," a delay that may result from needs for greater clarity about policy implications, lack of support from key stakeholders, or concerns about how federal programs affect local preferences.[66] The strategic delay in New York was facilitated by advocates who sought partisan advantage, made claims about home rule, or insisted on framing the issue of election administration in terms of civil rights.[67] As a result of compromises that ended the strategic delay—those already reached and those expected as a result of the federal court order—the administration of elections will be considerably centralized. Local boards of elections will continue to play consequential roles in the elections process. So, too, will the advocates for change in New York's system, whose voices throughout the implementation process were forceful and effective. Ultimately, however, HAVA's combination of mandates and funding incentives changed the agenda for election reform in New York.

For two years after the 2000 election, election reform in New York was mired in gridlock, a consequence of partisan divisions, a strong tradition of home rule, an entrenched de-centralized election system, and fierce advocacy groups. In 2002, HAVA—with its prospect of more than $235.6 million to replace New York's lever machines, educate voters, train election-day workers, and establish a statewide registration database—changed the terms and the pace of election reform. Though the state legislature missed the HAVA's deadline of January 1, 2004, for voter identification, Assembly Democrats and Senate Republicans reconciled their differences in time for the September 2004 primary elections.[68] It was a compromise between the Assembly Democratic majority's expansion of HAVA language to include 22 forms of acceptable voter identification (in light of its traditional base of poor, urban, minority voters, many of whom do not have a driver's license), and the Republican Senate majority's much less inclusive list responsive to its largely suburban base. The compromise included the HAVA language and allowed discretion for local elections boards to verify identification.

New York sought and received a waiver to January 1, 2006, for compliance with com-puterized statewide voter registration list and voting information requirements, and was faced with the same deadline for compliance with voting systems requirements. Partisan-ship and access advocacy were entangled in New York's responses to those HAVA mandates. Governor Pataki's designation of Peter Kosinski, Republican deputy executive of the state Board of Elections, as chief state elections official—bypassing Thomas Wilkey, the Democratic executive director of the state board—generated charges of partisanship.[69] Kosinski was criticized for "failing to represent adequately the diverse citizens of New York State, especially… racial, ethnic and language minority communities" in the 19-person Task Force he appointed, and for "preventing [the Task Force] from playing any significant role in the process of preparing the State Plan.[70] The plan filed in August 2003 with the Election Assistance Commission was intended by the State Board as a framework for "an ongoing process" within which to discuss and resolve specific issues; it was characterized by its detractors as full of good intentions, but failing to "articulate a true plan of action."[71]

Over the next two years, the Assembly Democratic majority and Senate Republican majority passed one-house bills, but failed to reconcile differences. Finally, with the January 1, 2006, HAVA deadline looming, the legislature unanimously passed major reforms in New York's election system in April, May, and June 2005. The Election Reform and Modernization Act, passed at the end of the 2005 session on June 25, contained the two most dramatic reforms—development, maintenance, and administration of a new statewide registration database by the state Board of Elections and replacement of lever machines with state-certified DRE or optical scan machines, each with a paper record of votes cast. Although the statewide database and new voting systems were nearly foregone conclusions by both houses of the legisla-ture by the time of adoption, the final bill reflected compromises that respected partisan positions, sensitivities of county boards, and concerns of watchdog groups and disability rights organizations.[72]

New York's lateness in adopting laws compliant with HAVA mandates bore out the prediction that failure of the State Plan in 2003 to resolve contentious issues "would push New York to the limit in 2006."[73]

VOTING SYSTEMS

The truncated timetable for replacing New York's lever machines in time for the September 2006 primary elections was unrealistic. "We think it's a massive project that requires time and care to get done and we would feel very anxious to have to run a couple of elections in a row with workers not familiar enough with these machines to carry it off without disenfranchising some people," a state board spokesman commented.[74]

The Election Reform and Modernization Act of 2005 stipulates that state-certified DRE or optical scan machines, with a paper record of votes cast, are to replace the lever machines. One voting machine or system at each polling place is to accommodate voters with disabilities or to permit alternative language accessibility. The state board published draft voting machine regulations on November 30, 2005, and held four public hearings in regions around the state in December and January. Civic groups, including the New York State Public Interest Research Group, Common Cause, and the League of Women Voters, reacted negatively to the draft regulations. Their comments included concerns about

lost votes and failure to assure full access to voters with disabilities and to protect language minorities.[75] "Voting Systems Standards," final regulations revised in response to those comments, were not issued by the state board until May 2006.

Implementation then shifted to a second state agency, the Office of General Services (OGS), charged with negotiating with and awarding contracts to vendors of HAVA-compliant machines. OGS issued requests for bids on June 1, 2006. After the award of contracts for a term of five years, the process will revert to the state Board of Elections for certification of the voting systems. At the same time, each county and New York City will begin its own machine selection and vender-negotiation processes. Finally, each local elections board will submit a plan to the state board detailing its preferred machine and how it will meet voter education, election worker training, and accessibility for persons with disabilities mandates in HAVA and New York State law. By mid-June 2006, some movement had occurred with regard to New York's voting systems. However, the basic charge of the U.S. Department of Justice against New York of failure to meet voting systems standards of HAVA still pertained. (See below for discussion of the lawsuit filed on March 1, 2006.)

THE STATEWIDE VOTER REGISTRATION DATABASE

The challenges of developing a statewide voter registration database were recognized from the outset at both state and local levels. They, too, were exacerbated by late adoption of state legislation to bring New York into compliance with HAVA. "Building a statewide database was supposed to be simpler than replacing our lever machines," one local elections commissioner observed. "It turned out to be more complicated."[76] "We knew we were going to be late," a state elections board official acknowledged, but also asserted, "We were not going to rush."[77]

After months of consultation by the state Board of Elections with elections experts around the country, OGS issued on May 22, 2006, a request for proposals (RFP) to build "NYSVoter," a statewide voter registration system. The broad parameters for a "bottoms-up" statewide database were specified in the 2005 New York Election Reform and Modernization Act: a system "whereby each of the 62 counties maintains its own local registration and election management system and feeds voter registration data to a statewide registration database." The state Board of Elections responded by adopting the "bottoms-up," two-phase process of the State of Washington.[78] As described in the 2003 Washington State Plan, the first phase was to "implement a single interactive state-wide voter registration database (VRDB) designed to interact with [existing] county election management systems and to interact in some fashion with commercial election management systems (EMS) operating at the county level."[79] The second phase, in cooperation with county officials, involved tight integration of VRDB and EMS, "allowing the state to provide greatly enhanced voter information services to the counties. This phase 'include[d] building an EMS in-house to replace county EMS systems, or building additional tools and linkage mechanisms.'"

The Washington State voter registration database was attractive to New York for several reasons. First, by obviating the need to "custom-build" or purchase a "commercial-off-the-shelf" solution, it could expedite the procurement and implementation processes. Second, it was cost-effective since Washington State both offered to transfer its database architecture and connectivity features and Microsoft, its software platform, without cost to New York. Proposals to OGS on the bid date of June 28, 2006, for systems integration implementation assistance for NYSVoter allowed bidders to "implement and modify the Washington transfer solution using... existing or... alternative technologies."[80]

VOTER EDUCATION AND ELECTION
WORKER TRAINING
Local boards of election are responsible for poll worker training and education of voters. The entire chain of steps for local installation of new voting machines was held up by late enactment of HAVA-compliant state laws. Without vendor contracts and certified voting systems, training of local elections officials, from commissioners to technicians to election inspectors, and outreach efforts to educate voters on new voting systems, could not be initiated. In brief, the ripple effects of the state legislature's lateness in bringing New York into compliance with HAVA came home to roost.

THE U.S. JUSTICE DEPARTMENT LAWSUIT
AGAINST NEW YORK
Although the state Board of Elections moved immediately to translate the Election Reform and Modernization Act into reality, it could not

move quickly enough to meet the HAVA compliance deadline of January 1, 2006. For two months after the deadline passed, the state board negotiated with the U.S. Department of Justice to develop a consent agreement on an implementation timetable.[81] "We thought we had an agreement; it was 99 percent worked out," stated Lee Daghlian.[82] The Department of Justice determined otherwise.

New York was the first state to be sued by the federal government for non-compliance with HAVA. Legal action was initiated on March 1, 2006, with the filing of a suit in U.S. District Court for the Northern District of New York (Albany) against the New York State Board of Elections, the co-executive directors of the board, and the State of New York. Two causes of action were specified in the lawsuit—the state's failure to implement a statewide voter registration database and to meet voting systems standards of HAVA (Sections 303 and 301, respectively). "Unless and until ordered to do so by the court," the Department of Justice stated in its petition to the court, "New York would not take timely action to ensure compliance" with these mandates of the Help America Vote Act.[83]

Shortly after the lawsuit was filed, a coalition of New York voters and civic groups, including New Yorkers for Verified Voting and the New York State League of Women Voters, filed a motion to intervene. The coalition was critical of the state for "having failed to comply with HAVA, when proper implementation could have led to proper elections" in 2006. However, the coalition contended that forcing New York to overhaul its voting systems before the September 26 primary would "throw elections into complete chaos" for voters and election-day workers using untested voting systems acquired in haste.[84]

Three weeks later, on March 23, 2006, U.S. District Court Judge Gary L. Sharpe ordered New York to submit by April 10, 2006, "a comprehensive plan for compliance with Sections 301 and 303(a) of HAVA," and the Department of Justice to respond to the state's proposed compliance plan 10 days later. At the same time, Judge Sharpe denied the coalition's motion to intervene.

THE NEW YORK PLAN FOR COMPLIANCE WITH HAVA

The New York Board of Elections responded to the court order with a proposed remedial plan in two-phases: interim compliance in 2006 and full compliance in 2007. Both phases concern HAVA's voting systems and statewide voter registration database mandates.[85]

- The Interim Voting Systems Plan focuses on steps to make voting devices accessible to persons with disabilities for the 16 September 2006 primary elections. Locations of such ballot-marking devices are to be determined on a jurisdiction-by-jurisdiction basis; most of the county boards of elections proposed to locate one machine at one central place (typically its central office) for all its disabled residents. Interim compliance with HAVA statewide voter registration requirements takes the form of initial steps to fully implement the Washington State "bottoms-up" model described above. The Interim Plan includes milestone tasks with target start and completion dates for voting systems and NYS Voter, the statewide database.

- The plan for full compliance in 2007 stipulates a chain of actions necessary to replace New York's 20,000 lever machines—from promulgation of regulations, certification of machines, contracts with vendors, to acceptance testing of voting equipment prior to use in an election—and to locate at least one HAVA-compliant voting system for individuals with disabilities in each polling place. The target for full compliance is the fall 2007 elections. Complete development and implementation of NYSVoter, is intended to be achieved by spring 2007. The Full Compliance Plan does not specify milestone tasks and target dates.

The response of the Department of Justice to the New York remedial plan was reluctant approval. The interim voting systems plan was characterized as "far less than even minimum compliance since [it] deals only with compliance with Section 301's requirements of voting system accessibility for individuals with disabilities and, even then, only provides for partial—and far from full—compliance." The department described the jurisdiction-by-jurisdiction plans as "for the most part, very poor [but] better than nothing." With "great reluctance" and the desire to avoid "overwhelming electoral chaos" if New York were to attempt "replacement of all lever machines and achieve complete voting systems accessibility by the fall," the department did not oppose the interim voting systems plan of the state board. Regarding the plan for full compliance in 2007, given New York's "record to date," the department requested the court to order the state board to submit by July 15, 2006 a "detailed schedule for long-term voting systems compliance." The department was less critical of the interim and long term plans for development and implementation

of NYSVoter, the statewide voter registration database, agreeing that, on full implementation, "New York should be in full compliance with Section 303 (a) of HAVA." Nonetheless, it requested that the state board submit a detailed scheduled by June 15, 2006, of implementation milestones to the court.[86]

Judge Gary Sharpe accepted the remedial plan submitted by the state Board of Elections on June 2, 2006, viewing it as leading, "upon full implementation, to full compliance with HAVA." "The actions that the State and local jurisdictions in New York to partially comply with HAVA for the fall 2006 elections," he wrote, "will provide a practicable measure of compliance tempered by the need to ensure that the right of every voter to vote is not impaired and that the orderly conduct of the election process itself is not in any manner jeopardized." At the same time, retaining the court's jurisdiction, he ordered more submissions by the state board than were requested by the Department of Justice. They were four separate filings, in June, August, and September 2006, of efforts by each county and New York City to ensure privacy of the individual vote of each voter with disabilities, a detailed schedule for replacing all lever machines, regulations for NYSVoter, and a detailed schedule to develop and implement the statewide registration list. Finally, he ordered the state Board of Elections to submit bi-weekly reports through November 7, 2006, and monthly reports thereafter of progress in implementing his Remedial Order.[87]

GETTING HAVA RIGHT
AND ON TIME

"New York," an elections official observed, "has been more concerned about getting HAVA right than doing it on time." Filtered through the lenses of partisanship in the legislature, demands by advocacy groups, and local claims for election control, "getting HAVA right" was inextricably linked to strategic delays in implementation. The federal court order has changed the timetable for implementation. New York must now not only "get it right," but "do it on time."

CONCLUSION

How did states with traditionally decentralized election systems respond to a law that requires greater state centralization in election administration? The short answer to this question is that they did so with difficulty and in different ways. Delays in Pennsylvania were largely a result of tensions between state and local officials, certification problems, and the magnitude of the task of replacing voting machines in 67 counties. The causes for delay in New Jersey depended on the issue. A lack of leadership at the outset of the process and functional problems later on stalled the effort to build a statewide registration database; partisan differences over voter identification prevented the state from meeting voter safeguard requirements on schedule; and unclear certification guidelines, problems with installing disabled access equipment, and apprehension over the VVPAT slowed the process of installing and upgrading voting equipment. Some observers suggest that the prevalent delays in implementing HAVA in New Jersey stem

from its institutional structure. New Jersey is the only state in which the attorney general is the chief elections official. In addition to commingling law enforcement with administrative functions, this arrangement may weaken the administrative capacity of the Division of Elections, as it competes with other priorities of the office.[88] New York suffered the longest delays in enacting enabling legislation, due to intense partisanship, local traditions, and advocacy group demands. Then, further complexity resulted from converting such legislation into new HAVA-compliant voting systems across the state and creating an operational statewide registration database in time for 2006 elections. If not for the force of a federal judge, the prospects for implementing HAVA in New York would still be dim.

A few common themes emerged with respect to the consequences of HAVA. First, though HAVA compliance required greater state responsibility over essential aspects of election administration, the federal legislation also served as a stimulus for innovation. These innovations varied across the states and they emerged in the context of HAVA requirements (such as the statewide databases, voter education, and voting system standards), and somewhat tangentially as a consequence of the increased attention to election reform. Second, compliance decisions and policy innovations were advanced through administrative, legislative, and legal channels, and in some cases through more than one of these. Those decisions required a blend of complex, technical information about tasks like programming a database or developing protocols for certification, philosophical and partisan debates over voter identification and access, and practical issues about the interaction of voters with election officials and poll workers. Third, because of the technical and practical issues, state-level policymakers had to engage local election officials who had the experience and expertise needed to gain HAVA compliance. HAVA unquestionably required greater state responsibility in election administration, but involving local officials in both legislative and administrative decisions was essential, particularly in the development of statewide voter registration databases. Fourth, delays in meeting HAVA deadlines for voting equipment normally resulted from state and local politics, the certification process, and the availability of machines. One could argue rea-sonably that, in specifying deadlines for HAVA compliance, Congress did not anticipate the enormous pressure the new law would put on administrators and manufacturers of voting equipment. Congress' failure to anticipate the VVPAT further complicated the situation. Finally, though partisanship does not pervade all aspects of election reform, party does matter in issues related to voter access and voter identification. Our state-by-state comparison provides evidence for the adage: "Democrats want every vote to count; Republicans want every vote to count once."[89] Let the counting resume, as election officials continue to work through the complex and challenging issues posed by the Help America Vote Act.

Notes

The authors express appreciation to the elected and appointed public officials and private citizens who shared their expertise on New Jersey, New York, and Pennsylvania elections. We also appreciate the research and editorial assistance of Worlanyo Kudonou and David Roberts. We are responsible for any errors of interpretation contained in the analysis.

1. Robert S. Montjoy, HAVA and the States," p. 17.

2. Sarah F. Liebschutz and Daniel J. Palazzolo, "HAVA and the States," *Publius: The Journal of Federalism* 35 (Fall 2005), p. 506.

3. Federal payments for these requirements are contingent upon the state submitting an implementation plan, including a commitment to match 5 percent of the total payments.

4. For a summary of provisions for HAVA and funding implications, see Robert S. Montjoy, "HAVA and the States," *Election Reform: Politics and Policy*, eds. Daniel J. Palazzolo and James W. Ceaser (Lanham, MD: Lexington Books, 2005), pp. 16–34.

5. For a review of HAVA compliance in all states, see Electionline.org, *Election Reform: What's Changed, What Hasn't and Why 2000–06*, (Washington D.C.: Electionline.org, 2006).

6. Electionline.org, *Election Reform 2004: What's Changed, What Hasn't and Why* (Washington D.C.: Electionline.org, 2004), p. 25.

7. For a review and analysis of election reforms in Pennsylvania, see H. W. Jerome Maddox, "Pennsylvania: New Policies, Old Politics," Daniel J. Palazzolo and James W. Ceaser, eds., *Election Reform: Politics and Policy* (Lanham, MD: Lexington Books, 2005), pp. 141–56.

8. Dan Seligson, "Ten States Still Debating Help America Vote Act Compliance Legislation," February 19, 2004, electionline.org, accessed March 9, 2006.

9. Electionline.org, *Election Reform: What's Changed, What Hasn't and Why: 2000–06*, p. 19.

10. Electionline.org, *Election Reform: What's Changed, What Hasn't and Why 2000–06*, p. 9.

11. Daniel J. Elazar, *The American Federalism: The Impact of Space, Time, and Culture on American Politics* (Boulder, CO: Westview Press, 1994), p. 241.

12. See Virginia Gray and Russell Hanson, *Politics in the American States* (Washington, D.C.: CQ Press, 2004), for ratings of competitiveness (p. 88), professionalism of legislatures (p. 158), and governor's powers (pp. 212–14).

13. Gray and Hanson, *Politics in the American States*, p. 54.

14. Electionline.org, *Working Together? State and Local Election Coordination* (Washington DC: electionline.org, September 2002).

15. For information on these three voting systems, see Electionline.org, *Election Reform: What's Changed, What Hasn't and Why 2000–06.*

16. Maddox, "Pennsylvania: New Policies, Old Politics," p. 141.

17. For elaboration of these points see Maddox, "Pennsylvania: New Policies, Old Politics."

18. Commonwealth of Pennsylvania, *State Plan as amended*, September 15, 2005, p. 22.

19. Electionline.org, *Election Reform: What's Changed, What Hasn't and Why, 2004–06*, p. 65.

20. Interview with William Boehm, Director of Policy, Bureau of Elections, Pennsylvania Department of State, March 21, 2006.

21. Interview with William Boehm.

22. Interview with Darlene Burnett, Wayne County Director of the Bureau of Elections, 16 March 2006.

23. Interview with Edgar Howard, Philadelphia Commissioner, March 21, 2006.

24. Interview with Edgar Howard.

25. Maddox, "Pennsylvania: New Policies, Old Politics," p. 147.

26. Commonwealth of Pennsylvania, *State Plan as amended*, p. 37.

27. Verbal observation by Doug Chapin, Director of Electionline.org, "Making Every Vote Count: A Colloquium on Election Reform Legislation," Princeton University, April 7, 2006.

28. Diana Reddington, "It's a go for new voting systems," *Philadelphia Inquirer*, March 3, 2006, p. B4.

29. Peter Hall, "Counties told to move on machines," *The Express-Times*, March 15, 2006. www.nj.com

30. Deborah DePaul, chief registrar in Northampton County, quoted in Peter Jackson, "Some Counties Struggle to beat May deadline for voting machines." Pennlive.com, April 11, 2006.

31. Hal Marcovitz, "Bucks only county to lose vote funds," www.mcall.com, May 11, 2006.

32. Interview with Darlene Burnett, June 2, 2006.

33. Mark Belko, "Allegheny County gives good grade to new voting machines," www.post-gazette.com, May 8, 2006.

34. Commonwealth of Pennsylvania, *State Plan as amended*, p. 4.

35. Commonwealth of Pennsylvania, *State Plan as amended*, p. 30.

36. Interviews with Michael Gallagher, New Jersey HAVA administrator, March 27, 2006; Steven Finkel, Assistant Attorney General in New Jersey and Director of Legislative Affairs, March 30, 2006; Joanne Armbruster, Atlantic County Supervisor of Elections, March 17, 2005; and Ingrid Reed, Director of the Eagleton New Jersey Project, Eagleton Institute of Politics at Rutgers University, March 30, 2006.

37. Interview with Reed; Dana Convoy, Policy Advisor, New Jersey Assembly Republican Office, March 24, 2006; and anonymous local election official, March 27, 2006.

38. "The States Tackle Election Reform Summary of 2003 Legislative Action" May 11, 2004, www.ncsl.org/programs/legman/elect/taskfc/03billsum.htm, accessed March 10, 2006.

39. Dan Seligson, "Ten States Still Debating Help America Vote Act Compliance Legislation," *electionline Weekly,* February 19, 2004, www.electionline.org, accessed March 10, 2006.

40. Votes on final passage in the Assembly (June 17, 2004) and the Senate (March 22, 2004). Data provided by Dana Conrad, Policy Advisor, NJ Assembly Republican Office (March 22, 2006).

41. The bill ensured that polling places complied with the Americans with Disabilities Act and established voting accessibility advisory committees at the county level to inspect polling places for disability access. For county committees, see www.state.nj.us/lps/elections/voter_advisory_committees_doe.html.

42. Interview with Armbruster.

43. Interview with Armbruster.

44. For specific protocol, see, for example, "SVRS Decision Matrix," New Jersey Office of the Attorney General, HAVA Unit-SVRS Project Management Office, www.state.nj.us/lps/elections/svrs/resources/decision-matrix-6-15-05.pdf; for references to communications from the attorney general's office, see www.state.nj.us/lps/elections/svrs/index.html, both accessed March 20, 2006.

45. Interviews with Arbruster and Michael Gallagher, New Jersey HAVA administrator, March 27, 2006.

46. Interview with Gallagher.

47. Interview with Gallagher.

48. New Jersey Help America Vote Act (HAVA), New Jersey Office of the Attorney General. At: www.state.nj.us/lps/elections/hava-info/p8.html, accessed March 26, 2006.

49. Office of the Attorney General, "New Jersey HAVA State Plan: Improving the Shape of New Jersey's Voting Experience," p. 25. www.state.nj.us/lps/elections/hava_plan.html, accessed March 20, 2006.

50. Interviews with Feehan and Reed. See also, Erica Zarra, "Ballot of the Ballot Boxes Rages on: Representatives, Political Activists Continue to Study Voting Options," *The Montclair Times,* November 2, 2005, http://montclairtimes.som/

page/php?page=10706, accessed 20 March 2006. See also, Electionline.org, "What's Changed What Hasn't and Why: 2000–06," p. 9.

51. Legislative Fiscal Estimate, No. 33 State of New Jersey 211 Legislature, May 19, 2005, www.njleg.state.nj.us/2004/Bills/A0500/33_EI.PDF, accessed March 26, 2006.

52. Jeffrey T. Zaino, "Voting Officials Challenged to Provide Paper Backup," *Asbury Park Press,* August 2, 2005, www.app.com/apps/pbcs.dll/article?AID=/20050802/ OPINION/508020329/1030/ POLITICS, accessed March 7, 2006.

53. Though municipal clerks in New Jersey were required to take classes in order to be certified under state law prior to HAVA, county election officials were not given formal training in election administration. Office of the Attorney General, "New Jersey HAVA State Plan: Improving the Shape of New Jersey's Voting Experience," p. 22, www.state.nj.us/lps/elections/hava_plan.html, accessed March 20, 2006.

54. "Attorney General Peter C. Harvey Announces New Jersey's Inaugural County Elections Officials Training Program," News Release, Office of the Attorney General, January 6, 2005, www.state.nj.us/lps/newsreleases05/pr20050106b.html, March 20, 2006. Interview with Professor Earnest Reock, Center for Government Services, March 8, 2006.

55. Interview with Armbruster.

56. New Jersey Office of the Attorney General, press releases, May 13, 2003, "Volunteer New Jersey Elections Reform Committee Meets for First Time; Membership Includes Local Elections Officials, Leaders of Advocacy Groups," www.state.nj.us/oag/newsreleases03/pr20030513a.html, accessed March 28, 2005.

57. Office of the Attorney General, "New Jersey HAVA State Plan: Improving the Shape of New Jersey's Voting Experience," p. 19, www.state.nj.us/lps/elections/ hava_plan.html, accessed March 20, 2006. A subsequent attorney general report placed voter outreach ahead of statewide registration databases and voting equipment in order of importance in terms of HAVA compliance. New Jersey Attorney General, New Jersey Help America Vote Act (HAVA), www.state.nj.us/lps/elections/hava-info/p12.html, accessed March 20, 2006.

58. Stated in the testimony of Doug Chapin, director of electionline.org, "Testimony concerning the implementation of the federal mandates imposed by the Help America Vote Act and its impact on the administration of elections in New Jersey." February 9, 2004, www.njleg.state.nj.us/legislativepub/pubhear/afr020904.pdf, accessed March 23, 2006.

59. Kevin Riordan, "N.J. hopes stars can convince young people to vote," *Courier-Post Column,* July 22, 2004, www.courierpostonline.com/columnists/cxri072204a.htm, accessed March 21, 2006.

60. Michael Eisen, "Excerpt from "Giants Tee Off for Charity," *Giants.com.* www.state.nj.us/lps/elections/interview_ag-ph-nfl-com_060204.html, accessed March 21, 2006.

61. News release, New Jersey Office of the Attorney General, "Russell Simmons and the Hip-Hop Summit Action Network Invites the Public to Attend the New Jersey Hip-Hop Summit, Combining Hip-Hop Culture, Music, Young People," September 21, 2004, www.state.nj.us/oag/news releases04/pr20040921b.html; Help America Vote Act, New Jersey Performing Arts Center, April 7, 2004 *NJEDge.Net,* www.njedge.net/njhava/index.html, accessed March 21, 2006.

62. Sandy McClure, "Harvey's hip-hop voting ads a $3M buy," *Courier News,* c-n.com, January 15, 2006, www.c-n.com/apps/pbcs.dll/article?AID=/20060115/NEWS/ 601150356, accessed March 15, 2006.

63. The report indicated that in the 2004 election, 460,000 new registered voters, 232,000 individuals voting for the first time, 5 million individuals in New Jersey (the highest number in history), and voting turnout among 18–24 year olds increased from 35 percent in 2000 to 50 percent in 2004. www.state.nj.us/lps/elections/hava-info/p37.html, accessed March 25, 2006.

64. Both quoted McClure, "Harvey's hip-hop voting ads a $3M buy."

65. For the vote on final passage of A35, (June 20, 2005) all Democrats in the Assembly and only five Republicans voted for the bill; 24 Republicans voted against it. The Senate vote on final passage was less divisive: Republicans voted 10–4 in favor of the bill and all Democrats voted in favor. Data provided by Dana Conrad, Policy Advisor, NJ Assembly Republican Office (March 24, 2006).

66. For more on the concept of strategic delay, see Malcolm Goggin, et al, *Implementation Theory and Practice: Toward a Third Generation* (Glenview, IL: Scott, Foresman/Little Brown, 1989).

67. Liebschutz argues that New York's delay was strategic in Sarah F. Liebschutz, "The Implementation of HAVA in New York: From Antiques to High Tech," *Publius* 35 (2005), p.597–98.

68. New York has long allowed for provisional voting, so that was not an issue in HAVA compliance.

69. Wilkey, a nationally regarded elections specialist, was named the first executive director of the federal Election Assistance Commission in 2005.

70. New York State Board of Elections, *State Implementation Plan,* August 2003, p. 45; New York State HAVA Implementation Task Force, *Minority Report in Response to the State Implementation Plan,* p. 3.

71. *Minority Report,* p. 3; Interview with Peter Kosinski, deputy executive director, New York State Board of Elections, January 14, 2004.

72. For an analysis of the compromises in the New York HAVA legislation, see Liebschutz, "The Implementation of HAVA in New York: From Antiques to High Tech," pp. 611–613.

73. Electionline.org, "In Focus This Week: Critics say New York HAVA Plan is 'No Plan at All,'" October 30, 2003, www.electionline.org.

74. M. Mindy Moretti, "In focus this week," *election line Weekly,* March 23, 2006. www.electionline.org.

75. Common Cause/New York and New York Public Interest Research Group, "Civic Groups React to State Board of Elections Vote on New Voting Machines," November 2, 2005.

76. Interview with Peter Quinn, Monroe County, New York Elections Commissioner, March 3, 2006.

77. Interview with Lee Daghlian, director of public information, state Board of Elections, March 23, 2006.

78. Interview with Daghlian.

79. Washington State Board of Elections, *Washington State Plan* 2003, p. 10, www.secstate.wa.gov.

80. New York State Office of General Services, "Request for Proposal No. 1235," May 22, 2006.

81. Wan J. Kim, assistant United States attorney general, in a letter dated January 10, 2006 to Eliot Spitzer, New York state attorney general, and Todd Valentine, general counsel, New York State Board of Elections, expressed the hope that "we will be able to resolve this matter through a negotiated consent decree rather than through costly and protracted litigation."

82. Interview with Daghlian.

83. U.S. District Court, Northern District of New York, *United States of America v. State of New York, et al.,* Civil Action No. 06-CV-0263.

84. U.S. District Court, *United States of America v. Larry Rockefeller, et al.,* Civil Action No. 06-CV-0263, *Memorandum in Support of Intervention.*

85. New York State Board of Elections, *Plan for Compliance with the Help America Voter Act and Chapters 24 and 181 of 2005 Laws of New York,* April 10, 2006.

86. *United States' Response to State of New York's HAVA Remedial Plan,* April 28, 2006.

87. *Proposed Remedial Order,* June 2, 2006.

88. New Jersey Citizen's Coalition on Implementation of the Help America Vote Act, *Making New Jersey's Votes Count,* New Jersey Citizen's Coalition on Implementation of the Help America Vote Act (Newark: New Jersey Appleseed Public Interest Law Center, 2004), p. 15).

89. We are not sure where this phrase originated, but we trace it at least to Cokie Roberts, see James W. Ceaser and Andrew E. Busch, *The Perfect Tie* (Lanham, MD: Rowman and Littlefield, 2001), p. 9.

The Legitimacy of Imperfect Elections: Optimality, Not Perfection, Should Be the Goal of Election Administration

Edward B. Foley
Moritz College of Law,
Ohio State University

The title of this conference is "Making Every Vote Count," and I have been asked specifically to address the topic of "Equity in HAVA Implementation." But what do these terms really mean? What would it mean to achieve true equality of voting rights in election administration, and is "making every vote count" really the same as counting every vote and doing so accurately? I want to suggest that there is an inevitable gap between the idealism of our "equal voting rights" rhetoric and the reality of whatever the best designed and best implemented system of electoral administration is capable of achieving.

My thesis is that we have not yet come to grips with this gap, although it is imperative that we do so. We must figure out a way to modulate our idealism. We must ratchet down public expectations of what the optimal electoral system can deliver—so that if and when we actually put the optimally feasible system into place, we can say that it is entitled to public acceptance and appreciation as satisfying the highest possible standard of demographic legitimacy, rather than being condemned as inadequate in failing to live up to our professed ideals of equal voting rights.

Our nation by no means yet has achieved an optimal electoral system. There is still much, much work to be done, as avoidable errors abound. In a recent primary election in Cleveland, for example, local election officials lost 70 computer memory cards containing vote totals from 14 percent of precincts, and even a full week after the election these officials did not know how many of these lost cards had been recovered and, conversely, how many remained missing.[1]

But even if we ever get to optimality, it would not satisfy the rhetorical aspirations of "making every vote count" and would not guarantee complete equality of voting rights for all citizens, as that phrase is often used. Thus, we need a new way to define and describe the optimally feasible system, and as society we have hardly started to tackle this essential task.

I will begin by describing the problem in some more detail, illustrating it with several examples. Then, I will offer a tentative solution, or at least a way to begin thinking about a solution.

THE PROBLEM OF PERFECTIONIST EXPECTATIONS

Our "equal voting rights" rhetoric, as well as the understanding of democracy it reflects, demands perfection from the electoral system.

But perfection is unattainable, and not just because of technological limitations or the inevitability of human error, but because there are other important human values that necessarily compete with the ideal of "making every vote count." As a society we appropriately will not give up our commitments to those other human values, and yet we are not yet willing to admit to the existence of this values conflict and the sacrifice it demands to the achievement of equal voting rights.

Think of an election which is decided by just one vote, but we know that two ballots cast for the losing candidate that should have been counted were not. Perhaps they were misplaced provisional ballots, or provisional ballots that were not properly checked against original registration forms, as occurred in the State of Washington during its 2004 gubernatorial election.[2] If this occurs, we say that the election process malfunctioned: the wrong candidate won. Indeed, we have procedures designed to rectify this error. It is in this important sense that our conception of democracy demands perfection, and it demonstrates what we mean when we say that we are committed to making every vote count. If we find out that just two provisional ballots were mishandled, in an election decided by only one vote, we demand that the result be overturned and that the true rightful winner be declared victor and installed in office.

Consider, as an illustration of this point, an editorial in the *Boston Globe* concerning the wrongly rejected provisional ballots in the Washington gubernatorial election. Entitled "One Person, One Vote," thus invoking the most fundamental mantra of perfectionist rhetoric, the editorial observes that the voters themselves "had done nothing wrong" and, therefore, it was proper for the judiciary to insist that these erroneously excluded votes be added to the final official tally, even as the consequence would be to flip the positions of the winning and losing candidates. Then, fully embracing the standard of perfection in the counting of votes, the editorial concludes: "[M]istakes that allow losers to win because legitimate votes are not counted must be squeezed out of the system. The cause of each mistake should be tracked down and eliminated."[3] The message of this editorial is crystal-clear: not a single outcome-determinative mistake is tolerable.

The same demand for perfection exists if two votes cast for the winning candidate were ineligible ballots, when the margin of victory is again just one vote. Perhaps a married couple voted by absentee ballot—and then again in person—as occurred in a local election in Ohio a couple of years ago.[4] This outcome is equally flawed, and equally in need of rectification. Two votes must be removed from the result. And if these two extra votes were for the candidate who won by just one vote, well then the wrong candidate prevailed. Democracy—the commitment to equal voting rights—demands reversal of the result. Again, in this situation, for the election to be fair it must be perfect.

Yet we know there is no such thing as a perfect election. Any election administrator will tell you that. Or, as a recent comprehensive GAO report on the 2004 election summarized, "[t]he administration of election systems will never be error free or perfect."[5]

So why does our rhetoric and our understanding of democracy demand the impossible standard of perfection? It may come from the original town meeting idea of democracy. Or from our image of voting as it occurs among members of a legislature. If a senator's vote is not counted, or a representative votes twice, and either error makes the difference in whether a law is enacted by Congress, we would say that the voting process in the legislature malfunctioned, with the error needing to be rectified. But in a town meeting or a legislative session, democracy occurs on a scale small enough for perfection to be a reasonably attainable ideal. Not so in the context of a modern mass democracy, where millions cast votes for governor or president.

ACCURACY AND EQUALITY CONFLICT WITH OTHER ESSENTIAL VALUES

Perfection is not just unattainable in practice; it is unattainable in principle. Thus, the task is not merely to build better vote-counting machines, ones with fewer error rates than the infamous punch-card ballots used in Florida during the 2000 presidential election. Nor would it suffice to improve the hiring and training of poll workers and other election officials, so that these individuals made fewer mistakes in the handling of ballots and the counting of votes. To be sure, vast improvements still could be made in both these respects, especially in terms of increasing the skill and performance of election personnel, and one can only speculate about how much healthier our democracy

would be if the nation's electoral systems were to operate in accordance with the "Six Sigma" standard adopted by many businesses and other sectors of public administration.[6]

Six Sigma is a management protocol that seeks to reduce the rate of error in a system's operation to 3.4 incidences per million. Pioneered by Motorola and championed by General Electric, among other major corporations, Six Sigma derives its name from the mathematical symbol for the statistical concept of six standard deviations from the mean. If applied in the context of elections, Six Sigma would require fewer than four vote-counting errors (ballots either erroneously included or excluded from the certified total) for each million voters who attempt to cast a ballot. In the 2000 presidential election, where approximately six million ballots were cast in Florida (5,963,070 according to official results[7]), compliance with Six Sigma would have produce a margin of error of 20 votes, well below the 537-vote margin in favor of then-Governor Bush, according to the state's certified results. Even the 129-vote victory for Christine Gregoire in the 2004 Washington governor's race, out of total of 2,808,341 ballots in the state's certified results,[8] would have been well beyond the 10-vote margin of error called for by Six Sigma. Consequently, even though Six Sigma could not guarantee absolute perfection—the proverbial one-vote margin of victory where just two ballots were wrongly included or excluded would escape Six Sigma's strictures in an election with more than one million voters—it would be an extraordinarily rare statewide race that would fail the Six Sigma standard. As a nation, we might have to wait another several centuries for such an event to occur.

But the Six Sigma standard is likely to be unattainable for elections not simply because we are unwilling to devote the financial resources that would be necessary to achieve it, or because we lack the political will to implement effective management practices in the sphere of electoral resources. Instead, important social values that we are unwilling to sacrifice require us in the context of elections to tolerate the risk of error rates that are significantly higher than what Six Sigma would call for. To understand this inevitable values conflict, it is useful to consider some examples from different areas of election administration.

REGISTRATION

Deadlines

There needs to be enough time to evaluate the eligibility of new registrants. If officials try to do this before election day, so that the new registrants can vote a regular ballot rather than a provisional ballot, then the system needs a cut-off date for closing the door on new registrants. For example, 30 days. But then anyone who changes residence after 30 days is shut out of the election.

The consequence of the cut-off date is most vivid if we imagine someone who moved to the state 25 days before election day and then goes to the polls in the patriotic hope of participating in the election of the nation's president. (Turnout, after all, is to be encouraged.) Assuming that this new resident receives and casts a provisional ballot, this provisional ballot would not count because the resident was not properly registered within the deadline for doing so. Perhaps we would not consider the exclusion of this provisional ballot erroneous, but a more lenient deadline (say 15 days, instead of 30) would have enabled this citizen to participate in the franchise, as he or she wished to do.

To avoid this denial of the right to vote, six states permit same-day registration, whereby a new voter can both register and vote on election day.[9] The elimination of any pre-election registration deadline, however, increases the risk that a person appearing at the polls is ineligible to vote but that this ineligibility will be undetected. The person might be underage or a non-citizen or might even have voted previously in another polling place. The risk of erroneously included ballots as a result of same-day registration might be relatively small —perhaps not much more than 100 per million[10]—but a state might wish to avoid even this amount of risk by imposing some form of pre-election registration deadline.

The same kind of timing trade-off exists with respect to the purging of voter registration lists. If the purging occurs too close to election day, the purged voters do not have enough time to contest the inaccuracy of the purge. Conversely, if the purging occurs too far in advance of election day, the purging will fail to remove the names of individuals who have died, moved out of state, or (where applicable), been convicted of a felony after the purge has occurred. Either way, there is some inevitable risk of inaccuracy in the content of the voter registration database. Even as a state endeavors to minimize that risk, it must balance the extent to which it prefers the risk of erroneously retained or erroneously purged names. Arguments can be made that it is better to permit an ineligible individual to vote than it is to deny an eligible individual the right to vote—just as it is better to let the guilty go free than it is to convict the innocent—but ultimately this value choice must be made by the democratic process itself, as reflected in legislation adopted by Congress or the states (unless it is possible for the judiciary to tease out this value choice from the bare text of the U.S. Constitution's Equal Protection Clause).

Identification

An early registration deadline and a late purging deadline will reduce the risk of ineligible individuals being registered to vote. But these deadlines will not reduce this risk to zero. Instead, if a state really wished to eliminate this risk entirely, or at least to come as close as possible in accordance with the Six Sigma objective of approximating perfection, the state would have to adopt a voter identification requirement much more stringent than anything either previously adopted or even currently contemplated.

A policy of zero tolerance of ineligible registrants would mean that every citizen, to enter the state's database of registered voters, would need to produce a birth certificate or naturalization papers as proof of citizenship. Moreover, there would need to be in place a mechanism incontrovertibly linking these proof-of-citizenship documents to the individuals who hold them, in order to avoid the possibility that they were fraudulently obtained or conveyed. Perhaps a genetic test, both at birth (or naturalization) and at time of registration, to establish that the DNA of the registrants matches the DNA of the citizens they purport to be, would suffice to rule out fraud. Assuming that the error rate of the DNA-testing laboratories as well as the error rate of the election officials who reviewed the lab reports would be less than one in a million, then in theory the risk of an erroneous election caused by ineligible registrants could be reduced to within Six Sigma standards.

But would any state tolerate a system of universal DNA testing, so that the government can maintain a database of every citizen's DNA to make sure that no non-citizen registers to vote and no citizen registers more than once? Certainly not. Not even the ideal of "making every vote count" would be worth that invasion of personal privacy and affront to personal dignity.

Nor do Arizona's new registration rules attempt to go so far. While Arizona is seeking to impose the obligation to show proof-of-citizenship documents at the time of registration, a requirement that the U.S. Election Assistance Commission has determined to be inconsistent with the National Voter Registration Act (NVRA or "Motor Voter"),[11] Arizona makes no effort to use biological evidence to link these citizenship papers with the individuals who possess them. Therefore, even if Arizona enforces its new requirements, the state cannot be sure that its registration database actually will contain only eligible citizens.

Consequently, we can imagine a situation in which as few as 20 individuals, out of the more than two million who vote in Arizona elections, fraudulently register to vote based on forged or borrowed citizenship papers. Yet we can also imagine a closely contested statewide race in Arizona being decided by fewer than 20 votes. In this hypothetical situation, the accuracy of the election would have been compromised by the inability of the state to eliminate entirely the risk of ineligible registrants.

But the lesson to be learned from this thought experiment is not to increase the stringency of Arizona's identification requirements even further, by mandating a DNA match between time of birth (or naturalization) and time of registration. Instead, the lesson is to accept the inevitable imperfectability of the electoral system, recognizing that the harm to privacy and dignity from such DNA matching trumps the importance of electoral accuracy. Simply put, it is better to risk an erroneous election, even with the wrong candidate being installed into office, than it is to impose a draconian system of DNA testing in an effort to eliminate this risk.

Indeed, it is far from clear that one would want a court to overturn the results of this hypothetically erroneous election, even if evidence came to light that 20 individuals voted fraudulently. Although it is hardly desirable to let stand the results of an election tainted by fraud, it might be even less palatable to permit elections to be challenged afterwards based on claims that some voters should not have been permitted to register in the first place. Arguably, one might say that the time

to challenge the eligibility of a registered voter is in advance of the election and, therefore, if the election occurs without a challenge of this kind, then a vote cast by a registered voter cannot subsequently be nullified.[12]

PROVISIONAL VOTING

Perfectly accurate voter registration lists would reduce, although not entirely eliminate, the need for provisional voting. (For example, there would still be the need for provisional ballots in the not-infrequent situation in which a harried poll worker cannot find an individual's name of the voter registration list even though it is there—like failing to find a name in a phone book because of a mental error concerning alphabetical order.) And, of course, registration lists will never be perfectly accurate: there will always be some names improperly excluded because of erroneous purging or an erroneous failure to add the names of new registrants to the list.

Provisional voting, therefore, is a welcome addition to the electoral process. But it, too, cannot function as a perfect "fail-safe," despite the promises that are sometimes made on its behalf. One reason is that the time available for verifying the eligibility of provisional voters is necessarily limited in the aftermath of the election, and the verification process may be shut down before there is enough time to check all the available records to see if some provisional voters who superficially appear ineligible are in fact eligible.

As common sense would indicate, available evidence shows that a higher percentage of provisional ballots are verified in states that spend more time verifying provisional ballots. In 2004, according to research conducted by the Eagleton Institute of Politics at Rutgers University, 61 percent of provisional ballots were verified in states that spent over two weeks at this task, whereas only 47 percent of provisional ballots were verified in states spending between one and two weeks. Furthermore, the percentage of verified provisional ballots decreased to 35 percent in states spending less than one week at this effort.[13]

Recalling the problems that occurred in the 2004 Washington gubernatorial election, we can easily understand why this relationship between verification rates and time spent at verification would exist. Some provisional ballots were initially ruled ineligible based on an incomplete review of the election board's records; only after litigation required these officials to take another look did they discover the documentation that demonstrated the voters' eligibility. Somewhat more surprising, perhaps, it was not until after completion of the manual recount of Washington's ballots that officials unearthed several provisional ballots that had never been processed previously—because they had been erroneously placed in a pile of empty envelopes or erroneously left sitting at the bottom of a box.[14]

The manual recount of Washington's gubernatorial election, however, was not complete until eight weeks after the election: Gregoire was certified the winner on December 30. Moreover, litigation over her 129-vote victory, which included a dispute over 252 provisional ballots that were counted but concededly should not have been, did not end until June 6,

2005, over seven months after election day, and the litigation stopped then only because Gregoire's opponent decided not to appeal the trial court's decision that refused to nullify the election notwithstanding the inclusion of more invalid ballots than her margin of victory. After all, Gregoire had already been serving as governor for six months by the time of the trial court's ruling, and it was impossible, once the improperly included provisional ballots had been commingled with other votes, to determine whether these ballots had been cast for Gregoire or her opponent.

Thus, even if not entirely accurate, the process of verifying provisional ballots must—as a practical matter—come to an end before inauguration day. Indeed, in a presidential election, this process must finish within five weeks of election day, because the fifth Tuesday after election day is the "safe harbor" deadline set by Congress, meaning that any state wishing its Electoral College votes to be immune from subsequent challenge in Congress must resolve any disputes over those votes by this deadline. As one will recall, in *Bush v. Gore*, the U.S. Supreme Court halted any recounting of votes in Florida because of this deadline.[15] Presumably, then, in any future presidential election involving a dispute over the verification of provisional ballots, the Supreme Court will terminate the verification process on the fifth Tuesday after election day, so that the state whose provisional ballots are in dispute can take advantage of the congressional safe-harbor deadline. Yet if the process of verifying provisional ballots in Washington had shut down after only five weeks in 2004 (three weeks before the certification of Gregoire's victory), not only would there have been a lot of errors left uncorrected, thereby disenfranchising over 500 eligible voters, but a different governor would have been installed into office.[16]

Even with improvements to the process of verifying provisional ballots that have been adopted in Washington and elsewhere in the wake of the 2004 elections, five weeks may be an insufficient amount of time for the verification process to satisfy the Six Sigma standard. If a state averages 100,000 provisional ballots per election, Six Sigma would find acceptable only one erroneous eligibility determination for every three elections (which is mathematically equivalent to a 0.34 error rate for each election involving 100,000 ballots).[17] The task of processing 20,000 ballots per week is daunting enough, especially once one recognizes that the initial administrative review of these ballots needs to be finished even earlier if there is to be any time within this five-week period for litigating in court the validity of these administrative determinations. The idea that a combined administrative and judicial review of 100,000 provisional ballots within a frenzied five-week period could occur without a single error in two out of every three elections seems fanciful.

But this conclusion does not imply that Congress should extend the safe-harbor deadline beyond the five-week period.[18] Even if Congress and the states were to rethink the time between election day (or the end of a multi-day voting period) and inauguration day, it would seem unlikely that this period would be extended beyond eight to 10 weeks. After all, it is often said that a defeated incumbent sits too long in office before the elected successor takes over. Thus, the implication instead is that it is necessary to accept an increased risk of error in order to serve the important societal interest in "electoral finality"—meaning that the results of the election are final soon after voting ends.

In sum, we could guarantee more accurate election results if we took longer to evaluate the eligibility of provisional ballots after they have been cast. If we stop the process after five weeks, we may leave hundreds of provisional ballots uncounted that should have been included, and we may also count hundreds of provisional ballots that should have been excluded. As a result, in a close election, the "wrong" candidate may be declared governor—or even president. Even so, it would be worse to let the process for fighting over disputed provisional ballots to drag on indefinitely, after the time has come for the winner to take office. Thus, the counting and re-counting must stop, within a few short weeks after the voting is over, even if the count remains inaccurate. The Six Sigma standard must yield to the need for finality.

ABSENTEE BALLOTS

The biggest obstacle to an error-free electoral system, or at least one that satisfies the Six Sigma standard, remains to be considered. As is widely known among election officials, absentee ballots present the greatest threat to the accuracy and integrity of an election's results. This is true because absentee ballots present all the problems associated with polling-place ballots—they must be counted, the individuals who cast them must be eligible voters, there must be a match between the ballots cast and the registered voters who received them—and then some.

Control over the chain-of-custody of absentee ballots is obviously much harder than with polling-place ballots. With polling-place voting as it is commonly practiced, it is necessary to observe that the individual who has checked in and signed the poll book is the same person who casts the corresponding ballot, and after the ballot is cast it is necessary only to keep track of the voting machines and accompanying paper or electronic records. If registration databases and voting machines were to be become technologically integrated, so that an electronic pollbook that each voter signed (using an electronic pen similar to ones now in many retail stores) also functioned as an electronic ballot, then the chain-of-custody issue for polling-place voting would become even easier. (Obviously, this system would need to be designed in such a way as to preserve ballot secrecy, so that once a ballot is cast, it no longer can be specifically traced to the voter who cast it.) As there would be no more custodial gap between the check-in process and receiving a ballot, there also would be no more risk of a discrepancy between the number of ballots cast and the number of signed pollbook entries (a discrepancy which, regrettably, occurs with considerable frequency today).

By contrast, with absentee voting, there is the "outbound" fact that the ballot is mailed to an individual who requested one and, then, the "return-trip" fact that the ballot, after being cast, is mailed back to the board of elections for counting. Who can know for sure what happens to that ballot while en route in either direction? It might have been intercepted before reaching the individual who requested it, and filled out fraudulently in that person's name, or perhaps it might have been caught in transit on its way back and either altered, destroyed, or replaced with a fraudulent substitute. Imagining these possibilities is not to say that they are likely, although history shows that such illegalities have occurred.[19] Rather, the point is that, because they are conceivable, in a close election the losing candidate may be able to raise a plausible question about the integrity of some absentee ballots, thereby casting doubt on the ability of the electoral system to make sure that every valid vote counts, and counts equally, in a particular race.

Even if the absentee ballot gets without incident to and from the person who requested the ballot, it is also harder to verify that this person is an eligible voter than it is if the same person must show up at a polling place to cast the ballot. The reason, of course, is that at the polling place the flesh-and-blood person can be examined in comparison with whatever documentary evidence of eligibility might be required: the individual can be asked to produce a signature to be checked against one on file, the individual's visage may be compared against a photo either on record or in hand, or a fingerprint of the individual can be taken on the spot to be checked against a fingerprint collected at time of registration. But none of these methods works as well in the context of absentee voting: even if the absentee voter is asked to supply a signature, photo, or fingerprint, these forms of identification could have been forged; unlike with polling place voting, there is no way to check for sure that the individual filling out the absentee ballot is the same one whose signature, photo, or fingerprint is supplied along with the ballot. (And even if it is, there is a greater likelihood that the individual submitting the absentee ballot is not an eligible voter: a person who can both register and vote by mail is more likely to do so even if not qualified than if the same person must go in person to either register or vote; the prospect of having to break the law while directly engaged in a face-to-face encounter with government officials tends to deter the unlawful conduct.)

There is yet another major problem with absentee voting that does not affect polling-place voting. Absentee ballots are not necessarily secret. Anyone might watch an individual fill one out: a spouse, a friend, a partisan operative. Therefore, even if there is no doubt about the eligibility to vote of the individual who casts an absentee ballot, the integrity of that ballot is compromised if the individual, while being watched, casts that ballot for a particular candidate because of coercion or pressure to do so. The influence of the observer may be subtle ("Everyone at our church is voting for Smith") or blatant ("We'll break your kneecaps if you don't vote for Jones"). Or the observer may even pay the individual $20 to vote as instructed. In any of these situations, the absentee ballot is hardly a reflection of the individual's own free will, as the vote would have been had it been cast in secrecy behind the curtain at a polling place.

Despite the potential for these kinds of abuses, absentee ballot laws are rapidly being liberalized, with many states adopting so-called "no-excuse absentee voting," meaning that individuals can choose to mail in their votes from home for no other reason than it is more convenient to do so. Consequently, the risk that the outcome of a close election will be tainted by improperly cast absentee ballots is increasing, not decreasing. If one-quarter of all ballots are mailed in from home, rather than less than 10 percent, there is a significantly greater chance that the outcome of a close election will depend upon the resolution of a dispute over questionable mailed-in votes.[20]

This observation does not necessarily mean that the liberalization of absentee ballot laws should be opposed. On the contrary, the convenience of on-demand at-home voting may be a societal value that outweighs the increased risk of erroneous election results. The point simply is that society must recognize the inevitable trade-off between liberalized absentee voting and the goal of reducing error-dependent election results.

In an election where the margin of victory is 100 votes, what happens if there is evidence that 1,000 at-home voters were each paid $20 to vote for the apparently winning candidate? Should a court void the election result, tossing out all the ballots that had been bought, and declare the other candidate to be the rightful winner? How strong does the evidence of the vote-buying scheme need to be, and what if there is testimony that the persons who received payment would have voted for the same candidate anyway—that $20 was merely a way to solidify their inclinations? Suppose, further, that the vote-buying scheme comes to

light only after the absentee ballots, for purpose of counting, have been commingled with
regular ballots, or otherwise de-linked from
the individuals who submitted them, thereby
negating any ability to prove with certainty
which absentee ballots were compromised by
the payment scheme. Should a court still void
the election and order a new one, in the hope
that it will not be similarly tainted?

Alternatively, what if the evidence is not of
vote-purchasing, but instead of more subtle
manipulation of mail-in votes? Suppose, for
instance, that a church-affiliated group holds
an end-of-campaign-season supper party and
quietly suggests that attendees can bring their
absentee ballots with them, so that they can
ask each other any questions they might have
about how to fill them out. Church volunteers,
of course, will be ready to help in this regard.
Should these ballots be voided, and perhaps
with them the entire election, if this form of
assistance comes to light?[21]

To salvage the ideal of "making every vote
count" in the context of widespread at-home
voting, it may be necessary to rule off-limits
challenges to the validity of a vote, as long as
that vote was cast by a qualified voter. In other
words, an at-home vote is properly included in
the certified results of an election even if there
is evidence that the registered voter who cast
the ballot was manipulated into doing so in a
particular way. This ballot may be a tie-break-
ing one. Even so, the system will not entertain
the possibility of voiding the ballot just because
there is evidence that the voter's wife threatened to leave him if he didn't cast his at-home
ballot for her preferred candidate. Or the

voter's priest told him that he could no longer
receive communion at church if the priest
saw that his absentee ballot had been cast for
such a sinful candidate. Or even if the voter's
neighbor and coworker told him that he would
lose his job if he did not vote for the pro-labor
candidate at the top of the ticket.

To consider such challenges to the validity of
absentee ballots may expose the electoral system to too much uncertainty and instability. It
may be better, on balance, to accept the results
of an election as conclusive and unimpeachable
than to permit the results to be questioned on
the ground that absentee voters would have
voted differently had they not been pressured
into voting the way that they did. This value
judgment, however, may bring about a reduction in erroneous election results, but only
because the concept of an electoral error has
been redefined more narrowly.

No matter what the value judgment, there
is little likelihood that a system of absentee
voting could be administered in accordance
with the Six Sigma standard. Even if the trend
toward on-demand at-home voting were
abandoned in favor of returning to a regime
of absentee ballots being available for a strictly
limited list of legitimate causes, and even if
the integrity of an absentee ballot could not
be challenged on the grounds of improper
influence, but solely on the grounds that it
was cast by an ineligible individual, the extra
chain-of-custody problems associated with
the absentee voting would seem to put its
administration out of Six Sigma range. As we
have seen with provisional ballots, if a state has
an average of 100,000 absentee ballots cast

each election, then Six Sigma would permit a single erroneous determination concerning an absentee ballot's eligibility only once every three elections. In other words, in two out of every three elections, the state must be absolutely perfect in counting every absentee ballot cast by an eligible voter and excluding every absentee ballot cast by an ineligible voter. In these elections, not a single fraudulently cast absentee ballot could escape undetected. It seems an impossible standard to meet.

Yet obviously we cannot abandon absentee voting entirely. The need for absentee ballots, even when they are strictly limited to the circumstances in which they have historically been provided, is too great: voters away from home on business, voters serving overseas in the armed forces, voters hospitalized or otherwise unable to go to the polls because of illness or infirmity, and so forth. Simply put, we would not permit the disenfranchisement of these citizens just because of their unavoidable inability to get to a polling place on election day. As a result, whether or not states choose to liberalize absentee voting, they must accept some irreducibly significant risk of electoral error caused by the necessity of even strictly limited absentee voting.

TOWARD A RESOLUTION OF OUR VALUES CONFLICT

In sum, three essential elements of our electoral system—registration, provisional voting, and absentee voting—all point to the same problem: in even the best designed and implemented electoral system, there is a real risk that some eligible citizens will be denied the opportunity to cast a ballot that counts (and thus will be disenfranchised in the election), while at the same time some of the ballots that are actually counted will have been cast by individuals who are ineligible to vote. This risk exists even if voting technology works perfectly and there is no human error by poll workers in the distribution and collection of conventional ballots at the polling places. Even more discouragingly, the unavoidable risks of errors with respect to each of these three essential elements of the electoral system cannot be considered in isolation, but instead must be taken together, thereby compounding the likelihood that the outcome of a close election will be tainted by cumulative errors affecting the electoral process as whole.

We can easily imagine, in other words, 50 fraudulent registrations, 70 misplaced or otherwise mistreated provisional ballots, and 90 improper absentee ballots combining to cloud the outcome of an election with a 100-vote margin of victory. We want every vote in this close election to count—and to count equally. We want every provisional ballot cast by an eligible voter to be included in the total, because each one might make a difference to this razor-thin result. We want every ballot cast by someone who registered fraudulently to be excluded, even though there are just a few of them, because they, too, could make a difference in the outcome, depriving each valid vote of its equal right to determine the winner. Likewise, we want to exclude any absentee ballots that were illegally intercepted and fraudulently filled out by a partisan imposter, for any election in which these improper absentee ballots determined the winner would be considered a stolen election.

We want all this, but we cannot guarantee it, because we have no way to reduce the risk of these problems to the point that they approach the perfectionist aspiration of the Six Sigma standard. We cannot reduce this risk to a Six Sigma level because of countervailing considerations built into these three essential features of our electoral system. Our process of registering voters cannot demand a DNA-matching identification requirement that would violate privacy and dignity even though that would be the only way for a state's registration database to satisfy a perfectionist standard of accuracy. Our process of verifying provisional ballots must come to an end before there is sufficient time to achieve a perfectionist count of these provisional ballots. And because our electoral system cannot negate the need for at least some absentee voting, it cannot eliminate the distinctive risks of fraud that are inherently associated with absentee ballots.

What, then, are we to do about this inevitable conflict between our professed ideal of electoral perfection and these other values that we are unwilling to sacrifice? Simply put, we need to abandon electoral perfection as our standard of democratic legitimacy, and develop instead a standard of electoral optimality, a standard that is feasible and reflects our best judgment on how to compromise among our competing important values. Here are some thoughts about how we might begin to understand electoral optimality:

1. We should stop placing so much emphasis on the desirability of closely competitive elections.[22] It is actually better for electoral results to be clear-cut and decisive. It would be far from ideal if each election were decided by just one vote. Although that situation would mean that the competing candidates were always expert in appealing to the proverbial "median voter," the clouds of uncertainty that would hang over each election as both sides went to court to fight over who really won each race would be destabilizing. Democracy in this society would soon disappear. Therefore, we should hope instead that the process of campaigning causes in each election a sufficient swath of undecided middle-of-the-road voters to develop a distinct preference, with the result that the winner prevails by at least one percentage point (which in an election with one million votes would amount to a 10,000 vote victory).

2. Equality of voting rights can be meaningful even when an individual's vote is unable to be counted properly in order to be decisive in an extremely close election. Much of the value of voting is the symbolism of equal citizenship that results from casting a ballot that is expected to be counted along with all other valid votes. When African Americans, women, and other previously disenfranchised groups can go to the polls and proudly cast their ballots shoulder to shoulder with every other U.S. citizen, the victory for democracy is clear. To be sure, if some of these ballots inadvertently fail to get counted, that disenfranchisement is a clear harm to democracy, but when that inadvertent failure goes undetected it cannot undercut the democratic value that resulted from the equal casting of the ballots in the first place. Symbolism is not the same as reality. Nonetheless, the equal entitlement of all citizens to cast a countable ballot is symbolically important and not to be underappreciated despite the inevitable inability to make sure that every ballot is properly counted.

3. There is a crucial difference between the problems of Florida 2000 and Ohio 2004. Florida 2000 involved a razor-thin result that likely would have been within the margin of error even if the system had been well designed and well implemented. Ohio 2004, however, turned out to be not that close—118,599 votes separated Bush and Kerry in the end[23]—and yet the system

showed itself to be horrendously designed
and riddled with implementation errors.
Our immediate goal as a nation should
be to design and implement an electoral
system that avoids the problems of Ohio
2004. In other words, we should start by
hoping for an electoral system that at least
is capable of working well in a race that is
not so close. For now, and perhaps forever,
it will be too much to expect that our
electoral system will operate with sufficient
accuracy to produce an unimpeachable
result when one million votes are cast and
the margin of victory is less than 1,000 (or
0.1 percent of the total).

4. The inevitability of some irreducible margin
   of error in a well-designed and well-imple-
   mented electoral system should not be
   shocking or disturbing. We understand the
   existence of margins of error in all sorts
   of other human endeavors, from flying
   airplanes to operating nuclear reactors. We
   should, therefore, determine an acceptable
   margin of error for an electoral system and
   then hold the system accountable to that
   standard. For the reasons I have elaborated,
   the acceptable error rate cannot be the
   Six Sigma standard that is suitable for some
   industrial or other administrative processes.
   The more interesting question, in my judgment, is whether it would be appropriate
   for an electoral system to hold itself to
   an error rate of 0.01 percent, or only 100
   errors out of one million voters, rather than
   the less ambitious standard of 0.1 percent
   (1,000 errors per million voters).

5. It is important, too, that errors be randomly
   distributed, that there is no systematic bias
   built into the electoral system that would
   make one group of voters more likely to
   suffer from counting errors than other
   voters. As long as errors are truly random,
   then voters can accept the results of a
   close election as fair and legitimate, even
   if the system is unable to guarantee that
   all eligible ballots were properly counted
   and no ineligible ballots taint the result.
   Conversely, if errors are non-random and
   fall predictably on one segment of society
   (African Americans below the poverty line,
   for example), then even the symbolic value

of casting a ballot would disappear. An
electoral system with a built-in bias against
counting the votes from one particular
demographic group cannot pretend to
honor the democratic ideal of equal citizenship, not even in the breach.

6. This criterion of democratic legitimacy is the
   crucial test of an electoral system. It is necessary that a properly functioning process
   work as expected, the way it is supposed
   to. Yet sometimes even the best designed
   and best operated process results in error.
   In this sense, the erroneous result is sometimes expected, and the system still works
   as intended even if we are understandably
   disappointed when it produces its expected
   error. In this way, an erroneous result may
   still have a legitimate democratic pedigree
   and be acceptable to the public as such.

7. As a consequence of this possibility, it is
   necessary to develop the attitude that,
   should a random error unfortunately occur
   in a close election (despite the proper
   functioning of an optimal process), the
   solution is to wait for the next election in
   the recurring operation of democracy. If the
   results of Florida 2000 (or the governor's
   race in Washington in 2004) were so
   hard to take, it was because the system
   was so egregiously flawed and the errors
   were hardly random. But if we can decide
   democratically what an optimal electoral
   system would look like, and if we properly
   implement this optimal system, then when
   it produces a randomly erroneous result
   according to the design specifications we
   gave it, we at least know that it worked as
   well as could have been expected, and we
   will live to see it operate properly again.

In the end, we must acknowledge this simple
truth: democracy always produces winners
and losers, and a fair democratic process—in
addition to treating both sides fairly with
respect to the inevitable margin of error—
gives the side that came up short this time a
fair chance to prevail next time around.

Notes

Director, Election Law @ Moritz, and Robert M. Duncan/Jones Day Designated Professor of Law, Ohio State University. This paper was presented at "Making Every Vote Count: a Colloquium on Election Reform Legislation," held at Princeton University on April 7, 2006. I am very grateful to Tom O'Neill, Tova Wang, Michael McDonald, Rick Pildes, and other conference participants for their helpful suggestions. Likewise, I received extremely valuable feedback on an earlier draft from Dan Tokaji, Steve, Huefner, Terri Enns, and the students in my Election Law seminar during the spring 2006 semester.

The earlier draft is available at http://moritzlaw.osu. edu/electionlaw/freefair/060502.php.) Thanks also to Sara Sampson and Kathy Hall of the Moritz Law Library for their research assistance in connection with this paper, as well as all members of the Election Law @ Moritz team whose ongoing work in this field informs my understanding of this topic. All errors in this inevitably imperfect paper are, of course, solely my own, although I hope that they do not detract from the legitimacy of my basis thesis.

1. See Edward B. Foley, *Electoral Laments in Major and Minor Keys, Free & Fair* (May 9, 2006), available at http://moritzlaw.osu.edu/electionlaw/comments/2006/060509.php; Joan Mazzolini, "Election Board Opens Probe Into Voting Fiasco," *The Plain Dealer* (May 9, 2006).

2. Democrats in Washington initially brought suit to identify which provisional ballots had been improperly disqualified. *Washington State Democratic Central Committee v. King County Records* (Nov. 16, 2004), http://moritzlaw.osu.edu/electionlaw/docs/WSDCC/WSDCCorder2.pdf. Local election officials went back and discovered their errors, and the Washington Supreme Court ultimately confirmed the need for them to rectify their mistakes. *Washington State Republican Party v. King County Division of Records*, 103 P.3d 725 (Wash. 2004). If one wishes to get a full picture of the administrative errors that beset the Washington governor's race in 2004, one can review the daily news coverage of the post-election turmoil during November and December in the *Seattle Times* and the *Seattle Post-Intelligencer*.

3. Editorial, "One Person, One Vote," *Boston Globe*, December 24, 2004, p.A18.

4. Holly Zachariah, "Couples' 4 Ballots Stirs Chaos in London," *Columbus Dispatch*, November 17, 2004, p.1A.

5. GAO, "The Nation's Evolving Election System as Reflected in the November 2004 General Election" 31 (June 6, 2006).

6. For background on Six Sigma, see Mahesh S. Raisinghani, Six Sigma: concepts, tools, and applications, 105 *Industrial Management & Data Systems* 491 (2005); Navin Shamji Dedhia, Six Sigma Basics, 16 *Total Quality Management* 567 (2005). Thad Hall and Mike Alvarez, among others, has suggested applying Six Sigma to elections. See more on Lean Six Sigma and "Lean" Voting, *Election Updates* (November 1–2, 2005), available at http://electionupdates.caltech.edu/2005_10_30_archive.html.

7. National Archives (www.archives.gov/federal-register/electoral-college/2000/popular_vote.html).

8. Official results of second recount in 2004 election for governor, Washington secretary of state (http://vote.wa.gov/Elections/Results/Results.aspx?e=fe7e6b45-e39d-4959-95c7-9e27cf6e0b59&j=a1c5db0b-5cf2-4016-abe9-b5dfdb0f4fec&o=a8327ef7-2f99-40a3-85c9-ef-641023cc0f).

9. Idaho, Maine, Minnesota, New Hampshire, Wisconsin, Wyoming.

10. Reports from Wisconsin, a state with same-day registration, indicate that in the 2004 election over 300 ineligible ballots were cast, out of a total of approximately three million (2,997,007). Greg Borkowski, "Inquiry Finds Evidence of Fraud in Election," *Milwaukee Journal-Sentinel*, May 11, 2005, p. A1; National Archive (www.archives.gov/federal-register/electoral-college/2004/popular_vote.html).

11. See Daniel P. Tokaji, "EAC on Arizona Registration Requirements" (03/07/06), *Equal Vote*, available at http://moritzlaw.osu.edu/blogs/tokaji/2006/03/eac-on-arizona-registration_07.html.

12. For further thoughts on whether the accuracy of a state's voter registration database should be subject to challenge in the aftermath of an election, see Edward B. Foley, "The Promise and Problems of Provisional Voting," 73 *Geo. Wash. L. Rev.* 1193, 1203–04 and n.69 (2005).

13. David Andersen, *Relationship Between Time Allotted to Verify Provisional Ballots and the Level of Ballots that are Verified,* The Eagleton Institute of Politics (on file with author).

14. David Postman, "Reed says county has right to fix error, tally 735 ballots," *The Seattle Times,* December 21, 2004, p. A1 (describing how seven provisional ballots "had been mistakenly put in a pile of empty envelopes and not discovered until after the first recount"); see also David Postman, "It's Gregoire by 130; is it over?", *The Seattle Times,* December 24, 2004, p. A1 (describing two provisional ballots "that had been left in locked compartments of voting equipment after the election").

15. 531 U.S. at 9–10: "Because the Florida Supreme Court has said that the Florida Legislature intended to obtain the safe-harbor benefits of 3 U.S.C. § 5," which "requires that any controversy or contest that is designed to lead to a conclusive selection of electors be completed by December 12," and [b]ecause it is evident that any recount seeking to meet the December 12 date will be unconstitutional for the reasons we have discussed, we reverse the judgment of the Supreme Court of Florida ordering a recount to proceed."

16. Gregoire's opponent led after both the initial count of ballots and the first machine count, and she did not overtake him until December 22, at the end of the manual recount. See David Postman, "Gregoire leads by 10," *The Seattle Times* (December 23, 2004), p.A1.

17. Washington had almost 93,781 provisional ballots cast in 2004; Ohio had over 157,7140. See U.S. Election Assistance Commission, *Election Day Survey,* Chapter 6 Data Tables, available at www.eac.gov/election_survey_2004/toc.htm.

18. My colleague Steve Huefner explores this possibility in *Reforming the Timetable for the Electoral College Process* (11/30/04) , http://moritzlaw.osu.edu/electionlaw/comments/2004/041130.php.

19. See, e.g., *Pabey v. Pastrick,* 816 N.E.2d 1138 (2004) (recounting egregious facts of partisan abuses of absentee ballots).

20. In states with "no-excuse absentee voting" in 2004, 20 percent of registered voters requested absentee ballots (making these ballots an even larger percentage of ballots cast, since not all registered voters cast ballots). By contrast, in states without "no-excusive absentee voting in 2004, only 5 percent of registered voters requested absentee ballots. See U.S. EAC, *Election Day Survey,* Chapter 5, p. 5–10, available at www.eac.gov/election_survey_2004/doc/EDS-chap percent205 percent20 absentee percent20ballots.doc.

21. For a more general discussion of these remedial concerns, see "Voting and Democracy," 119 *Harv. L. Rev.* 1127, 1188–1200 (2006) (describing and discussing the concept of "remedial deterrence" as applied to election administration); see also *id.* at 1155–1164 (discussing remedial difficulties when the number of illegal votes exceeds the margin of victory yet it is unknowable for which candidate the illegal votes were cast).

22. Of course, the intentional stifling of electoral competition to serve the interests of incumbents is an evil in need of a remedy. See, e.g., Richard H. Pildes, "The Constitution and Political Competition," 20 *Nova L. Rev.* 269 (2006).

23. National Archives, 2004 Presidential Election, Popular Vote Totals, available at www.archives.gov/federal-register/electoral-college/2004/popular_vote.html.

Appendix A: Commentary and Panel Discussion Summaries

Commentary: DeForest B. Soaries Jr.

Thank you so much, and thank you for gathering here to discuss this very important subject matter, and for inviting me to share this time with you.

Dr. Wuthnow is one of my intellectual mentors. Before I was in seminary, while I was in seminary, and since I finished seminary, his writing and his insight have served as guiding lights for me, and to have met him, after having read and having been instructed by him from afar, was one of the great privileges of my life. When I saw that he was introducing me here today, I was somewhat intimidated. I admire him so much for what he does, and want to thank him for his friendship.

I want to thank Princeton for hosting this important meeting. The policy people here are to be commended for allowing us to gather here, because these are important times, this is important subject matter, and Princeton, for me, is the right place to have it.

Of course, the Brennan Center is very, very important to me personally. When I was chairman of the Election Assistance Commission during 2004, we got started so late, we had so little funding, that we just didn't have the capacity to produce even the most basic tools that we felt were needed to get us through the 2004 election effectively. The Brennan Center really came alongside us, and produced tools that enhanced our capacity. By the time the U.S. Election Assistance Commission produced its best practices documents, we were able to include in our best practices references to the Brennan Center's work that they had done throughout the year. I think this work was absolutely critical. They were particularly insightful and proactive as we considered some of the implications of electronic voting. When you talk about HAVA, hopefully you'll talk about the impact of electronic voting on the democratic shifts that are happening in the country. The Brennan Center was very helpful in articulating methodologies and challenges that we face, and solutions: many people can cite problems, but few people bring with those problems solutions, and the Brennan Center did a fine job. I'm so happy that the Brennan Center is still actively involved in this analysis.

The Fels Center out at Pennsylvania played a critical role that hopefully will guide democratic practice for decades, in that for the first time, citizens in the country had a central way of accessing the most fundamental informa-

tion that we need to vote—that is, where
to go to vote. I'm so happy to see my friend
Ken Smukler here, and his affiliation with the
Fels Center, I think, makes this combination of
Princeton, and Brennan, and Fels—New York,
New Jersey, Pennsylvania—a very, very blessed
trinity.

So many people are here that I know—Frank
Askin is one of my early heroes; we were
organizing tenants back in the early 1970s,
whose landlords thought it was alright to
collect rent without providing any services at
all. Frank Askin became one of my chief legal
resources, and has been the conscience of
so many seasons of political leadership, and
continues to be on the cutting edge, the front
lines of very important battles, as we fight
continuously to level the playing field in every
aspect of our society. I'm so honored to see
you, Frank. And of course, my friends from
Eagleton are here—I feel like I'm home.

* * *

I was minding my business, I was at home, it
was a bad-weather day in New Jersey, March
of '03, and the White House called me, and
I thought it was a prank. The call came, not
from the Office of Protocol, which is the office
that invites you to social functions. It was the
Office of Personnel.

My assumption—after I got over the thought
that it was a prank—was that they were calling
me to get a reference for someone who had
applied for a job. What they told me was that
the president wanted me to serve on the new
Election Assistance Commission. Of course,

I thought the commission had already been
formed—it was created in legislation that
responded to the problems encountered during the presidential election in 2000. And here
it was the year 2003, and they were starting
the process of looking for the commissioners.
This was quite alarming on its face.

So I went to Washington, and I met with
the policy staff at the White House, I read
the legislation, I had followed some of the
negotiations—and I said to the young people
with whom I was talking, I said: Listen, two
things. One, I served in the administration of
Christine Todd Whitman. She was governor,
I was appointed by her. And her invitation
came to me just like the president's did: I need
your help. I would advise you to call Governor
Whitman, to ask her what help from me
looks like. Because my first press conference
as secretary of state was to disagree with the
governor on the issue of racial profiling. Cabi-
net members don't usually disagree with the
governor publicly.

I wanted the White House to understand that
if they wanted help from me, that help came
wrapped in a very particular kind of package.

The second thing I said—I said, therefore, I
will do this. If you're serious, I'm going to get it
done. If I discover that you're not serious, I will
be a problem for you.

I found that they were not serious.

When we look at making every vote count,
and we consider the issues of campaign
finance, the Help America Vote Act, which has

to do with election administration, or Voting Rights, which has to do with justice, one would think that we have a national consensus on the proposition of voting.

Whether we consider history and watch democracy evolve in the country, or whether we consider contemporary reality, where voting is really assigned to political consultants, we have to assume that democracy is more a philosophical passion than it is a practical goal in the country.

That's why this meeting is so important.

Historically, we have to concede that the only time politicians have been effective at expanding democracy is when that particular political party perceived that such expansion would benefit it. So whether it's Democrats or Republicans, democracy and democratic practice and voting have now been reduced to computer models and producing the voters who voted in the last two elections in a particular way.

When we consider the matter of disenfranchisement, it is somewhat amusing that the Democrats like to argue that the problem with voting in America today is that Republicans like to suppress the vote; the problem to solve is voter suppression. And Republicans are preoccupied with the notion that Democrats are passionately committed to voter fraud. So when the Democrats have their way, they want to make sure there are enough lawyers available to ensure that everyone has access to the ballot; and when the Republicans have their way, they want to make sure there are

enough safeguards in place to stop these illegal people from voting, even at nursing homes—the nursing home seems to be the real pet peeve of the conservative movement.

And in the meantime, there are big questions to answer: What do we do about 40 percent voter turnout? What do we do about polling places that are not accessible for people that are physically challenged? What do we do about the fact that all of us who measured phone calls on Election Day, 2004—whether it was the EAC, with our eight-person call center, or whether it was the University of Pennsylvania that took in millions of calls—what do we do about the fact that the average person on Election Day has as their chief problem just finding out about where to vote? What do we do about the fact that there are parts of this country where the elections administrators are so underfunded that they keep voter registration applications in a shoebox under their desk? What do we do about the fact that there's no formal training for elections administration, so that if you want to be an airplane pilot, you go to school; if you want to be a barber, you go to school; but if you want to be an elections administrator, you just have the right political contact in the right place?

While the political apparatus is fighting over the minutiae, the big picture is not being discussed by those who have the power to change it.

When I got to Washington in January of 2004, ostensibly to lead the first government-sponsored effort to oversee elections administration in the history of the country, I had a budget to operate that agency that is smaller than my church, which is 14 miles north of Princeton University on Route 27. Further, the two billion dollars that Congress had appropriated to distribute to the states to buy new equipment and to upgrade the administration of elections could not be released until we published every one of the state HAVA plans in the Federal Register. And publishing the states' plans in the Federal Register cost $700,000. Now the Federal Register is owned by Congress. So Congress passed a law forbidding release of the money to the states until EAC published the states' plans in the Federal Register but Congress did not think to put enough money in our budget to publish the plans in their Federal Register. So tell me—who really wanted the states to get this money?

And this was a bipartisan consensus—or conspiracy.

Within one week of going to Washington in 2004, I went to the White House with my resignation. I said, "You people aren't serious, and I told you if you weren't, there'd be a problem."

My problem was that if I had gone through with my resignation, the commission would now be at 75 percent capacity, and any failure in November could be attributed to my behavior. So I stuck it out, painfully, for a year, asking God every morning, "Should I tell everything I know?"

My point is that I don't want you to assume that your meeting is taking place within the context of a national consensus that these issues are priorities. I do not want you to believe that if we can just fix a few things, everything will be alright. We are not here deliberating voting rights and campaign finance and HAVA within the context of a national consensus. The goal of most politicians, essentially, is to produce the same people who voted for them last time, hoping that the opposition will do the same, and therefore they will be returned to office. As we moved around the offices of Democrats and Republicans, ranking members and new legislators, what we discovered was that most of them felt there was very little wrong with the voting process, because after all, it produced them.

If persons like yourselves, and institutions like these, do not develop the capacity to challenge the political status quo, then this time in history will reveal perhaps the greatest contradiction in the history of this country. We are spending a billion dollars a week under the banner of helping to facilitate democracy in the Middle East, and at the same time, can't figure out a way to have satellite voting for people displaced by a natural disaster in our own country.

I was invited to come to New Orleans and do something relative to the municipal elections, and I've opted not to go—because you don't need to be in New Orleans to monitor the elections in New Orleans. Most of the people who live in New Orleans aren't in New Orleans. The chief elections officer who will certify the election is running for mayor. The justice department—and the state legislature —is not concerned at all.

Let me say—I think my introductory time is up—let me say that this is not a casual matter. There is a sense of urgency, and somewhere from beyond government and politics, we need an emergence of young people and scholars, independent thinkers and community-based organizations and activists, who will not be bound by any particular partisan outcome. If partisan politics remains the only player on the political field, then we've all lost. Someone's got to function as an honest broker between the mythology and the reality of democracy.

I went to Vienna to speak for the country at a European conference on democracy. Bulgaria was there, and Romania was there, Poland was there, Russia was there… I was embarrassed. At first, when I got there, a member of the State Department staff gave me my speech— you know, I'm a preacher, nobody writes my sermons for me—and I said, I'm not reading any speech written by the State Department. And then after I went to the deliberations and realized I had to give the closing remarks, I was so embarrassed, not wanting to cause an international crisis, I just read the speech. Because if I had said what I saw—what I felt—the Department of Homeland Security might not have let me back in the country.

This is urgent.

And I'll just—again—give you one example of the urgency. The majority of the people on Election Day who call and ask a question—of anybody—ask the question, "Where do I go to vote?" They called Washington, they called our office in Washington, and asked, "I don't know where to vote." On Election Day. Yet we can't get the Democrats and Republicans to agree that it's worth investing in helping people know where to vote.

What I've discovered is that the political process wants every vote cast for them to count, and to hell with the rest. Whoever the rest are—felons, immigrants, urban, doesn't matter. It does not matter.

The challenge we have is that the people who have the power to solve the problem are the people who care the least.

I'm hoping that out of this deliberation will come not only great ideas, but some strategic thinking, about how to market the notion that we're living at a time of great contradiction.

At least—in 1965, kids were dying in Vietnam, but at least we passed the Voting Rights Act… also. In 1970, Vietnam was still going on, but at least we renewed the Voting Rights Act… also. In 1968, Dr. King was killed, but at least we passed the Fair Housing Act… also. History has a way of at least having some balancing acts so that great tragedies are accompanied by great victories. We have great tragedy going on right now, as we speak, without any significant victory to balance that which undermines who we say we are.

I'm not interested in America being who I think America should be. I'm only interested in America being who America says America will be.

If we don't get a Voting Rights Act that focuses

on issues far beyond language; if we don't
get HAVA right, which focuses on equipment
heavily, but also needs to focus on enforcement—there's no real enforcement capacity
in HAVA at all; if we don't get national voter
registration right, where people can register
easily; if we don't get this voter ID issue
right—then what we will have is a country that
has practiced the greatest hypocrisy of any
nation on the planet Earth in history. How can
you blow up hospitals and schools and muse-
ums and libraries and disrupt weddings and
families and have casualties that you can't even
count, in the name of helping people learn
how to vote, and right here in your own country, you turn a blind eye to everything that
would enhance people voting? It's an absolute
contradiction, and it's embarrassing that we're
not more upset about it.

I told Frank that if I had said everything I knew,
leading up to the November election in 2004,
it would have been a national disaster, because
perhaps no one would have voted.

And the dirty little secret about Florida 2000
is that we got caught then. But Florida 2000
wasn't unique at all. In fact, there was a particular secretary of state on election night in
2000 who was thanking God that the press
didn't come there. We lost more votes in that
state in 2000 than we lost in Florida 2000—
it's just that that state didn't have the perfect
storm of electoral votes, election return
timing, and election administration challenges.
And let's not even talk about New Jersey—
we're in New Jersey right now—today.

I really came, not to inform you—you've got
enough scholars and experts here—I came
to beg you to take this issue seriously. In small
rooms like these, with gatherings of equal size,
great ideas have emerged to fuel great movements.

I don't think we can afford to compromise on
the integrity of our democracy. We can debate
about effective approaches of providing afford-
able housing, we can debate about economic
theory, we can debate about whether or not
we should continue space exploration—there
are a lot of things that reasonable people can
debate and even disagree about. But about the
fundamental tenets of democracy, and about
the willingness of this society to guarantee the
rights of everyone to vote, and about ensuring
that the methodology is in place to protect
that vote, and about ensuring that every vote
counts—reasonable people in this country
cannot and should not disagree.

* * *

If you fail to do your jobs, write your books,
do your op-eds, do your research, and testify
at hearings, then this country will be the
greatest mockery ever to masquerade under
the title of a democratic nation. So that's your
challenge.

Thank you.

Commentary: Ray Martinez III

"Prudent Steps Toward Improving Voter Confidence"

"[T]he protection of the voting process is as important for the well-being of the body politic as is protection of public health and safety for the bodies of our individual citizens."

Let me start this afternoon by thanking our gracious hosts from the the Policy Research Institute for the Region here at Princeton University and in particular, its director, Tony Shorris. My thanks also to Andy Rachlin for his assistance in bringing us all together and assembling a fine mix of academics, advocates, and practitioners. I am honored to be here. This happens to be my first visit to this wonderful university and already, I am in awe of both its beauty and its rich history and tradition. Your outstanding commitment to research excellence and undergraduate education has ensured that your motto of "… being in the nation's service" is not only well-earned, but well-deserved. Let me also say how pleased I am to travel yesterday from our nation's current capitol to this campus, which of course, briefly hosted the Continental Congress back in 1783 and in so doing, served for a brief period as the capital of the United States. (Is there any chance we can move it back to Nassau Hall so that I can just stay here?)

Let me also thank Myriam Gillies for your very kind introduction, the Fels Institute of Government at the University of Pennsylvania, and the Brennan Center for Justice at New York University School of Law for sponsoring this important conference. (Michael Waldman, executive director, Brennan Center, is my former colleague on the White House staff during the Clinton administration.)

I want to also publicly acknowledge my good friend and former colleague, the Reverend DeForest "Buster" Soaries, who was your keynote speaker yesterday. Although I was unable to make it here in time for his remarks, I understand that he was as dynamic and insightful as always. Reverend Soaries is an outstanding national leader who worked diligently during his tenure as chairman of the EAC to bring appropriate attention and resources to the efforts of our agency to make a difference in improving the process of election administration—I'm honored to follow him at this podium. Likewise, I would be remiss if I did not take this opportunity to publicly thank several individuals in attendance at this conference who, throughout my time on the EAC, have been gracious in providing me advice and counsel on a variety of important policy matters—in particularly, Professor Ned Foley, the director of the electionlaw@ Moritz program at the Moritz College of Law at Ohio State University; Doug Chapin, executive director of electionline.org; and Christina Galindo-Walsh, senior attorney, National Disability Rights Network.

INTRODUCTION

With your indulgence, I'd like to take a few minutes this afternoon to share with you some personal thoughts I have on the current state of election reform and to humbly offer some ideas to improve the underlying confidence in the integrity of election administration.

Yesterday's focus on campaign finance and the Voting Rights Act allowed us to consider the important policy decisions that will need to be made in the near future regarding further implementation of BCRA and the re-authorization of the Voting Rights Act.

And yet, as significant as these two topics are—and I can think of nothing more important that re-authorization of the Voting Rights Act—there is, as you know, a third aspect to election law that has become increasingly central to ensuring fundamental fairness on Election Day. And, of course, that third aspect is election administration and the Help America Vote Act. In order to ensure that we are improving how we conduct our elections—which is, after all, the promise of HAVA—we must not be afraid to have candid discussions about our progress and to shine a constant spotlight on our actions. Which is why I am so delighted to be here today.

ERODING VOTER CONFIDENCE

Perhaps one of the most alarming trends in our country, at least from my perspective, is the continual erosion in voter confidence in the process of election administration. Various independent polls taken over the last several years indicate a precipitous decline in the level of confidence that an average voter has in the accuracy of tabulated results. As Professor Rick Hasen and others have noted, the problems in election administration since the 2000 presidential election—including allegations of

fraud, claims of voting system manipulation, and the perception of partisanship by election administrators—have adversely affected the opinions of many Americans regarding the fundamental fairness of our electoral process. A *Wall Street Journal–NBC News* poll, for example, taken shortly after the 2004 presidential election, showed that more than 25 percent of those surveyed worried that the vote count in the 2004 presidential race was unfair. More recently, the American Bar Association, at its 2005 summer meeting in Chicago, released a nationally commissioned poll showing that some 20 percent of Americans surveyed had lingering doubts that their vote was accurately counted in the 2004 presidential election. Clearly, what I refer to as the "voter confidence meter" is trending in the wrong direction.

I must also say that these days, it seems like nearly everyone—from the mainstream media to the fringes of the "blogosphere"—is talking almost exclusively about real or perceived deficiencies in voting system technology. Are electronic voting machines safe? Can they be manipulated, thereby affecting their reliability and accuracy? Should DRE's be used only with a voter-verifiable paper audit trail, if used at all? Despite warnings by election administrators and public interest advocates alike regarding the lack of attention to the "people" aspect of election administration, our collective national attention has not strayed too far since November 2000 from the "technology" we use in casting and counting ballots.

To be sure, I am not suggesting that this important national debate on the integrity of electronic voting machines be in any way curtailed or even discouraged, especially in light of the financial incentives given to state and local governments under HAVA to purchase new voting equipment. Because of HAVA, election administrators throughout the country have been put in the unenviable situation of having to make difficult policy decisions regarding the purchase and use of electronic voting systems during a climate of relative uncertainty and looming federal deadlines.

Clearly, the American public ought to be informed—and vocal—in their opinions about these key technology decisions regarding the means by which we capture and count our ballot choices. And yet, focusing almost exclusively on "technology" will only get us so far in accomplishing meaningful election reform. Moreover, regardless of how one feels about the reliability and integrity of electronic voting machines, one result of this contentious and at times, highly partisan national debate, has been to further erode the confidence of the American public in our election outcomes. Given that this national debate on electronic voting machines is unlikely to fade any time soon, it is all the more imperative that we concurrently examine other means by which to afford the American public with a renewed sense of optimism in the fundamental fairness of our electoral process.

RECOMMENDATIONS FOR GREATER IMPARTIALITY

When it comes to considering ways to improve the perception of fundamental fairness in election administration, I am guided primarily by my professional experiences as a lifelong student of both politics and public policy, as well as by the perspective I have been privileged to gain while serving as an EAC commissioner. The continued partisan wrangling and controversy associated with our nation's last two presidential elections have placed a tremendous obligation upon election officials at all levels of government to improve upon each aspect of election administration—including, but especially, the technology we use, the policies and procedures which govern our elections, and of course, the people who administer the entire process.

I believe we are making significant progress in all three areas. For those of you not familiar with the work of the EAC, it is worth noting that in our short two-year history, we have fully distributed all HAVA funds to every jurisdiction in the country; we have developed and adopted—after much deliberation and extensive public comment—the first set of revised voluntary voting system guidelines governing the accessibility and security of electronic voting systems; we have issued voluntary guidance regarding statewide voter registration lists; we are poised, in the coming months, to transfer the national voting system certification program from the National Association of State Election Directors (NASED) to the EAC; we have developed significant research and data collection regarding various aspects of election administration; and perhaps most important, we have worked diligently to achieve genuine collaboration and partnership with all HAVA stakeholders, which in turn, has allowed the EAC to become a legitimate and credible voice in the arena of election administration and election reform.

Progress is also due in no small part to the efforts of state and local election administrators throughout the country. In my many years of working in the public sector, I have never met a group of individuals as universally committed to fairness and integrity in the process as are state and local election officials. There are certainly differences of opinion in this group as to numerous policy issues and how best to achieve meaningful election reform, but there is never any wavering in their universal commitment to continual improvement in the conduct of free and fair elections.

And yet, while we are making progress in enhancing all phases of election administration, the pace of this steady improvement, in my opinion, does not appear to be keeping stride with the persistent erosion in voter confidence. That is, while election reform legislation at the state and federal levels—such as HAVA—will take years to fully implement, the growing contentiousness and litigious nature of our election process is creating additional doubts with each passing election cycle. It is true that there is little we can do to diminish the controversy associated with close elections, nor the courtroom battles that sometimes ensue—moreover, our great democracy is clearly capable of withstanding such difficulties. And yet, the continued attrition in voter trust ought to concern not only the election administration community, but all Americans.

There are four restrained and reasonable steps that can be taken today, which will, in my view, begin to stem the flow of voter trust.

First, as Professor Rick Hasen has already suggested, I believe it is imperative for states to perform an "election law audit" on a routine or periodic basis to determine whether there exists any lingering ambiguities or outright inconsistencies in the current policies and procedures governing the administration of elections for that particular jurisdiction.

For example, language in HAVA required that each state adopt a "uniform and nondiscriminatory" definition of what constitutes, and what will count as, a vote for each type of voting system used in that state. This requirement, a clear attempt by Congress to address the difficulties encountered by Florida in the 2000 presidential election, caused state legislatures to examine their respective election codes with a collective discerning eye towards "voter intent."

Likewise, in my view, state legislatures should periodically turn such collective scrutiny toward all aspects of their statutory and administrative election policies and procedures, not just voter intent. And, this election law audit should be done in a fully transparent and collaborative manner, much like the development of the respective "state plans" under HAVA. In fact, the very same planning committees that were statutorily mandated to develop a state's HAVA plan—many of whom are now either dormant or disbanded—should be reconstituted for the very purpose of conducting a periodic election law audit on a state-by-state basis.

In addition to assessing ambiguities and confusion in state policies and procedures, a periodic election law audit will also allow state policymakers to better understand how the various election procedures operate, who has discretion or responsibility to implement such policies, and perhaps equally important, what election-related policies and procedures are not currently, but should be, written into state law.

For example, one of the most controversial aspects of the 2004 presidential contest was the casting and counting of provisional ballots, an issue that was extensively litigated right up to Election Day. In conducting such an election law audit, a state may determine that the policies and procedures governing provisional voting should be largely codified by the state legislature rather than administratively promulgated by a state chief election official who was likely elected or appointed to that office on a partisan basis. At a minimum, if state legislatures were to institute a periodic, transparent and collaborative review of statutory and administrative election laws and procedures, such an assessment will at least deter the perception by some that the "rules of the game" are being made up in the middle of an election contest.

Second, while many respected academics and commentators have articulated a compelling rationale for state chief election officials to be appointed on a nonpartisan basis and confirmed by a super-majority vote, I believe that calls for such an approach are premature. Like a majority of members of the National Association of Secretaries of State, I happen to believe that chief election officials who are elected to their positions—as most are—will make decisions knowing that the ultimate

accountability for their actions will be decided by voters on Election Day. Thus, before we take steps that could decrease such accountability, we should consider whether voter confidence can be strengthened through a less drastic step.

Accordingly, I believe the time has come for adoption, on a state-by-state basis, of a limited, yet strong, conflict-of-interest requirement for all state chief election officials—whether elected or appointed. In the current environment of close public and media scrutiny over election administration, clearly, the momentum is building for such a development. Recently, two statewide chief election officials—Secretaries Bruce McPherson of California, a Republican, and Bill Bradbury of Oregon, a Democrat, issued a joint pledge to carry out their duties in an "independent and non-partisan manner that is beyond question" and to not "serve in any ongoing official capacity" on a campaign supporting any candidate. Others have expressed similar support for political impartiality by a state's chief election official, including former NASS president Mary Kiffmeyer, who currently serves as the elected secretary of state in Minnesota.

Let me be clear in stating that I do not believe that when a state's chief election official chooses to engage in a partisan contest, such political involvement necessarily leads to any partisan advantage. Every statewide chief election official—such as a secretary of state—takes an oath of office pledging to implement the laws of that jurisdiction in a fair and impartial manner. And yet, I am in agreement with those—such as Secretaries McPherson and Bradbury—who have concluded that the issue of public perception when such a conflict-of-interest is present is simply too compelling to ignore.

In short, removing the perception of partisanship by requiring a state's chief election official to refrain from serving, whether actual or honorary, on a campaign or committee supporting any candidates and to remain neutral on any referendums, measures, propositions, recalls, or initiatives unless they relate directly to the official duties and responsibilities of the chief election official seems to me a restrained, and yet significant step, toward restoring the public's faith in the underlying fairness of our election system.

Although voluntarily adopting such a restriction is certainly prudent—as many current secretaries of state have done—in my view, such conflict-of-interest provisions should be legislatively debated and enacted into state law. One state in the country has done so, by the way, which is Colorado. There are several benefits to codifying such a provision. First, the public input and discussion that would be generated by having a state legislature debate this important topic would, in my view, serve to increase public confidence in the electoral process, regardless of what language, if any, is finally adopted. Second, while a voluntary pledge of neutrality accomplishes the same result as one that is statutorily enacted, the voluntarily pledge is only as good as the official who makes it. In other words, any successor is not bound by the incumbent's pledge. Finally, and perhaps most important, adopting a conflict-of-interest provision into state law

would help remove the political pressure to participate in party politics that may be felt by a state's chief election official who is appointed or elected on a partisan basis. That is, having the ability to point to a provision in state law that restricts such activity is an enormously useful tool for a statewide chief election official who may be under great pressure to engage in partisan activity, particularly if that individual happens to be the highest-ranking statewide elected official for a particular political party.

Let me also say that I strongly believe that the genesis of such efforts for legislatively enacted conflict-of-interest provisions ought to come directly and solely on a state-by-state basis. Other than utilizing the "bully pulpit," as I am doing today, the EAC should play no role in effectuating this particular outcome. In my view, the best way to develop a meaningful conflict-of-interest provision applicable to a state's chief election official is through discussion and deliberation in each respective state, which will need to take into account various factors, such as state-specific constitutional, statutory, and regulatory provisions.

My third recommendation for improving the public's confidence in our election outcomes involves an increasingly essential player in the process of election administration—the vendors of election equipment. Given the important—and significantly direct—role that voting machine vendors play in our political process, I believe they too, have an obligation to take necessary steps toward greater neutrality. While I suspect the days of voting system company CEO's publicly pledging to deliver votes for a particular political candidate have long since passed, nevertheless, election equipment vendors must also consider adopting strong conflict-of-interest provisions to help restore confidence in the integrity of our electoral process.

As with the election community, many of the major election equipment vendors have voluntarily adopted company-specific ethical standards. This is a positive development. And yet, while each company having a specific policy is important, I believe an industry-wide conflict-of-interest provision is necessary, which, at a minimum, should include a prohibition on all company officers and executives from endorsing, assisting, or contributing to, candidates, political parties, or political organizations.

While I am concerned about the First Amendment implications of such a strict ethical standard, the special trust that is placed in an election equipment vendor by a jurisdiction that purchases its equipment—and then, in most cases, must rely on the vendor's technical expertise to set up and operate the voting systems—is quite compelling. In many ways, that particular vendor has just as much obligation—if not more so—to act with integrity, impartiality, and fundamental fairness as does a public officer, such as a state's chief election official or local election administrator. Therefore, in this particular circumstance, I am persuaded that the benefits of producing greater public confidence in the fairness of our election process in adopting such a strict political neutrality restriction outweighs the loss of individual rights for those election equipment company officers and executives that would be impacted by this provision.

At least one major election equipment vendor agrees. Diebold, Incorporated has adopted a policy prohibiting its chief executive officer, president, and chief financial officer, as well as company executives with oversight of election system companies and employees of those companies from making contributions to any political candidate, party, election issue or cause, or participate in any political activities, except for voting. Accordingly, I think the time has come for the election equipment industry to immediately implement a strict, industry-wide conflict-of-interest provision regarding political neutrality for, at a minimum, all senior company executives and officers.

Finally, as a means to further protect the public interest in such a key governmental function as is the fair and impartial administration of elections, I propose that, as a condition of state voting system certification, states require disclosure to appropriate state officials of certain key information from the vendor, such as: (1) details concerning past or present criminal or corruption investigations or prosecutions involving a vendor's employees or officers; (2) disclosure of financial information of the vendor pertaining to bankruptcy, insolvency, or reorganization; and (3) disclosure of all litigation in which the vendor is, or has been, a party within the past five years.

There is precedent for such a requirement. For example, many states currently require voting system vendors—as a condition of state certification—to deliver to state officials copies of the software and source code for electronic voting systems that are being certified for use in that particular jurisdiction. We ought to do the same in requiring key information from voting system vendors.

Let me also say that as the responsibility over federal voting system certification transfers from the National Association of State Election Directors (NASED) to the EAC, I believe it would be prudent for the EAC to adopt a similar disclosure requirement upon voting system vendors. In fact, having this criminal, financial, and litigation information disclosed at the federal level—to be shared with relevant state officials when necessary—may be a more efficient way to implement this disclosure proposal, rather than having the vendor do so each time it applies for state voting system certification.

While it is true that past conduct—whether meritorious or lamentable—is no definitive predictor of future behavior, nevertheless, the public, through its state election officials, has a right to know such details, particularly at a time of heightened public scrutiny and anxiety regarding the use of certain election technology. In my opinion, such transparency will ensure that state officials have adequate information to assess the integrity, reputation, and reliability of voting system vendors that wish to do business in that particular state. More importantly, this should serve as another small, yet significant step, toward improving the confidence of the American public in the process of election administration.

CONCLUSION

Let me conclude by saying that the four steps that I have proposed today—periodic election law audits, implementation of state-specific conflict-of-interest requirements for state chief election officials, adoption of an industry-wide political neutrality requirement for senior executives and officers of voting system vendors, and disclosure of certain criminal, financial, and litigation information by election equipment vendors to relevant state officials as a condition of voting system certification—serve as measured, yet, in my view, sound and prudent steps toward achieving a greater sense of voter confidence in our election procedures and outcomes. Moreover, none of these proposals require any additional authority or responsibility to be given to the EAC. I truly hope that all HAVA stakeholders will take these proposals in the spirit in which they are offered—not to upset the delicate federal/state balance that has been achieved with the passage of HAVA and the creation of the EAC, but as observations from an EAC commissioner who has been privileged to sit at a unique vantage point from which to view—and comment upon—the progress of election reform.

I will end my remarks today simply by stating that, as we move forward with HAVA implementation in the months and years to come, the EAC must diligently stick to the task it was assigned in HAVA—to distribute appropriated federal HAVA funds in a timely manner, as we have done; to provide timely voluntary guidance on matters related to the election technology and administrative requirements in HAVA; to act as a national clearinghouse on information and research pertaining to election administration; to assist in implementing important federal voting laws, such as NVRA and UOCAVA; and to develop a program of certification of voting systems in this country—together with strong and transparent voting system standards—that we can all have faith in. And, we must do all of the above in a transparent and collaborative manner while taking into account the great history in our country of election administration being a responsibility largely reserved—appropriately, in my view—to state and local governments.

I am honored to be here will you all today. Thank you.

Appendix A (continued): Panel Discussion Summaries

Panel Discussion Summary: Day One Report

Opening Session

Anthony Shorris, Director of the Policy Research Institute for the Region at Princeton, opened the conference by noting that election reform comprises many cross-boundary and cross-disciplinary issues, and is a particularly timely topic for discussion. Since the Bipartisan Campaign Reform Act (BRCA, McCain-Feingold) was passed, sweeping election law reforms are going on. And the Voting Rights Act (VRA) is in the news because it is now up for reauthorization. Shorris called 2006 "a make-or-break year."

BRCA and Beyond: Campaign Finance Reform in the States

The first session featured a presentation by Richard Briffault (Visiting Fellow, Program in Law and Public Affairs, Princeton University; and Joseph P. Chamberlain Professor of Legislation at Columbia Law School), entitled *Stepping Out of the Federal Shadow: Campaign Finance Law in the States.*

Briffault highlighted four main issues. First, he said there is "both an extensive opportunity for and a widespread practice of state and local campaign financing," since only about 1

percent of federal offices are elected offices; 99 percent are state and local.

Secondly, federal campaign law has only a limited effect on the states. IRS code section 527 and BRCA are the two that do. BRCA provides "for extensive regulation of the electioneering activities of state and local parties."

Third, federal constitutional law doesn't distinguish between state and federal elections. Indeed, the Supreme Court has held that campaign contributions and spending and election-related speech are protected by the First Amendment, and that this applies to both state and local campaign finance laws.

Finally, contribution limits and public funding programs need to be revised. Until BRCA automatically indexed contributions to increases in the cost of living, federal limits remained constant, thus becoming eroded by inflation. Changes in campaign costs should be considered in revising the limits on contributions. Another factor that should be considered is the different sizes of constituencies for different offices. Now maximum contribution limits set by federal law are the same for candidates for the House, the Senate, and the Presidency.

Briffault concluded that "money is not evil; money is good. It just needs to be spread around more equally and detached from its donors." He called public funding the "most constitutionally attractive option."

A panel, moderated by Larry Bartels, Donald E. Stokes Professor of Public and International Affairs; Director, Center for the Study of Democratic Politics, Princeton University, responded to the presentation. Nick Nyhart, Executive Director of *Public Campaign,* a Connecticut political action committee, said that money is increasingly central to "what a candidate needs to do to run a winning campaign." While BRCA is finely tuned and was carefully considered, problems still exist.

The good news is that well-functioning local and state models do exist. Nyhart called the New York City model the best example of the matching-funds system, but there are nine models of "clean money" or "clean elections systems." In these models, candidates who want to participate and get public money gather large numbers of small contributions, which they turn in to get grants. Then if large amounts of private money are given to opposing candidates, matching funds (or "rescue money") are made available, thereby protecting the "clean elections" candidate. These systems are in effect in Albuquerque, New Mexico, and Portland, Maine. New Jersey is considering such a system in two districts. And in New York, a bill for a clean-elections system is pending in the legislature.

Such systems change the dynamics of elections. The first step in campaigning becomes approaching small donors, giving them equal clout and standing. "It pushes candidates out to ordinary voters," Nyhart said. Candidates can do less fundraising, instead "spending time with voters instead of dialing for dollars." He concluded that federal campaign laws, when eventually passed, will be better because of these experiences in the states.

Suzanne Novak, Deputy Director, Democracy Project, Brennan Center for Justice, New York University School of Law, addressed three issues: the electioneering communications aspect of BRCA; "pay-to-play" regulations; and legal challenges to public-financing systems in the states.

She noted that BRCA spells out the types of communication that can be regulated—"the magic words test"—which includes "vote for," "vote against," and "support." Regulation can be averted by avoiding the use of those words. Or candidates can make ads that focus on "genuine issues," without an attempt to influence an election. She recommended that states consider "broadening their definition of what it means to conduct electioneering."

"Pay to play" regulations apply specifically to lobbyists, state contractors, or regulated industries. Sometimes these increase the threshold of disclosure of contributions. Others put lower limits on contributions, but some ban contributions entirely. Lower limits have been upheld by the Supreme Court, but bans are "more dangerous constitutionally," Novak said, because they can be interpreted as "limiting association" with a candidate.

Some public-financing laws have been challenged, usually on grounds that they violate the First Amendment, or are vague, unreasonable, or coercive. Courts have mainly upheld the laws, saying these schemes expand speech instead of restricting it.

Questions and comments from the audience followed.

One questioner asked, Should campaign finance reform laws emphasize simplicity or detail? Nyhart said what is really needed is "reality-based crafting" of laws to make sure the "floor" is high enough. The presidential voting system currently provides a very low floor. Briffault added that the basic approach is to institute "ceilings," with the result that very large gifts from individuals have mainly disappeared. The value of putting more money into the system is that it increases competition and indirectly promotes anticorruption laws by providing candidates with other sources of money. He pointed out that the rise of the Internet and blogging as campaign tools means that money that is not going into direct donations is going into these new kinds of speech.

Another participant asked whether use of the Internet and blogs is tied to the great variation in campaign sizes seen at state and local levels. Legal models seem to focus on the bigger races. Briffault said we haven't really seen definitively how the Internet works in campaigning. It works well for facilitating fundraising, as Howard Dean showed, for "people who know who they want to give money to." But the Internet also makes it harder to draw some lines between regulatable and nonregulatable speech.

An audience member asked, "Why is there so little public enthusiasm for campaign finance reform?" Nyack replied that campaign finance reform is not a "well-staged debate." With the biggest opponents to it being incumbents and big contributors, you can only fix the system "by pulling together a very broad coalition that goes beyond the usual suspects."

Evolving the VRA

The second presentation of the day was given by Guy Charles, James S. Carpentier Visiting Professor of Law, Columbia Law School; and Russell M. and Elizabeth M. Bennett Associate Professor of Law, University of Minnesota Law School. His talk was entitled, *Evolving the VRA.*

Charles pointed out that the VRA is "at an evident crossroads." It created, he said, an invasive regulatory regime that has been immensely successful in increasing voting by people of color; it has achieved much of its purpose since 1965; and the types of discriminatory practices that gave rise to the VRA (political violence on the basis of race, etc.) have nearly been eradicated. But the VRA's regulatory component has been hampered by the Supreme Court's interpretation of it, which has narrowed the reach of the act and which "might destabilize the foundational nature of the act itself."

So how should the VRA be considered and restructured going forward? The political reality is that advocacy groups advocate for the current model, even though it is not as effective as it could be and not focused on the problems of the 21st century. Can we develop a theory, Charles asked, for developing a new model of the VRA that is more broadly oriented toward consequential political participation and not just as a reaction against discrimination?

Race should, of course, be considered, but there are other issues to think about as well. For example, why shouldn't the VRA address felon disenfranchisement, which has huge racial implications? Voter identification likewise requires "a broader national conversation," as do uniformity of ballots and redistricting. These are, Charles said, "structural issues that affect voters of color but also voters more generally."

Mark Posner, Adjunct Professor, Washington College of Law at American University, responded by trying to frame the issues that are critical to renewal of the VRA. He noted that there are three basic parts of VRA. These include prohibitions on discrimination in voting (Section 2). Some VRA provisions are temporary and will sunset unless Congress renews them. These include Sections 203 and Section 5. Section 203 requires certain jurisdictions to provide ballots in languages other than English and to provide assistance to voters. Section 5 applies mainly in the South. It stipulates that if a jurisdiction acts to change something like a polling place or redistricting, that jurisdiction must get federal approval from the Department of Justice or a federal court in Washington, D.C.

Do we still need these provisions? 99 percent of the time, Posner said, jurisdictions do go to DOJ, but DOJ objections are now virtually nonexistent. Section 5 should be renewed but

needs to recognize its own success. "Special preclearance provisions need to be ramped down in some way," Posner said, perhaps excluding polling-place changes, instead focusing on more major changes.

Gregory Harvey, Partner, Montgomery, McCracken, Walker & Rhoads, LLP, reviewed lessons from the case of *United States v Burks County.* Burks County (37 percent Hispanic, of which 63 percent are Puerto Rican) surrounds Reading, Pennsylvania, which is not subject to Section 203 of the VRA (it applies only if a language minority of the voting-eligible population exists and the level of illiteracy is above the national average; in Pennsylvania, only Philadelphia meets these criteria). However, Spanish-language ballots are provided to protect the rights of Puerto Ricans, who are U.S. citizens. But election observers said Puerto Ricans were treated hostilely at the polls, there was a lack of bilingual helpers and ballots, assistance in voting was denied, and the Board of Commissioners did nothing about these problems. The court ultimately handed down these remedies: if the polling place had more than 5 percent Hispanic voters, one bilingual person had to be hired; if more than 40 percent, two bilingual persons, etc. A procedure was set up to receive complaints, an educational program was instituted, a coordinator was hired, and reports were filed with DOJ.

Phil Olaya, an attorney for the Asian American Legal Defense and Education Fund (AALDEF), discussed why reauthorization of Section 5 is important (more important than Section 203) for Asian Americans. On the issue of election protection, AALDEF objected to the way

Asian-American voters in New York City's Chinatown were treated during local elections that had to be rescheduled after the terrorist attacks of September 11, 2001. A large polling place in Chinatown had been taken over by the Federal Emergency Management Agency, and voters were not given notice of the change; there were no newspapers ads and no community notification. AALDEF was able to force the board of elections to comply with the provisions of Section 5. It was also able to demand a preferential-voting system, with the result that Asian-American candidates were successfully elected to the school board. Now AALDEF wants to expand the language-assistance provisions of the act for the Asian-American population, which now stands at 12 million and growing, by lowering the trigger from 10,000 people to 7,500. This change would affect 17 jurisdictions around the country.

Beyond HAVA and VRA

The first afternoon session, *Beyond HAVA and VRA*, featured a presentation by Richard Pildes, Sudler Family Professor of Constitutional Law, New York University School of Law. Pildes said we are unlikely to have serious policy reform in voting rights, and that there is little national legislation dealing with voting rights. The 2000 election, which stunned many Americans, revealed our "pathologically decentralized" election system. As a result, he said, "we're reverse engineering our way out of this."

VRA and HAVA are the two most significant national legislative efforts since the Civil War designed to bring uniformity to national elections. But they embody two radically different philosophies. The VRA is a narrowly targeted, selective statute that does not protect the right to vote as such but does protect against racial discrimination in voting practices.

HAVA, which was passed after the 2000 election, demonstrates a shift from an anti-discrimination model to a set of guarantees for the right to vote. Which model, VRA or HAVA, should prevail for the future?

Pildes suggested that geographic targeting in VRA doesn't make sense for the future, since today issues are not confined to region and not easy to predict in advance. We should instead trade the model of geographic targeting, which reflects a past era of voting rights, for more federal legislation modeled on HAVA. But Pildes predicted that Congress will most likely reauthorize Section 5 in its present form. "It will be the preservation of the past," he said.

In the panel discussion that followed, Frank Askin, Professor, Rutgers University Law School, and General Counsel for the ACLU, speaking for himself and not the ACLU, agreed that Section 5 would likely be renewed but would have little impact in the real world. He noted that, as felon disenfranchisement prevents millions of blacks from voting, invalidation of those laws "should be a slam dunk under Section 2 of the VRA."

Edward Hailes Jr., Senior Attorney, The Advancement Project, said that most people do not know that the U.S. Constitution does not contain an express right to vote. He suggested the VRA be amended to include such a provision, by stating, "all citizens of the United States who are 18 years of age or older shall have the right to vote in federal elections in the jurisdiction where the citizen resides."

Juan Cartagena, General Counsel for the Community Service Society, disagreed with Pildes, saying we must have national standards, especially with respect to felon disenfranchisement. It makes no sense, he said, to let states pick and choose who can vote. Cartagena pointed out that HAVA was not the first attempt to regulate federal elections. The National Voter Registration Act (NVRA) of 1993 regulated elections and established important rights (an affirmative obligation to register voters, elimination of the nonvoting purge, establishment of mail-in registration, etc.). And when some states refused to implement it, the DOJ enforced the law's provision. Using NVRA as a model creates a "floor" of principles on the national level and provides a specific tie-in with VRA.

Questions from the audience followed. *One person asked about the tradeoffs between the broad reach but weak enforcement provisions of HAVA vs the narrower reach but stronger enforcement provisions of VRA.* Pildes responded by saying that HAVA is a "symbol of nationwide protection of the right to vote," and that he was skeptical about abandoning a private right of action. Do we have to choose between VRA and HAVA?

Closing Session
In the day's closing remarks, Michael Waldman, Executive Director, Brennan Center for Justice, New York University School of Law, said the real question is, How can we make democracy and the fight for it at the center of politics in this country now? He suggested that four things are necessary to create real change: some sort of scandal or crisis, good ideas at the ready, disaffected voters, and a sense of urgency underpinned by the notion of a living constitution (in contrast to the originalist philosophy propounded by Justice Antonin Scalia). He quoted the architect Daniel Burnham, who said, "Make no little plans; they have no magic to stir men's blood."

Panel Discussion Summary: Day Two Report

HAVA in the States

The second day of the conference focused on HAVA. A panel of election administrators detailed how their states are responding to and implementing HAVA provisions. Stanley Zalen, Co-Executive Director, New York Board of Elections, said because of a lawsuit by DOJ, New York State's goal is to implement HAVA as fast as possible. By 2007, the state is expected to have a fully interactive and HAVA-compliant registration system.

The State of Delaware, according to Howard Sholl, Deputy Administrative Director, Department of Elections for New Castle County, has, in contrast to New York, a top-down system, in which all voting is run by the state. He noted, however, that it has taken years to develop and implement a statewide voting system.

Michael Gallagher, New Jersey's HAVA administrator, said HAVA "has been a challenge in New Jersey without question," and more time is still required to implement the law. The state is not yet compliant with all HAVA provisions, including the statewide registration system, which requires bringing 21 counties into a single system. "I've learned a whole new meaning of the word 'complex'," Gallagher said, but "in the end, we will have a system that not only works but will be the model for the nation, God willing."

There was much discussion of the deadlines imposed by HAVA, whether they were workable, and how they affected strategies for implementation, especially with respect to IT and training issues. The moderator, Doug Chapin, Director of Electionline, noted that the deadlines have motivated and shaped change but have not necessarily defined it.

MyVote1 in Action

Technology was the focus of a second presentation, by Christopher Patusky, Executive Director, Fels Institute of Government, University of Pennsylvania, and Ken Smukler, President of Voterlink. Patusky said the 2000 election showed that there is no national election system. One solution, called MyVote1, is to use technology to assist voters (a national toll-free hotline with an automatic poll locator and automatic transfer to a local county hotline) and to diagnose the election system (by recording data such as transfer success rate, complaints, requests, etc.) (A full report of MyVote1 can be found at www.fels.upenn.edu/FGRS/Final MyVote1 Report 11.1.05.pdf.) The most frequent voter complaint is registration: people don't know where to vote, they don't have easy access to the information that would tell them, and counties don't answer their hotlines. Smukler noted that one solution is Web-based information about poll locations, but only 9 or 10 states have this technology.

Complying with HAVA Funding Guidelines

In the concluding panel, moderated by Christopher Sheridan, Policy Director, The

Committee of Seventy, presentations focused on compliance with HAVA funding guidelines.

In a paper prepared by Sarah Liebschutz, Distinguished Service Professor Emeritus, State University of New York–Brockport, and Daniel J. Palazzolo, Professor of Political Science at the University of Richmond, the presenters said experience in New York, New Jersey, and Pennsylvania shows what happens to federal law when it is translated into reality. HAVA is a direct mandate from the federal government to the states and requires compliance, but there is a $700 million dollar gap between what was mandated and what has been appropriated for implementation.

Panelists representing specific states and groups responded.

Rachel Leon, of Common Cause New York, warned of looming problems in New York State stemming in part from lack of representation from citizens. "We've all failed in New York State," she said, "and the people who're going to pay the price are voters in the fall."

Renée Steinhagen, Executive Director, New Jersey Public Interest Law Center, asked whether New Jersey has achieved "real systemic structural change." She said that HAVA imposes on states a duty to maintain an accurate database and an obligation to ensure uniformity in elections. States have to rely on local officials who are juggling multiple responsibilities: New Jersey's chief election administrator is accountable to the public, acts as a liaison to the legislature, and has the capacity to issue administrative rules. She said

data are needed from other states that have an elected chief election officer.

Christina Galindo-Walsh, Senior Attorney, National Disability Rights Network, said that HAVA is not just about election reform but about civil rights. It gives people with disabilities the opportunity to cast an independent vote.

Patricia DeConstanza, Supervisor of Elections for Bergen County, New Jersey, the largest county in the state, said that her state's HAVA plan was written by the state attorney general, and that election officials, "who do the job," disagreed with much of it. She said officials needed more time to implement a centralized voter registration system. "There will never be a perfect election," she declared, "but there will be a fair one."

Equity in HAVA Implementation

A panel on equity in HAVA implementation followed, moderated by Thomas O'Neill, Director, Provisional Voting Project, Eagleton Institute of Politics, Rutgers University. Edward Foley, Professor of Law, Moritz College of Law at the Ohio State University, posed the central question: What would true equality in voting rights mean? And how can we have systems that guarantee this?

Current problems Foley highlighted include: extremely close local elections, which can be decided by one or two votes; registration databases and registration processes (even an optimally designed system would not be perfect if it had to contain every single name of every person who would be eligible to vote and not to contain any names of people who were not eligible); cutoffs for registration and provisional voting; and absentee voting. Foley said we should strive for "a notion of optimality and therefore of fairness and legitimacy," and for a system that is itself a product of democratic deliberation.

Responses from panelists followed. Tova Wang, Fellow, The Century Foundation, said that voter identification, which has opened a floodgate of legislation, is not the answer to systemic voting problems. We should concentrate instead on cleaning up statewide voter registration databases, increasing penalties for committing voter fraud, and making absentee ballots more secure.

Michael McDonald, Visiting Fellow, the Brookings Institution, highlighted the issue of provisional balloting. According to information from a 2004 Election Day survey, 1.9 million provisional ballots were cast, of which 1.2 million were verified. A problem that remains is that higher rates of provisional ballots are cast in areas where education and income are lower, indicating that minorities cannot interface effectively with the electoral system. McDonald noted that one benefit of statewide databases is their lower rates of provisional balloting.

William Baroni, Professor, Seton Hall Law School, and Assemblyman, New Jersey State Assembly, discussed the problem of partisan beliefs about who is manipulating elections. Democrats, he said, are always thought to be stealing elections in urban areas, and Republicans are always said to be keeping people of color from voting. Technology, especially provisional balloting, will allow us to get around these two partisan objections.

Closing Session

Donald Kettl, Director, Fels Institute of Government, University of Pennsylvania, made some closing remarks. He emphasized the critical role of technology as the source of both the deepest problems and the most interesting solutions to election reform. A fundamental issue is the central role played by how voting is administered, and the belief held by some that people who can't figure out the voting process don't actually deserve to vote. Finally, he said, election reform requires weaving together technology, administration, and academic research. The issues discussed here are "fundamentally important not only for the conduct of elections but for the role of elections in American public life."

Appendix B: Agenda

MAKING EVERY VOTE COUNT:
A Colloquium On Election Reform Legislation

APRIL 6–7, 2006

Sponsored by the Policy Research Institute for the Region at Princeton University, the Brennan Center for Justice at New York University School of Law, and the Fels Institute of Government at the University of Pennsylvania

Opening Session
Welcoming Remarks
> **Anthony Shorris**, Director, Policy Research Institute for the Region, Princeton University

BCRA and Beyond: Campaign Finance Reform in the States
Presentation
> **Richard Briffault**, Visiting Fellow, Program in Law and Public Affairs, Princeton University; Joseph P. Chamberlain Professor of Legislation, Columbia Law School

Moderator
> **Larry Bartels**, Donald E. Stokes Professor of Public and International Affairs; Director, Center for the Study of Democratic Politics, Princeton University

Panelists
> **Suzanne Novak**, Deputy Director, Democracy Project, Brennan Center for Justice, New York University School of Law
>
> **Nick Nyhart**, Executive Director, Public Campaign

Evolving the VRA
Presentation
> **Guy Charles**, James S. Carpentier Visiting Professor of Law, Columbia Law School; Russell M. and Elizabeth M. Bennett Associate Professor of Law, University of Minnesota Law School

Moderator
> **David Epstein**, Professor of Political Science, Columbia University

Panelists
> **Phil Olaya**, Attorney, Asian American Legal Defense and Education Fund
>
> **Mark Posner**, Adjunct Professor, Washington College of Law at American University
>
> **Gregory Harvey**, Partner, Montgomery, McCracken, Walker & Rhoads, LLP

Lunch and Keynote

Introduction
> **Robert Wuthnow**, Adlinger Professor of Sociology; Director, Center for the Study of Religion, Princeton University

Speaker
> **DeForest Soaries**, Senior Pastor, First Baptist Church of Lincoln Gardens

Beyond HAVA and VRA

Presentation
> **Richard Pildes**, Sudler Family Professor of Constitutional Law, New York University School of Law

Moderator
> **Justin Levitt**, Associate Counsel, Brennan Center for Justice, New York University School of Law

Panelists
> **Juan Cartagena**, General Counsel, Community Service Society
> **Frank Askin**, General Counsel, American Civil Liberties Union; Professor, Rutgers University Law School
> **Edward Hailes Jr.**, Senior Attorney, the Advancement Project

Closing Session

Closing Remarks
> **Michael Waldman**, Executive Director, Brennan Center for Justice, New York University School of Law

Opening Session

Opening Remarks

Anthony Shorris, Director, Policy Research Institute for the Region, Princeton University

HAVA in the States

Moderator

Doug Chapin, Director, Electionline

Panelists

Stanley Zalen, Co-Executive Director, New York Board of Elections

Howard Sholl, Deputy Administrative Director, Department of Elections for New Castle County, State of Delaware

MyVote1 in Action

Presentation

Ken Smuckler, President, Voterlink

Christopher Patusky, Executive Director, Fels Institute of Government, University of Pennsylvania

Lunch and Keynote

Introduction

Myriam Gilles, Visiting Fellow in the Program in Law and Public Affairs, Princeton University; Professor, Benjamin N. Cardozo School of Law

Speaker

Ray Martinez, Vice Chairman, Election Assistance Commission

Equity in HAVA Implementation

Presentation

Edward Foley, Professor of Law, Moritz College of Law, Ohio State University

Moderator

Thomas O'Neill, Director, Provisional Voting Project, Eagleton Institute of Politics, Rutgers University

Panelists

Tova Wang, Fellow, The Century Foundation

Michael McDonald, Visiting Fellow, The Brookings Institution

William Baroni, Professor, Seton Hall Law School; Assemblyman, New Jersey State Assembly

Complying with HAVA Funding Guidelines

Presentation

Sarah Liebschutz, Distinguished Service Professor Emeritus, State University of New York–Brockport; Daniel J. Palazzolo, Professor of Political Science, University of Richmond

Moderator
Christopher Sheridan, Policy Director, The Committee of Seventy

Panelists
Renée Steinhagen, Executive Director, Public Interest Law Center of New Jersey
Rachel Leon, Executive Director, Common Cause New York
Christina Galindo-Walsh, Senior Attorney, National Disability Rights Network

Closing Session

Closing Remarks
Donald Kettl, Director, Fels Institute of Government, University of Pennsylvania

Appendix C: Participant Biographies

Frank Askin
Professor of Law and Robert E. Knowlton Scholar, Rutgers School of Law–Newark; General Counsel, ACLU

Frank Askin has served on the National Board of the American Civil Liberties Union for 33 years, and has served as one of the ACLU's general counsel since 1976. He is the author of *Defending Rights: A Life in Law and Politics,* published in 1997 by Humanities Press.

Askin has been a member of the Rutgers Law School, Newark, faculty ever since his graduation from there in 1966, following an earlier career as a newspaper reporter. He teaches in the areas of constitutional law, federal courts and procedure and election law.

Askin founded Rutgers's pioneering Constitutional Litigation Clinic in 1970. He has interspersed his academic career with stints as a Congressional counsel. In 1976–77, he served as special counsel to the House Labor-Management Subcommittee; and from 1987 to 1992 served as a consultant to Rep. John Conyers and the House Government Operations Committee on issues relating to national security and civil liberties.

He was the unsuccessful Democratic candidate for Congress in 1986 in the 11th Congressional District.

At Rutgers, Askin has combined the teaching of constitutional law with the active defense of civil liberties, litigating, with his students, many significant cases on behalf of the ACLU.

In *Council of Alternative Political Parties (CAPP) v. Farmer,* Askin won a ruling from the New Jersey Appellate Division that members of alternative parties could register on the voting rolls as members of their own party. As a consequence, the voter registration lists in New Jersey now include designations in addition to Democratic, Republican, Independent, and unaffiliated. He recently failed in an effort to re-enfranchise felons on parole and probation under the New Jersey Constitution.

He is listed in Woodward & White's Best Lawyers in America and as one of New Jersey's Super Lawyers.

William Baroni
Professor, Seton Hall University; Assemblyman, New Jersey State Legislature

William Baroni is serving his second term in the New Jersey State Legislature and is a member of the Education and Higher Education Committees and the Joint Committee on the Public Schools. He also serves as a member of the New Jersey Citizens' Clean Elections Commission.

Assemblyman Baroni is an adjunct professor at Seton Hall University Law School, where he teaches education law, voting rights, and campaign finance law and was named Adjunct Professor of the Year in 2004.

Baroni is also an accomplished attorney and committed community volunteer. Referred to as a "voluntary quartermaster" for the New Jersey National Guard by a local newspaper, Baroni has offered his office as a clearinghouse for items to be sent to troops serving overseas. He has helped residents send holiday packages, facilitated the donation of 10,000 audiobooks, and hosted a Pancake Breakfast to raise money for the families of New Jersey National Guard members serving overseas.

Baroni currently serves on the Board of Trustees for the Hamilton Area YMCA, Visitation Home and Project Freedom, which build homes for New Jerseyans with disabilities. He also serves on the Board of Trustees of the New Jersey Symphony Orchestra, where he has worked to enhance music education programs for students in Central New Jersey.

He previously served as chair of the Mercer County College Board of Trustees and the Foundation Boards of both the College of New Jersey and Mercer County Community College.

Baroni graduated from the University of Virginia School of Law and George Washington University, where he majored in history, and graduated magna cum laude with special honors and was a Rhodes Scholar state finalist.

Baroni currently resides in Hamilton, New Jersey.

Larry M. Bartels
Donald E. Stokes Professor of Public and International Affairs, Princeton University

Larry M. Bartels received his B.A. and M.A. degrees from Yale University in 1978 and his Ph.D. in political science from the University of California–Berkeley in 1983. He taught at the University of Rochester for eight years before moving to Princeton in 1991. He has published numerous articles on electoral politics, public opinion, the mass media, and political methodology in *The American Political Science Review, The American Journal of Political Science,* and other leading scholarly journals, and in a variety of edited volumes. His current research focuses on the American electoral process, the political economy of inequality, and democratic theory.

Bartels's first book, *Presidential Primaries and the Dynamics of Public Choice* (Princeton University Press, 1988), received the Woodrow Wilson Foundation Award for the year's best book on government, politics, or international affairs. He has been the recipient of major grants and fellowships from the Carnegie Corporation, the Center for Advanced Study in the Behavioral Sciences, the John Simon Guggenheim Memorial Foundation, the National Science Foundation, the Pew Charitable Trusts, the Russell Sage Foundation, and the Social Science Research Council. He was elected a Fellow of the American Academy of Arts and Sciences in 1995. Bartels served as chair of a national task force on campaign reform and co-edited (with Lynn Vavreck) the task force's report, *Campaign Reform: Insights and Evidence* (University of Michigan Press, 2000). In 2001 he served as the pivotal non-partisan member of the New Jersey Legislative Apportionment Commission and was a defendant in a major federal voting rights case, *Page v. Bartels*. In 2003–04 he was a member of the American Political Science Association's Task Force on Inequality and American Democracy. He has also served as chair of the Board of Overseers of the American National Election Studies, president of the Methodology Section of the American Political Science Association, and chair of the Princeton University Committee on Public Lectures, and on a variety of other departmental, University, and professional boards and committees.

Richard Briffault
Vice Dean and Joseph P. Chamberlain Professor of Legislation, Columbia Law School

Richard Briffault's primary areas of teaching, research, and writing are state and local government law and the law of the political process. He received his B.A. from Columbia University, and his J.D. from Harvard Law School. He is the co-author of a casebook, *State and Local Government Law;* the author of *Balancing Acts: The Reality Behind State Balanced Budget Requirements;* and *Dollars and Democracy: A Blueprint for Campaign Finance Reform,* the report of the Commission on Campaign Finance Reform of the Association of the Bar of the City of New York. He is also the author of numerous law review articles on local government law, state-local relations, campaign finance reform, and voting rights. While at Princeton, he will work on a book on campaign finance regulation.

Juan Cartagena
General Counsel, Community Service Society

Juan Cartagena has served as general counsel at the Community Service Society (CSS) since 1991. His overall responsibilities include directing the legal department in public interest litigation on behalf of the poor in the areas of voting rights, education, housing, health, and environmental issues.

Prior to joining CSS, Cartagena was the legal director in the New York Office of the Department of Puerto Rican Community Affairs in the U.S. Commonwealth of Puerto Rico and an attorney at the Puerto Rican Legal Defense and Education Fund. He also served as a municipal court judge in Hoboken, New Jersey.

From 1992 to the present, Cartagena has been a part-time lecturer at Rutgers University in the Department of Puerto Rican and Hispanic Caribbean Studies. He teaches the course "Law and the Latino Community in the U.S."

Cartagena received his J.D. from Columbia University School of Law and his B.A. from Dartmouth College.

Doug Chapin
Director, electionline.org

Doug Chapin, director of electionline.org, has worked on both the legal and policy aspects of election issues for more than 15 years. Chapin's campaign experience, as well as his experience at the Federal Election Commission and Election Data Services, Inc., equipped him with a background in election issues including redistricting, election administration, the census, and campaign finance. Before becoming electionline.org's first director, he worked at Skadden, Arps, Slate, Meagher & Flom LLP, counseling clients on compliance with federal, state, and local laws regulating campaign finance, lobbying, gifts to public officials, and conflicts of interest. From 1997 to 2000, he served as elections counsel to the Democrats on the U.S. Senate Rules Committee, where he worked on election issues within the committee's jurisdiction, including the disputed 1996 senate election in Louisiana. At Dickstein, Shapiro, Morin & Oshinsky LLP, Chapin established the firm's disclosure program under the Lobbying Disclosure Act and litigated redistricting cases in state and federal court. Chapin received a law degree from Georgetown University Law Center, a master's in public administration from Harvard's Ken-

nedy School of Government and a B.A. in politics from Princeton University. He is active as a volunteer coach and teacher in his hometown of Vienna, Virginia.

Guy-Uriel E. Charles
Russell M. and Elizabeth M. Bennett Professor of Law, University of Minnesota Law School

Guy-Uriel E. Charles joined the University of Minnesota Law School in the fall of 2000. He clerked for the Honorable Damon J. Keith of the United States Court of Appeals for the Sixth Circuit. While at the University of Michigan, he was the editor-in-chief of the *Michigan Journal of Race & Law*. From 1995–2000, he was a graduate student in political science at the University of Michigan. Prior to joining the law school, he taught as an adjunct professor at the University of Toledo School of Law.

Charles teaches and writes in the areas of constitutional law, civil procedure, election law, law and politics, and race. His articles have appeared in *Constitutional Commentary, The Michigan Law Review, The Michigan Journal of Race and Law, The Georgetown Law Journal, The Journal of Politics, The California Law Review, The North Carolina Law Review*, among others. He was the Stanley V. Kinyon Teacher of the Year 2002–03 at the University of Minnesota Law School.

Charles was a member of the National Research Commission on Elections and Voting and the Century Foundation Working Group on Election Reform. He is a frequent television, print, and radio commentator on issues relating to constitutional law, election law, campaign finance, redistricting, politics, and race.

In spring 2006, Charles was the James S. Carpentier Visiting Professor of Law at Columbia Law School.

Edward B. Foley
Professor of Law, Moritz College of Law, Ohio State University

Edward B. Foley (whose nickname is "Ned") is a professor of law at the Ohio State University, where he specializes in the fields of constitutional law, education law, and election law.

His publications have addressed the issues of campaign finance, school finance, Establishment Clause jurisprudence, and principles of constitutional interpretation, and have appeared in such journals as the *Columbia Law Review, Fordham Law Review, Stanford Journal of Law and Policy,* and *Constitutional Commentary.*

Foley recently returned to the University after a two-year leave of absence, when he served as state solicitor of Ohio. That position, in the office of the attorney general of Ohio, is responsible for supervising the state's appellate litigation and major constitutional cases.

In that capacity, Foley was the principal attorney for the state on a wide variety of cases in the U.S. Supreme Court and the Ohio Supreme Court. He also briefed and argued the Cleveland school voucher case in both the federal district court and court of appeals.

Before arriving at Ohio State in 1991, Foley practiced law in Washington, D.C. with the firms Wilmer, Cutler & Pickering and Jenner & Block. In addition, he served as a law clerk to Justice Harry A. Blackmun of the U.S. Supreme Court and Judge Patricia M. Wald of the U.S. Court of Appeals for the D.C. Circuit.

A graduate of the Columbia University School of Law in 1986, Foley served as writing and research editor for the *Columbia Law Review* and was a recipient of several academic awards. He received his B.A. in history, magna cum laude, from Yale University in 1983.

Luis Fuentes-Rohwer
Associate Professor of Law, Indiana University–Bloomington

Luis Fuentes-Rohwer's research and teaching interests include voting rights, judicial independence and accountability, legal ethics, and democratic theory. Before coming to Indiana, he was a visiting associate professor at Chicago-Kent College of Law, where he taught Voting Rights, Race and the Law, and American Legal History. Prior to his time at Chicago-Kent, he was a fellow at Georgetown University Law Center.

Fuentes-Rohwer holds a B.A., J.D., and Ph.D. from the University of Michigan and an LL.M. from the Georgetown University Law Center.

Christina Galindo Walsh
Senior Staff Attorney, National Disability Rights Network

Christina Galindo-Walsh oversees all of the voting training and technical assistance the National Disability Rights Network (NDRN) provides to the attorneys and advocates that are part of the congressionally mandated Protection and Advocacy Systems (P&As). She has spearheaded the efforts of the P&As under the Help America Vote Act of 2002 (HAVA) to ensure election access to individuals with disabilities. During the 2004 presidential election, she served as the disability commander in the Election Protection Program, a nationwide effort coordinated by the Lawyers' Committee for Civil Rights Under Law and People for the American Way. Galindo-Walsh also specializes in Titles II and III of the Americans with Disabilities Act (ADA).

Prior to joining NDRN, she worked as a litigation associate in Miami, Florida, focusing on litigation under the ADA and before law school she worked in various special education classrooms in Miami-Dade and Leon counties, Florida. Galindo-Walsh received a law degree and B.S. in mental disabilities from Florida State University.

Myriam Gilles
Professor of Law, Benjamin N. Cardozo School of Law

Myriam Gilles is a professor of law at Benjamin N. Cardozo School of Law in New York City. She received an A.B. in history and literature from Harvard College and a J.D. from Yale Law School. Her areas of interest include tort and litigation reform, class action practice, and civil rights and structural reform litigation. Her articles have appeared in the *Columbia Law Journal*, the *California Law Review*, and other scholarly journals. In 2004, she was a visiting professor at the University of Virginia Law School. While at Princeton as a fellow with the Program in Law and Public Affairs for the spring 2006 semester, she explored the concept of entrepreneurial litigation in contemporary American legal practice by considering the ways in which entrepreneurism influences substantive legal doctrine and procedure, effects the way lawyers are perceived by the public, provides a target for litigation reformers, and blurs the traditional lines between plaintiffs' and defendants' counsel.

Edward A. Hailes Jr.
Senior Attorney, The Advancement Project

Edward A. Hailes Jr. is an experienced civil rights attorney and an ordained Baptist minister. He formerly served as the general counsel for the United States Commission on Civil Rights, directing the federal agency's historic investigation into allegations of voting irregularities in Florida during the November 2000 presidential election and the commission's high-profile hearing on police practices and civil rights in New York City after the police shooting of Amadou Diallo. Hailes also served for 10 years as a legal, then legislative, counsel for the NAACP, gaining a remarkable record of success in civil rights litigation and

legislative advocacy on behalf of the
organization. A graduate of Howard University
School of Law, he also earned his undergraduate degree at Howard University as an Honors
Program graduate. Reverend Hailes is the
assistant to the pastor of Mt. Moriah Baptist
Church in Washington, D.C.

Gregory M. Harvey
Partner, Montgomery, McCracken, Walker & Rhoads, LLP

Gregory M. Harvey is a partner in the litigation department of Montgomery, McCracken,
Walker & Rhoads, LLP and is chair of the firm's
public election law practice. His practice has
resulted in more than 150 reported judicial
decisions and includes extensive experience on
appellate briefing and argument, First Amendment law, securities litigation, and public
election law. Harvey's First Amendment practice includes representation of several daily
newspapers, including the *Delaware County
Daily Times,* the *Bucks County Courier Times,*
the *Doylestown Intelligencer,* and the *Pottstown
Mercury.* His commitment to First Amendment
and public election law has earned him such
recognition as listing in *The Best Lawyers in
America* ("First Amendment Law"), the James
Madison Award of the Society of Professional
Journalist (Philadelphia Chapter), and the Judge
Learned Hand Human Relations Award of the
American Jewish Committee. Harvey was also
elected as a Fellow of the American College of
Trial Lawyers, an honorary association which
recognizes excellence in trial practice. Election
to membership is extended by the college only
by invitation, after careful examination of the

nominee's experience, skill, ability, and ethical
standards.

In Harvey's last nine appellate oral arguments,
six before the U.S. Court of Appeals for the
Third Circuit, two before the Pennsylvania
Superior Court, and one before the Commonwealth Court of Pennsylvania, Harvey's side
prevailed in eight of the nine appeals. The most
recent decision, *In re Combustion Engineering,
Inc.,* 391 F.3d 190 (Dec. 2, 2004), increased by
more than $200 million the funds to compen-
sate the parties for whom Harvey argued. In
the Commonwealth Court appeal, Harvey was
selected by PECO Energy Company to argue
for the constitutionality of Pennsylvania's Electric Competition Act, involving PECO's right
to recover over $5 billion in "transition costs"
as part of the transition toward competition in
retail sales of electricity. The significance of the
Commonwealth Court's unanimous decision
sustaining PECO's position is the subject of
Harvey's article published in *The Pennsylvania
Lawyer* (November–December 2001) titled
"Deregulation Done Right—How a different choice in the legal structure of electric
deregulation has so far saved Pennsylvania from
California's fate."

Harvey's other important appellate victories in
recent years include *In re CoreStates Trust Fees
Litigation,* 39 F.3d 61 (3d Cir. 1994), affirming
837 F. Supp. 104 (E.D. Pa. 1993)(putative class
action challenging bank's trust fees could not
be maintained under either the diversity or
federal question jurisdiction of the federal
courts, notwithstanding that there was no
right to conduct a class action in the state
court having exclusive jurisdiction of fiduciary

trusts); *Costello v. Ocean County Observer,* 136
N.J. 594, 643 A.2d 1012 (1994)(summary
judgment granted to newspaper defendants
by intermediate appellate court affirmed on
federal constitutional grounds despite exceptionally unfavorable facts); *Jubelirer v. Singel,* 162
Pa. Cwlth. 55, 638 A.2d 352 (1994)(en banc),
and two related cases, *Donatelli v. Mitchell,* 2
F.3d 508 (3d Cir.), affirming 826 F. Supp. 131
(E.D. Pa. 1993), and *Greenwood v. Singel,* 1993
WL 77271 (E.D. Pa. 1993)(adjudicating various
state and federal constitutional issues arising
from a battle for control of the Senate of
Pennsylvania; Harvey was chief counsel in the
Jubelirer case and obtained a unanimous en
banc decision sustaining the constitutionality of
counting the vote of a senator elected under
disputed circumstances on the issue of his own
seating).

As in these recent decisions, earlier cases
argued by Harvey have established important
legal principles, such as *D. H. Overmyer Co. v.
Frick Co.,* 405 U.S. 174 (1972), resulting in a
unanimous decision sustaining the constitutionality per se of confession of judgment, one
of the few appellate decisions sustaining the
creditor position; *Garner v. Wolflinbarger,* 430
F.2d 1093 (5th Cir. 1970), argued by Harvey
for the American Bar Association as amicus
curiae and resulting in the reversal of a trial
court ruling that plaintiffs in derivative litigation
were entitled automatically to corporate attor-
ney-client communications because they were
shareholders; and *Intraworld Industries, Inc. v.
Girard Trust Bank,* 461 Pa. 343, 336 A.2d 316
(1975), tried and argued on appeal by Harvey
for the party seeking to obtain payment under

a letter of credit and still the leading case in
Pennsylvania sustaining the sanctity of such
instruments against efforts by bank customers
to enjoin their being honored. Harvey's cases
also include tenacious efforts to achieve justice
for his clients, as in *NABCOR v. Philadelphia
National Bank,* in which an $8 million verdict
entered under controversial circumstances
by a state court trial judge was ultimately set
aside and a new trial denied by the intermediate appellate court, and the judge himself was
both defeated by the voters for retention and
twice held to deserve disciplinary removal
from the bench (both instances occurring after
his electoral defeat).

Harvey's representations involving public election law have frequently been referred to in
the legal press and in *The Philadelphia Inquirer*
and the *Philadelphia Daily News,* e.g., "one
of the state's leading authorities on election
law" (*The Legal Intelligencer,* Sept. 28, 1999);
"a leading election lawyer" (*The Inquirer,* June
2, 1994); "state elections law expert" (*The
Inquirer,* May 29, 1993); "one of the state's
top election attorneys" (*Daily News,* May 14,
1991). Harvey also holds elective political
party office as a member and ward co-chair
of Philadelphia's 8th Ward (Center City West)
Democratic Executive Committee.

Harvey graduated with an A.B. degree in
1959 from Harvard University, where he was
a member of Phi Beta Kappa, and with a J.D.
degree in 1962 from Harvard Law School.

Donald F. Kettl
Director, Fels Institute of Government; Stanley I. Sheerr Endowed Term Professor in the Social Sciences and Professor of Political Science, University of Pennsylvania

Donald F. Kettl is a student of public policy and public management and specializes in the management of public organizations. He has regularly appeared on national television and contributed to op-ed pages in major newspapers. He is the author or editor of a dozen books and monographs, including: *System under Stress: Homeland Security and American Politics; The Global Public Management Revolution,* 2nd ed.; *The Politics of the Administrative Process* (with James W. Fesler), 3rd ed.; *The Transformation of Governance: Public Administration for the 21st Century;* and *Leadership at the Fed.*

He has twice won the Louis Brownlow Book Award of the National Academy of Public Administration for the best book published in public administration. Kettl has consulted broadly for government organizations at all levels, in the United States and abroad, and he is a regular columnist for *Governing* magazine, which is read by state and local government officials around the country.

Kettl was awarded a Ph.D. in political science from Yale University. Prior to his appointment at the University of Pennsylvania, he taught at Columbia University, the University of Virginia, Vanderbilt University, and the University of Wisconsin–Madison. He is a fellow of Phi Beta Kappa and the National Academy of Public Administration. He is also a shareholder in the Green Bay Packers.

Justin Levitt
Associate Counsel, Brennan Center for Justice; Adjunct Professor, New York University School of Law

Justin Levitt's work focuses on election administration, redistricting, and voting rights concerns. Before joining the Brennan Center, he was in-house counsel to a national voter registration and mobilization organization and the Director of Strategic Targeting for a national presidential campaign. A graduate of Harvard Law School and the Kennedy School of Government, he clerked for Judge Stephen Reinhardt of the U.S. Court of Appeals for the Ninth Circuit.

Sarah F. Liebschutz
Distinguished Service Professor Emeritus, State University of New York–Brockport

Sarah F. Liebschutz is a widely published scholar in American federalism and intergovernmental relations; her most recent books are *New York Politics: Competition and Compassion* and *Managing Welfare Reform in Five States: the Challenge of Devolution.* She and Daniel Palazzolo were guest editors of the fall 2005 special issue of *Publius: the Journal of Federalism,* on "The States and the Help America Vote Act."

Ray Martinez
Vice Chair, U.S. Election Assistance Commission (EAC)

Ray Martinez was nominated by President George W. Bush and confirmed by unanimous consent of the United States Senate on December 9, 2003, to serve a four-year term on the U.S. Election Assistance Commission (EAC). Martinez was elected Vice Chairman of the EAC for 2006. A bipartisan, independent federal agency, the EAC is responsible for assisting state and local governments to implement uniform requirements designed to improve the process of administering elections for federal office. Prior to his appointment to the EAC, Martinez practiced law in Austin, Texas, with a focus on legislative and regulatory matters and a client base consisting primarily of county governments and related public sector associations.

Martinez began his law practice after serving as deputy assistant to the president for intergovernmental affairs at the White House. In this position, he was responsible for assisting former President Bill Clinton with various policy issues affecting state and local jurisdictions. Additionally, while on the White House staff, Martinez assisted with the development of long-term strategies to stimulate economic growth along the U.S.-Mexico border region, and with the establishment of the U.S.-Mexico Border Health Commission.

Before serving as deputy assistant to the president, Martinez served as regional director for the U.S. Department of Health and Human Services in Dallas, Texas, where he focused agency resources on public health issues such as full implementation of the Children's Health Insurance Program. His federal government service began in 1993, when he was appointed White House liaison to the U.S. Department of Health and Human Services, and later as special assistant to the president in the White House Office of Political Affairs. Prior to his service in the federal government, he worked as a legislative liaison for the Texas attorney general's office.

Recommended to his current position by former Senate Majority Leader Tom Daschle, Martinez has promoted transparency and access in the voting process during his term on the EAC. He has lectured at law schools, continuing legal education forums, and major universities, and spoken at numerous election administration conferences and symposiums throughout the country. Martinez places particular importance on building partnerships with state and local governments, public interest organizations, and other key stakeholders in striving to improve the process by which America votes.

A native of Alice, Texas, Martinez received his law degree from the University of Houston Law Center and his bachelor's degree from Southwestern University.

Michael P. McDonald
Assistant Professor of Government and Politics, George Mason University; Visiting Fellow, the Brookings Institution

Michael P. McDonald received a Ph.D. in political science from the University of California–San Diego, held a one-year postdoc fellowship at Harvard University, and has previously taught at Vanderbilt University and the University of Illinois–Springfield. McDonald's research on voting, redistricting, Congress, and statistical methodology has been widely published. He works for the national exit poll service on election night, was a redistricting consultant in five states, and is active in current redistricting reform efforts, and he co-authored a report for the U.S. Election Assistance Commission on election administration in the 2004 election.

Suzanne Novak
Deputy Director, the Democracy Program, Brennan Center for Justice, New York University School of Law

Suzanne Novak focuses principally on the areas of campaign finance reform and government accountability, which includes government reform and redistricting. In those areas, she litigates, drafts, and counsels others drafting legislation, testifies before legislatures, and prepares studies and reports. Most recently, Novak has been active in counseling Connecticut with respect to their new campaign finance and government ethics laws, defending North Carolina's judicial public financing system, and lobbying for ethics and campaign finance reform in New York State. Prior to joining the Brennan Center, Novak was a staff attorney in the Domestic Legal Program at the Center for Reproductive Rights in New York, where she had previously been a Blackmun Fellow. She was also a litigation associate at Arnold & Porter in New York and a clerk for the Honorable Stephen M. McNamee of the U.S. District Court for the District of Arizona. Novak graduated with honors from New York University School of Law. She received a B.S. in economics, cum laude, from the Wharton School at the University of Pennsylvania.

Nick Nyhart
Co-Founder and Executive Director, Public Campaign

Nick Nyhart is a co-founder and the present executive director of Public Campaign, a national organization dedicated to winning comprehensive "clean money" campaign finance reform. As Public Campaign's field director from 1997–98, he worked extensively with reformers in Arizona and Massachusetts who won full public financing ballot initiatives two years ago. For five years previously, Nyhart directed a six-state campaign finance organizing project for Northeast Action. The project's work with money and politics activists across the Northeast has put the region in the national spotlight with its cutting-edge reform measures. A former community organizer, Nyhart is a veteran of grassroots issue and electoral coalition politics in Connecticut.

He has offices in Hartford, Connecticut, and Washington, D.C.

Phillip A. Olaya
Voting Rights Public Education Coordinator, Asian American Legal Defense and Education Fund (AALDEF)

Phillip A. Olaya coordinates AALDEF's multi-state public education effort on the impact of the federal Voting Rights Act on Asian Americans. He also conducts legal research to document the continued need for language assistance at the voting booth (Section 203) and the importance of federal review of voting changes in jurisdictions with a history of discrimination (Section 5).

Olaya has appeared in the ACLU's "Freedom Files" documentary series on the issue of language assistance under the Voting Rights Act, as well as numerous local television and radio programs to speak on reauthorization and the impact of the language assistance provisions on limited English proficient communities.

Olaya is a graduate of Rutgers University School of Law–Newark, where he was co-editor-in-chief of the *Rutgers Race & the Law Review,* and of Tulane University, New Orleans.

Thomas M. O'Neill
Director, Provisional Voting Project, Eagleton Institute of Politics, Rutgers University

Thomas M. O'Neill is a New Jersey-based consultant on public policy and related issues. For 20 years, he served as President of The Partnership for New Jersey, an association of chief executives from corporations, nonprofits, and higher education. He created and led its Leadership New Jersey program and founded urban leadership programs in Newark and Trenton. He also led programs in education reform, diversity management, and other critical issues. Before joining the Partnership, he served as a president of the Center for Analysis of Public Issues in Princeton and edited its monthly magazine, *New Jersey Reporter.* He was a lecturer and member of the research staff in the Center for Environmental Studies of the School of Engineering and Applied Science at Princeton, served in the New Jersey Department of Environmental Protection, and directed the Governor's Task Force on Energy during the 1973 oil embargo. He was for several years an election night analyst for New Jersey Network Television and for WNET-Channel 13 in New York. He received a B.A. with honors in political science at Wesleyan University and was a member of the Woodrow Wilson School's MPA Class of 1970.

Daniel J. Palazzolo
Professor and Chair,
Department of Political Science,
University of Richmond

Daniel J. Palazzolo teaches courses on American government, public policy, Congress, and campaigns and elections. He is author of two books and several articles on the U.S. Congress, and he is co-editor, with James W. Ceaser, of *Election Reform: Politics and Policy* (Lexington, 2005). He is also co-author of two recent articles on election reform, one with Sarah Liebschutz and another with Fiona McCarthy in *Publius: The Journal of Federalism.* He is also co-author of a forthcoming article, with Vincent Moscardelli, in *State Politics and Policy Quarterly,* on election reform in the states after the 2000 presidential election.

Christopher Patusky
Executive Director, Fels Institute
of Government, University of
Pennsylvania

Christopher Patusky is responsible for managing the full-time MGA program and the Fels Government Research Service. Patusky is a member of the Fels faculty and teaches the government law course, "Law for Public Managers." He also serves on the Advisory Board for the Penn Graduate School of Education's Teach for America teacher certification program.

Patusky's project work at Fels addresses elections and performance management. He has served as project director for the School-Stat, Philadelphia Workforce Development Corporation training evaluation, MyVote1, and HAVA Local Election Official Support projects, among others.

Prior to joining Fels, Patusky worked for 12 years as a lawyer. He clerked with the Honorable Benjamin Kaplan and Ammi Cutter of the Massachusetts Appeals Court before entering private practice with the Boston firm of Hill & Barlow. In 1995, Patusky co-founded the Washington, D.C., firm of Mahon Patusky Rothblatt & Fisher. Patusky's practice areas included business startups, administrative law, copyright, and litigation. He is a member of the bars of Pennsylvania, Maryland, Massachusetts, and the District of Columbia. In 2000, Patusky took a sabbatical from his law practice to obtain his MGA at the Fels Institute of Government and joined the Fels staff in 2002 upon graduation.

In addition to his responsibilities at Fels, Patusky serves as the vice chair of the board and lead director for United Therapeutics Corporation, a publicly traded biotech company. He is also the past president and chair of the Fairmount Community Development Corporation, a non-profit organization dedicated to improving the Fairmount neighborhood of Philadelphia where he lives with his wife and two children.

Patusky received a B.A. from Northwestern University, a J.D. from the Harvard Law School, and an MGA from the University of Pennsylvania's Fels Institute of Government.

Richard Pildes
Sudler Family Professor of Constitutional Law, New York University School of Law

Richard Pildes, a member of the faculty at New York University School of Law, is one of the nation's leading scholars of public law and a specialist in legal issues affecting democracy. In the area of democracy, Pildes, along with the co-authors of his acclaimed casebook, *The Law of Democracy: Legal Structure of the Political Process* (now in its second edition), has helped to create a new field of study in law schools. While issues of democracy have been in the background of many public-law courses, *The Law of Democracy* systematically explores issues of democratic theory in the concrete institutional, policy, and doctrinal settings in which they have arisen historically: issues such as the right to vote, the role of direct democracy, the appropriate role of political parties, the financing of democratic elections, and the representation of minority interests in democratic institutions. Pildes is widely considered one of the nation's leading scholars on such topics as the Voting Rights Act, alternative voting systems (such as cumulative voting), the history of disfranchisement in the United States, and the general relationship between constitutional law and democratic politics in the design of democratic institutions themselves. Respect for his expertise in these areas is reflected in frequent citations of his work in U.S. Supreme Court opinions, the publication of his work in several languages, and his frequent public lectures and appearances, including his nomination for an Emmy Award for his legal analysis during the 2000 presidential election litigation.

In addition to his scholarship on democratic institutions, Pildes has written on other theoretical and practical aspects of public policy. This work includes analysis of conflicts between expert and lay valuations of risks in the health, safety, and environmental fields, and the institutional mechanisms by which regulatory policy might address these conflicts. He has become, with a co-author, a major proponent of an approach to law and public policy that emphasizes the expressive dimensions of action as well as the more material consequences action produces. In a related vein, Pildes has long stressed the importance of attending to the "cultural consequences" of public policies, and his work has been one of the catalysts for the emerging scholarly emphasis on the relationship between formal law and informal social norms.

Pildes is also an engaged public intellectual and an active public-law litigator. He has written for the *New York Times*, the *Wall Street Journal*, the *New Republic*, the *American Prospect*, and similar journals. Apart from his academic work, he has also served as a federal court-appointed independent expert on voting rights litigation, an assistant to a special master for the redistricting of a state legislature, and has worked with the State of North Carolina in redistricting litigation before the United States Supreme Court. In addition to his course on "The Law of Democracy," Pildes also teaches courses in legislation, constitutional law, and administrative law.

Pildes received his A.B. in physical chemistry from Princeton, and his J.D. from Harvard. He clerked for Judge Abner J. Mikva of the U.S. Court of Appeals for the District of Columbia Circuit and for Justice Thurgood Marshall of the U.S. Supreme Court, after which he practiced law in Boston. He began his academic career at the University of Michigan Law School, where he was assistant and then full professor of law from 1988 until joining the New York University School of Law faculty. He has been a visiting professor at the University of Chicago Law School, Harvard Law School, the University of Texas Law School, and was a fellow in Harvard's prestigious Program in Ethics and the Professions from 1998–99.

Mark Posner
Adjunct Professor of Law, Washington College of Law, American University

Mark Posner teaches a course in election law, and also serves as an adjunct professor at the University of Maryland School of Law. From 1980 to 2003, he served in the Civil Rights Division of the U.S. Department of Justice. He worked in the Division's Voting Section from 1980 to 1995, and from the mid-1980s to 1995 he supervised the review of voting changes submitted for preclearance under Section 5 of the Voting Rights Act. From 1992 to 1995, he served as the Special Section 5 Counsel in the Civil Rights Division.

Andrew Rachlin
Program Associate, Policy Research Institute for the Region, Princeton University

Andrew Rachlin's prior experience includes a year as the director of the Latin American section of the Center for the Study of Terrorism and Political Violence, a think tank linked to the University of St. Andrews in Scotland, and several months on the policy staff of the Barend for Congress campaign in upstate New York. He was also a Guggenheim Fellow working out of the Red Hook Community Justice Center in Red Hook, Brooklyn, and a summer fellow at Fundação Casa Rui Barbosa, a Brazilian government research center in Rio de Janeiro. Rachlin holds a master's in international security studies and counterterrorism from the University of St. Andrews and an A.B. in politics, magna cum laude, from Princeton University.

Christopher B. Sheridan
Policy Director, The Committee of Seventy

Christopher B. Sheridan serves as the policy director for The Committee of Seventy, a Philadelphia based non-partisan, non-profit government watchdog organization founded in 1904. In this capacity, Sheridan serves primarily as in-house counsel, specializing in election law, voting rights, campaign finance law, and municipal governance issues. He has managed Seventy's non-partisan election oversight program since 2002, training hundreds of field and office volunteers, and he works with the Philadelphia City Commissioners, law enforcement agencies, political campaigns, political parties, and many others to ensure that public elections are conducted in a fair, efficient, transparent, and lawful manner.

As part of Seventy's civic education effort, Sheridan participates in a wide range of public programs and frequently volunteers with the International Visitor's Council of Philadelphia/U.S. State Department Leadership Program, which has given him the opportunity to discuss issues related to democracy and government integrity with young leaders from dozens of countries.

Prior to joining Seventy, Sheridan served as a judicial law clerk in the Superior Court of Pennsylvania and the Philadelphia Court of Common Pleas. He is a graduate of Tulane Law School and holds a master's in political science and a bachelor's in English from Villanova University.

Howard Sholl
Deputy Administrative Director, Department of Elections, New Castle County, Delaware

Howard Sholl was appointed administrative director for the Department of Elections for New Castle County in 1993. The following year, he was appointed deputy administrative director following the appointment of a commissioner of elections with a different political party affiliation.

He is certified as an election and registration administrator (2002 and recertified in 2006) and as a registered election official (2006—State of Delaware certification). Sholl is a member of the Election Center's National Task Force on Election Reform (2001 and 2005) and has been a participant in the Joint Election Official Liaison Committee (JELOC) since its inception several years ago. He chairs JEOLC's UOCAVA Committee and is a member from Delaware of the U.S. Election Assistance Commission's Standards Board.

Sholl served in the U.S. Air Force from 1968 to 1992, retiring at the rank of colonel. He served as an intelligence officer and a minuteman missile combat crew commander.

Sholl is the vice president of the Triange Neighborhood Association in Wilmington, Delaware, and a past president of the First State Chapter of the Virginia Tech Alumni Association. He holds a B.A. in political science and an M.S. in history from Virginia Polytechnic Institute and State University, and an MBA from the University of Missouri.

Anthony Shorris
Director, Policy Research Institute for the Region; Lecturer, Public and International Affairs, Woodrow Wilson School, Princeton University

Before joining the Woodrow Wilson School faculty, Anthony Shorris served as deputy chancellor for operations and policy at the New York City Board of Education, the nation's largest school system. Shorris has more than 25 years of experience in public and nonprofit management. He was appointed by the mayor as New York City's commissioner of finance and its deputy budget director, as well as by two governors as the first deputy executive director of the Port Authority of New York and New Jersey, the nation's oldest and largest public authority.

In the nonprofit sector, Shorris has served as executive vice president and chief operating officer of a billion-dollar health-care organization operating in New York and Pennsylvania, as well as been chair of the boards of organizations focused on areas as diverse as leadership development, prisoner re-entry, and the delivery of local social services. He has consulted on management and policy issues for national and international foundations and nonprofit organizations on topics including education, public finance, health care, tax policy, economic development, housing, and infrastructure. Shorris holds a B.A. from Harvard College and an MPA from the Woodrow Wilson School at Princeton University.

Ken Smukler
President, VoterLink Data Systems

Ken Smukler is the president of VoterLink Data Systems, a nationally recognized leader in the development of technologies for political and news/entertainment clients.

In 2004, VoterLink's subsidiary, Infovoter Technologies, produced the NBC Voter Alert Line (1.866.MYVOTE1)—a national hotline streaming exclusive wave file content to NBC. This content fed NBC's live broadcast from the National Constitution Center on Election Day, November 2, 2004, as well as NBC Nightly News broadcasts in the week leading up to the election. This technology, Vote411, also supports a second national Election Day hotline for a consortium of civil rights groups and labor organizations.

In 2003, VoterLink designed and produced election day coverage, called "The War Room," for, WPHT Radio, "The Big Talker" 1210 AM Philadelphia. The station, using VoterLink's Tracker technology, was able to deliver, for the first time in radio broadcast history, live real-time turnout tracking to a radio audience.

In 2002, VoterLink introduced two breakthrough technologies in the political marketplace: Robo+ customized automated telecommunications in the political marketplace; Tracker provided the capability to track Election Day turnout in real-time across state lines.

From 1995 through 2001, VoterLink, through its subsidiary, Black and Blue Communications, developed radio and television ads for political clients. Its television advertising campaigns received national attention in 1998 during the Clinton impeachment and in 2001 for a special congressional election.

In the 2000 campaign cycle, VoterLink's clients included campaigns, state parties, and political committees across the country. VoterLink technology anchored the field operations in both the Iowa and New Hampshire primaries for the Gore 2000 campaign. Later in the cycle, VoterLink assisted the coordinated campaigns for the New York, California, Wisconsin, Washington, and Florida Democratic parties and designed voter contact programs for the National Abortion Rights Action League (NARAL), People For the American Way (PFAW), and the National Association for the Advancement of Colored People (NAACP). In addition, VoterLink Data System technology anchored the field operations for some of the largest and most important campaigns in the country including Hillary Clinton for Senate (2000), and McGreevy for Governor (2001).

Smukler has been a regular contributor on MSNBC and FOX Cable News as well as a regular presenter for The Women's Campaign School At Yale University, the University of Pennsylvania's Fels' School of Government, George Washington University, and Columbia University.

DeForest B. Soaries Jr.
Senior Pastor, First Baptist Church of Lincoln Gardens

Since DeForest B. Soaries Jr. assumed the leadership of First Baptist in 1990, the church membership has grown from 1,500 to 6,000 members.

A pioneer of faith-based community development, Rev. Soaries has led First Baptist in the construction of a new $17 million church complex. He has also led the church in forming many not-for-profit entities to serve the community, including the First Baptist Community Development Corporation; the Renaissance Community Development Credit Union; CDC Properties Housing Corporation; Renaissance Education & Technology Academy; and Harvest of Hope Family Services Network.

Internationally renowned as a speaker, author, and advocate for youth, Rev. Soaries was invited by Coretta Scott King to be the featured speaker at the official Year 2000 Martin Luther King Jr. holiday celebration in Atlanta.

Prior to serving at First Baptist, Rev. Soaries was the assistant pastor of the Shiloh Baptist Church in Trenton, New Jersey. Active in community life since his youth, he worked for the Urban League and Operation PUSH while he was a college student.

From 1999 to 2002, Rev. Soaries served as New Jersey's 30th Secretary of State. Appointed by former Governor Christine Todd Whitman, he brought new energy to the Department of State and its mission to preserve the story of New Jersey and its citizenry through the arts, history, and culture of the state. Not only did he manage one of the premier departments of state government but he also served as an adviser to the governor on issues that transcended traditional departmental lines. Perhaps his most significant accomplishment was the creation and implementation of "V-FREE," an innovative, statewide, youth-led violence prevention strategy that contributed to a reduction in school violence.

An ardent believer in the power and importance of education, Soaries earned a B.A. from Fordham University; a master of divinity degree from Princeton Theological Seminary; and a doctor of ministry degree from United Theological Seminary. He has also received five honorary doctorate degrees from institutions of higher learning. Additionally, he has taught courses at Princeton Theological Seminary, Drew University Theological School, Kean University, and Mercer County College.

Soaries has received numerous awards for his leadership and community service. He was recently recognized by the Claremont School of Theology in Claremont, California, with the Kilgore Award for Creative Ministry. This award is presented annually for outstanding and innovative ministry.

Renée Steinhagen
Co-founder and Executive Director, New Jersey Public Interest Law Center

At the New Jersey Public Interest Law Center, Steinhagen has made election reform a critical piece of her agenda, authoring the pamphlet "Making New Jersey's Votes Count: New Jersey Citizen Coalition to Implement the Help America Vote Act" and serving as chair of the NJ Citizens Coalition on the Implementation of HAVA. Prior to her work with the center, she served as a professor at Seton Hall Law School and as an attorney at the Center for Constitutional Rights in New York City. She holds a B.A. from Williams College, magna cum laude and Phi Beta Kappa, an MPA from the Woodrow Wilson School of Public and International Affairs at Princeton University, and a J.D. from the University of Chicago Law School.

Michael Waldman
Executive Director, Brennan Center for Justice, New York University School of Law

Michael Waldman is a nationally prominent public interest lawyer, government official, teacher, and writer. He became director of the Brennan Center in 2005.

Waldman was director of speechwriting for President Bill Clinton from 1995–99, serving as assistant to the president. He was responsible for writing or editing nearly 2,000 speeches, including four State of the Union speeches and two Inaugural Addresses. Previously, he was special assistant to the president for policy coordination (1993–95). Waldman was the top administration policy aide working on campaign finance reform, one of the center's signature issues, and drafted the administration's public financing proposal.

He is the author of several books, including *My Fellow Americans: The Most Important Speeches of American Presidents* (Sourcebooks, 2003); *POTUS Speaks: Finding the Words that Defined the Clinton Presidency* (Simon & Schuster, 2000); and *Who Robbed America? A Citizens' Guide to the Savings and Loan Scandal* (Random House, 1990).

Prior to his government service, Waldman was the director of Public Citizen's Congress Watch, then the capital's largest consumer lobbying office. After leaving the White House, he was a lecturer in public policy at Harvard University's John F. Kennedy School of Government (2001–03), teaching courses on political reform, public leadership, and communications. Most recently he has been a litigator in private practice in New York. Waldman appears frequently on television and radio to discuss public policy, the presidency, and the law.

Waldman is a graduate of Columbia College (B.A., 1982) and New York University School of Law (J.D., 1987), where he was a member of the *Law Review.*

Tova Andrea Wang
Democracy Fellow, The Century Foundation

Tova Andrea Wang is a nationally recognized expert on election reform and also works on other issues related to civil rights and liberties. She was the executive director of The Century Foundation's Post-2004 Election Reform Working Group, comprised of many of the most preeminent election law scholars in the country. In 2001, she was staff person to the National Commission on Federal Election Reform, co-chaired by former Presidents Carter and Ford, of which The Century Foundation was a co-sponsor. She is the author of several election reform reports, and her commentary on this subject has appeared in the *Washington Post,* national Associated Press reports, the *Nation,* the *Los Angeles Times, Newsday,* the *New York Daily News,* the *St. Louis Post-Dispatch,* the *American Prospect, Campaigns and Elections,* and MSNBC.com, among other media outlets. She has been a featured speaker at a number of national elec-

tion reform conferences and forums, provided information and issue analysis to members of Congress, and given expert testimony regarding the new federal election reform law before the New York State Assembly, the New York State Senate, the New York State Board of Elections, and the New York City Council. She is a member of the Civil Rights Committee of the New York City Bar Association.

Prior to joining The Century Foundation, Wang was the deputy director of public policy at The Kamber Group, a public relations and political consulting firm. At Kamber, Wang consulted for political candidates, advocacy organizations, nonprofits, and labor unions. During that time, she was also deputy director of an investigation into misconduct and disciplinary practices at the New York City Police Department for the Office of the Public Advocate.

Before joining Kamber, Wang worked as an independent political consultant and campaign staff member for a number of national and statewide political and advocacy campaigns. She worked for the Reverend Jesse Jackson in his 1996 get out the vote effort, and in 1992 was Manhattan field director for the Clinton for President campaign.

Wang is an attorney and 1996 graduate of New York University School of Law, and a magna cum laude graduate of Barnard College, Columbia University.

Robert Wuthnow
Gerhard P. Andlinger '52 Professor of Social Sciences and Professor of Sociology; Director, Center for the Study of Religion, Princeton University

Robert Wuthnow (Ph.D., University of California–Berkeley) teaches sociology of religion and cultural sociology at Princeton, specializing in the use of both quantitative and qualitative (historical and ethnographic) research methods.

His recent books include *After Heaven: Spirituality in America Since the 1950s* and *Loose Connections: Joining Together in America's Fragmented Communities.*

He has also edited the recent *Encyclopedia of Politics and Religion.* Currently he is directing a Lilly-funded project on *The Public Role of Mainline* Protestantism in America since the 1960s.

Stanley L. Zalen
Co-Executive Director, New York State Board of Elections

Stanley L. Zalen graduated from Brooklyn College with a B.A. in political science in 1968, and from St. John's University Law School in 1972 with a J.D. Zalen was admitted to the New York State Bar in 1973, and also admitted to a variety of federal district courts, the United States Court of Appeals for the Second Circuit, and the United States Supreme Court. Zalen has litigated in all these courts, including the highest New York State Court, and without oral argument in the U.S. Supreme Court. He worked for the New York City Corporation Counsel until 1974, litigating more than 300 cases in Brooklyn Family Court. From 1974 to the present, he has been employed by the New York State Board of Elections. He originally was deputy counsel for enforcement, and became the board's counsel for enforcement in 1993. In that role he controlled all litigation involving financial disclosure requirements, acted as a hearing officer or counsel to the board in administrative hearings to determine the validity of nominating petitions, and frequently lectured on financial disclosure and other election areas, among other duties. In 2005, he was appointed to his current position of co-executive director of the board. Although this position involves a wide range of duties, to date the bulk of Zalen's attention is on the continuing saga of the Help America Vote Act. Zalen has authored several magazine pieces, and is also a co-author of *Ethics in Government. The Public Trust: A Two-Way Street* (2002).